THE AUTHOR

Tony Wilden was born in England in 1935. He emigrated to Canada in 1953, and became a Canadian citizen in 1959. He took his Ph.D. at Johns Hopkins University in Baltimore in 1968 and was appointed to the Literature Department at the University of California at San Diego. In 1971 and '72 he taught systems theory at the Ecole Pratique des Hautes Etudes in Paris and in Togo, Africa. In 1973-74 he worked on the practical applications of the theory of ecosystems at Michigan State University. In 1974 he joined the Communications Department at Simon Fraser University, where he is working today.

His publications include *The Language of the Self: The Function of Speech and Language in Psychoanalysis* (1968) with Jacques Lacan, and *System and Structure: Essays in Communication and Exchange* (1972; Second edition, 1980). An earlier version of *The Imaginary Canadian* was published in 1979 by Presses Comeditex, Quebec City, under the title *Le Canada imaginaire.*

THE IMAGINARY CANADIAN

BY

Tony Wilden

PULP PRESS

ISBN: 0-88978-088-9
0-88978-090-0 (PAPER)

THIS IS A PULP BOOK
PUBLISHED BY PULP PRESS
P.O. BOX 3868
VANCOUVER CANADA
V6B 3Z3

PRINTED AND BOUND IN CANADA

In Memory of

Dorephus Abbey

Duncan Anderson

Daniel Bedford

Christopher Buckley

Joseph-Narcisse Cardinal

F.-M. Thomas Chevalier de Lorimier

Albert Clark

Cornelius Cunningham

Amable Daunais

Pierre Théophile Decoigne

Joshua Guilam Doan

Joseph Duquette

Daniel George

Francois-Xavier Hamelin

Charles Hindelang

Joel Keeler

Sylvester Lawton

Lyman L. Leach

Samuel Lount

Hiram Lynn

Peter Matthews

James Moreau

Pierre-Rémi de Narbonne

François Nicolas

Amos Perley

Russell Phelps

Jacques Robert

Ambroise Sanguinet

Charles Sanguinet

Sylvannus Sweet

Nils Szoltevcky von Schoultz

Martin Woodruff

Contents

IV. CONSTITUTIONAL AND POLITICAL

Some of the Evidence

Introduction

Being Anglo-Canadian, some say, means being a distinctive blend of British and American—with more class than the Americans and less class conflict than the British. Others indignantly declare that Anglo Canada is neither British nor American. Some go so far as to say that Canadians, of whatever sort, do not exist; others make it plain that whatever 'Canadian' means, they want nothing to do with it. It is as if we dwelt in Notland, where 'being Canadian' means *not* being someone else—not English, not American, not Asian, not European, and especially not French.

These confusions and conflicts are understandable. The long trail of broken promises and official violence in our history has made Canadians both touchy and skeptical. We have been brought up with an artificial nation, a 'Canada' created by other countries for their own benefit. This Imaginary nation is not the same as the country we actually live in, nor the land we know: the entire 'consciousness industry' in Canada thrives on manipulating this national derangement.

In Imaginary Canada, everyone has 'equal opportunity' but everyone 'knows their place.' The domination of some groups of Canadians over other groups is explained away as being the result of the 'natural superiority' of those at the top. This makes Imaginary Canadians easy to recognize—by the number of 'other' Canadians they consider, consciously or unconsciously, to be inferior to themselves, and below them on the various social and economic scales. These 'others' include the Québécois, Canadians who don't speak English, and Canadians with 'foreign' accents; Maritimers, Westerners, Northerners, and Canadians from small towns; 'lower class' Canadian youth, non-white Canadians, female Canadians, and the Canadian working class.

Living with an Imaginary identity for so long has not been easy. Even in our victories, it has so far turned out that we were fighting other countries' wars. Take Canada's second Victoria Cross. It was won at the Relief of Lucknow, in 1857, during the 'Indian Mutiny'—as the British call it—by William Hall, a black Canadian seaman born in Nova Scotia. He now lies buried there, outside of Hantsport, in an unmarked grave.

Canada is, of course, a capitalist country, and dabbles in imperialism secondhand. But on top of that, although we are all expected to believe in Canada's identity as a nation, Canada is in fact a British-American colony. In the face of this apparent dilemma, it comes as a great relief to recognize our 'national identity' to be purely fictional. This realization gives us a chance to look around from a new perspective, to discover where and how we really live, and to make another start.

The British now see mainly to the exploitation of our traditions; the Americans attend to most of the economic and ecological exploitation of the country. But many Imaginary Canadians in positions of power insist that Canada is an independent, industrialized, democratic state. Others, a little less ignorant perhaps, but no less cynical, declare that if Canada is a colony, then that is what Canadians want. Others yet more extremist will say that this is the best Canadians can hope for or deserve. But we are not by birth or nature 'colonials.' We were not born with a 'colonial mentality.' We were brought up and trained to be this way, in our collective history as in our personal lives.

From looking at the experience of other countries, however, we know that it is not enough to recognize that Canada is a colony. This moment of understanding may also be another level of resistance to the full truth. 'Canada' and 'colony' may remain mere abstractions 'out there,' and apparently unrelated to our own being and behavior. The bullet we have to bite is that we are *colonized*—historically, economically, socially, politically, and personally.

Colonized peoples are taught Imaginary histories in which they play the role of the 'natural' inferiors. The result is a country of amnesia victims. We cannot know who we are unless we know what our domestic and 'external' relations actually were at different times in our history—the record of our social memory—and how those relations changed over time.

Practically all our multicultural ancestors were at one time or another conquered and colonized like ourselves, and some of them still are. Our major difficulty seems to be collective shell-shock. For over three hundred years, Canada has not had a moment's respite from war, from the *economic* warfare waged against its many different inhabitants by foreign powers and their agents. It began with the French; it continues today with the new empires of the multinational corporations.

Yet we have not entirely lost, even now, never having fully committed our real strategic and tactical reserves. As long as those survive, the war for Canada can still be won.

Our principal weapon is simply our supply of natural and human resources. We are, after all, the wealthiest colony in the American empire, and as such of vastly greater importance to the United States than it has ever been to us. Nonetheless, like any other Third World country—colonies, neocolonies, and 'ex-colonies' in similar and much worse circumstances—we have to learn how to put our resources to work for our own benefit. We are going to have to get a number of critical issues straightened out among ourselves, and between ourselves and the rest of the world, before our exploiters finally drain our wealth and abandon us to freeze in the dark.

Our colonial exploitation could not accomplished without the active and passive collaboration of Canadians in positions of power. But why is there no Canadian name for these overseers, these informers, these respectable quislings, these local Uncle Toms? Most colonized peoples on this planet have specific words for collaborators. Surely it is useful, in economic warfare as in other kinds, to have a vocabulary capable of distinguishing friend from foe. We, however, have nothing of the kind. Can it be that after all these years we continue to believe we have met the enemy—and that the enemy is us?

Imaginary Canadians in authority don't like this kind of talk. It sounds too much to them like the egalitarianism and insubordination we once took pride in. Today, egalitarianism is dismissed as 'typical Canadian whining'; insubordination is treated as violence against the state. What we know to be colonization they call 'typical Canadian complacency.' Fight back, and you will be accused of suffering from a (typically) Canadian 'persecution complex.'

Item 1: Absurd Notions

How quickly do mankind discover those things that gratify their vanity! Many of the emigrants I saw had been on shore a few hours only, during their passage between Montreal and Kingston, yet they had already acquired those absurd notions of independence and equality, which are so deeply engrafted in the minds of the lowest individuals of the American nation.

—John Howison, Esq.: *Sketches of Upper Canada* (1821)

But a persecution complex—also called a 'victim complex'—is not a thing we have; it is a relation we are in. A persecution complex consists of at least a persecutor, a persecutee, and a code of rules in a real environment. In our case, the codes used by the colonizers and their collaborators are hidden from us. Unless we can discover and interpret the written and unwritten codes of rules actually in use against Canadians today, we will never understand how this collective insanity —Imaginary Canada—was imposed on us against our will—or how to fight against it.

—Burnaby, British Columbia

Item 2: Colonized Truth

you can't win. A Canadian catch-phrase, dating since ca. 1950 and 'expressing the impossibility of coming out on top and the futility of kicking against the pricks' (Leechman).

—Eric Partridge: *A Dictionary of Slang and Unconventional English:Supplement*
Eighth Edition (1974)

PART ONE

Personal and Political

'Brother Canadians, do not let yourselves be deceived by fair promises. Trust in the sacredness of your cause. You have the full approval of your distant brothers.... Do not, therefore, believe that the working millions of England have any feelings in common with your oppressors.... May the sun of independence shine on your growing cities, your joyous hearths, your deep forests and your frozen lakes— such is the ardent wish of the Workingmen's Association.'

—Address of the London Chartists to the
Patriotes of Montreal in March 1837

'Our arms are now the argument of justice and reason. They can easily be changed for more decisive weapons, if the eyes of the invaders of our rights continue too dull to see and their ears too obtuse to hear... We desire, through your Association, to proclaim that whatever course we shall be compelled to adopt, we have no contest with the people of England. We war only against the aggressions of their and our tyrannical oppressors.'

—Reply of the Montreal *Patriotes*
to the Workingmen's Association, 1837

CHAPTER ONE

Law and Order

In the 1960s, many people in North America had brushes with many different kinds of law and order. In the United States, we were instructed how to protect ourselves against the police and other agents of the established order. We learned to put into practice the protections provided to us—resident aliens included—by the U.S. constitution, for example. To our surprise and delight, these protections often worked. The continued struggle for civil and economic rights by oppressed groups in the United States eventually made this 'constitutional' approach an ordinary part of one's defenses against the abuse of power in many different contexts.

On returning to Canada, I discovered to my surprise that 'civil rights', the 'rights of the individual,' and 'democratic liberties' do not have the same meaning in Canada as these expressions do in the U.S. As I soon learned, under the English constitutional system we use in Canada, only Parliament and the representatives of the monarchy have any constitutional rights. The people have only those rights which Parliament chooses to allow us to have.

In contrast, under the American system—a derivative of the British and French traditions—constitutional rights are vested in the people first, then delegated to the various governments. One result of this crucial distinction between the two countries is that the whole basis of political discussion and understanding changes every time you cross the border from one to the other.

A major reason for this difference is that Canada still remains suspended in limbo politically, outside the English, the European, and the American traditions. When the Stuart government of England, Scotland, and Ireland was overthrown and the king was executed (1649) in the English Revolution of the seventeenth century (1642-88), we were a colony of an absolute monarchy: the France of Louis XIV. The English invaded and conquered New France in 1759-60, during the Seven Years War. During the American War of Independence (1775-83), Canada was used as a fortified base by the British, and we were obliged to be at war with France. By the time of the French Revolution of 1789, we were thoroughly under British heels, and the official violence against French and Anglo democrats and dissenters continued well into the nineteenth century.

A significant symptom of the peculiar political mixture we were left with becomes apparent in discussions of oppression in Canada. Whether the discussion concerns discrimination, segregation, racism, sexism, class elitism, or any other such dangerous ills in our country, arguments about *individual* rights based on the democratic concept of the *people's* rights don't go very far, as yet, in Canada. They are usually met with a kind of concerned blankness: one of the many faces of colonial authoritarianism in this country.

In Canadian universities, these attitudes are visible in the behavior of many faculty members, besides administrators and others, notably in their attitudes towards students and clerical workers (they still call women 'girls'). They are also visible in the apparently benevolent but oppressive paternalism of many of the same people, both male and female, towards students as individuals, as well as in the passive acceptance by most students of the established chain of divide and rule.

It is true that more and more students are struggling for the recognition of their right to have an effective voice in their own education. It is also true that others do what they can to minimize the effects of the abuse of power by university authorities with power to abuse. But practically the only time when 'rights' are raised as an issue by management in our universities is when management is talking about itself. And when student rights are raised as a general issue by faculty members and administrators, it is not necessarily with the good of the students in mind. As we saw from the 1979 lockout of the Association of University and College Employees (Local 2) at Simon Fraser University, for example, the issue of student rights can be just one more weapon used in more general attacks by business and government on the rights of union members. In harmony with the anti-labor policies of the Liberals and Conservatives in Ottawa, and other political parties elsewhere, these attacks ultimately come down to a concerted assault on the right to strike, the basic democratic right without which work is reduced to outright economic slavery.

I did not understand the sources of these attitudes for quite some time. Nor did I realize at first the extent to which Canadian academia and its teachings—both in and out of the classroom—are representative of the colonization of Canada as a whole. One likely reason for this failure on my part is that I was teaching in California when the most significant recent indicator of the real character of Canada made itself plain: the carefully calculated invocation of the War Measures Act by the Liberal government in October, 1970.

In the United States, we were not told very much about this imposition of martial law and its consequences, and certainly not about the devious machinations leading up to it. Somehow this drastic contradiction of the Canadian image abroad was filed away as just a peculiar exception. It was implied that the whole business was the fault of the Québécois, anyway. No one told us that this government action is typical of the history of Canada, typical of the real Canada behind the imaginary one. The imaginary Canada is all peaceful, all orderly, all British freedom and justice, all scenery and royalty, all comfortable and quiet, all Mounties and mountains, and a fine upstanding member of the United Nations, an independent country much admired for its cooperation in peacekeeping around the world. As far as most foreigners are concerned, the biggest problem in Canada is the weather.

It was just at the point when the October Crisis of 1970-71 was beginning to fade from the memories of many Canadians outside Quebec that someone finally blew the whistle on the RCMP. Apart from the more spectacular of the terrorist activities allegedly associated with them, such as attempted bombings and the highly publicized barn burning in Quebec, we discovered that the political targets of the RCMP Security Services included the following groups of Canadians:

—political parties, such as the Parti Québécois and the New Democratic Party
—left-wing political groups in general
—nationalist movements, especially, but not exclusively, in Quebec
—the trade union movement, especially Canadian unions (rather than the American unions called 'international' unions)
—citizen committees, community groups, consumers' protection groups, legal aid and similar groups
—professional organizations, such as the Quebec Federation of Professional Journalists
—democratic rights defense groups, such as the Rights and Freedom League in Quebec, from whose 1978 newspaper, *Operation Freedom,* I am taking this information. (This group was formerly and inappropriately called the 'Rights of Man League.')
—the French-language press agencies and the French-language Canadian Broadcasting Corporation; certain English-language and Québécois publishing houses and bookstores
—students and teachers

—ethnic organizations and politically active immigrant groups
—women's groups
—protest and dissident groups in general.

As yet, we know little about the illegal ways in which the RCMP went about these activities, aided by provincial and city police forces. We do know that they included illegal wire tapping, 'black bag' burglaries, unwarranted force, the destruction of private property, the confiscation of business records for political reasons, theft (including the theft of dynamite later anonymously blamed on a target group in Quebec), the use of forged documents and messages said to have come from the Front de Libération du Québec, many other agent-provocateur tactics, constant harrassment of 'politicals' and 'suspects,' and persistent attempts to intimidate individuals into becoming police informers.

Item 3: "Law and Order on the March"

The new tempo of police politics does not stop with capital punishment. At almost every level, Canadian police forces are now engaged in a quest for more equipment, more personnel, more money and more power. Especially power. Among their specific demands: the right to open mail (with a judicial warrant); changes in the Human Rights Act, to prevent criminals [sic] from gaining access to federal police files; withdrawal of Ottawa's freedom-of-information proposals; enough federal aid to double the size of police intelligence units, to fight organized crime; and amendments to the Criminal Code that would make any car owner liable for all offences involving his vehicle—even if it were stolen . . .

. . . The campaign for extra [police] clout comes when the growth rate of crime itself is levelling off . . .

One category that shows an indisputable advance, however, is cannabis offences, which now account for one in every eight charges laid against adults (compared to one in 57 [in 1969]).

—*Maclean's Magazine:* Edition of October 2, 1978 (Report by Michael Posner)

Many other questions remain unanswered about the specific activities of the authorities before, during, and after the crisis of October, 1970: the activities of the military and military intelligence; the activities of provincial and city police forces, as well as the RCMP; the activities of the Liberal government in power in Quebec at that time.

One question concerns the failure of the authorities to prevent the kidnappings of the British diplomat, James Cross, and of the Quebec minister, Pierre Laporte (later murdered). Allegedly, the authorities were expecting the kidnappings before they happened. The street on which Cross lived had been under tight police surveillance—but not on the day of the kidnapping. Laporte was acting premier of Quebec—but without police protection when he was kidnapped five days after Cross.

These and other issues are raised in Pierre Vallières' 1977 book, *The Assassination of Pierre Laporte.*[1] Vallières provides evidence implicating the American CIA and the British MI-5 in the whole suspicious business. He raises again the question of who actually killed Laporte, and the question of whether the authorities 'allowed' him to be killed. Laporte was under investigation and active surveillance by the organized crime unit of the Quebec police when he was kidnapped. His close associates have since alleged that his death was the result of internecine warfare in the Liberal party machine in Quebec.

To return directly to the RCMP, the list of their political police activities is so long that a brief chronology of *known* 'security operations' by the RCMP between 1969 and 1977 in Quebec alone occupies five closely printed pages of Volume 1, Number 1, of *Operation Freedom* (February 1978).

As some bits and pieces of this information about the RCMP got through the ordinary censorship of the English-language news media in the West, some of us expected that there would be a public outcry, that the Opposition parties in Ottawa would close in for the attack, and that the Liberal government which is responsible for all these activities would

---

[1] Vallières is the author of *White Niggers of America.* The book was written while he was held in prison without bail for three years on charges of which he was later acquitted—except for the charge of contempt of court. (He and Charles Gagnon were arrested in New York in September 1966 while demonstrating in front of the United Nations building, and deported back to Canada.) In one of its judgments, the Quebec Appeal Court indicated that Vallières had in effect been put on trial for his political beliefs. He was interned with many others minutes after the War Measures Act was proclaimed on October 16, 1970—on charges that were later quashed or dropped. In October, 1972 he received a one-year suspended sentence after pleading guilty to three charges of counselling criminal acts in letters he wrote from his prison cell in 1968 (Vallières, 1977: pp. 191-2).

move quickly to cover its tracks by bringing the state police under open and responsible control.

Nothing of the sort happened. Aided by the prejudices of too many non-French Canadians—who apparently believe that the Québécois get

---

Item 4: October, 1970

1970

October 5 British Trade Commissioner James Cross is kidnapped at his Montreal residence by four gunmen identified later as members of the 'Liberation Cell' of the Front de Libération du Québec.

October 10 Pierre Laporte, Quebec's labor minister and deputy premier, is kidnapped in front of his St. Lambert home by four gunmen belonging to the self-styled 'Chénier Fund-Raising Cell' of the FLQ.

October 15 Thousands of troops are rushed to Montreal and other centers across Quebec under terms of the National Defence Act.

October 16 The Canadian government proclaims the War Measures Act, suspending civil liberties and banning the FLQ. About 250 Québécois are interned without charges in a single day, another 250 later.

October 17 Laporte's body is found in the trunk of the car used a week earlier to kidnap him, abandoned at the heavily guarded St. Hubert air base.

December 2 The Canadian Parliament passes the Public Order Act, extending most provisions of the War Measures Act for five months.

December 3 Lawyers arrange the release of James Cross in return for a military flight to Cuba for his kidnappers.

December 28 Three suspects in the Laporte assassination are arrested in a farmhouse south of Montreal.

1971

January 4 The armed forces' intervention in Quebec comes to an end.

July 31 Remaining charges against 32 suspects are dropped. Of the 497 persons interned under the emergency laws, fewer than 20 are convicted, most of them pleading guilty to reduced charges in return for light sentences.

—Pierre Vallières: *The Assassination of Pierre Laporte (1977)*

the kind of police behavior they deserve—the Liberal government came out in support of the RCMP. They used every means possible to hinder the inquiry into the RCMP's activities, denying both knowledge of, and responsibility for, them (so much for our charade of 'responsible' government). Thus they proved that they knew much better than we did just what governments can get away with in Canada (cf. Item 63). The reaction of the Anglo and Anglicized population as a whole was to support the RCMP—which makes very good sense, in retrospect, since the carefully cultured image of these noble warriors is one of the few characteristics of Canada that anyone outside the country knows anything about.

Outside of Quebec and other places (such as the Interior of B.C.) that know the RCMP only too well, the truth about the RCMP came as a surprise to many people, thus making fools out of those who believed in the tradition. But the real crux of this matter has to do with the ambivalent attitudes of the colonized towards the symbols and the agents of the colonizing power (Britain in this instance). For many Canadians, the RCMP are Canada's cross between Scotland Yard, the Grenadier Guards, and the Household Cavalry. The image projected by the Mounties has become part of Canada's imaginary identity as a nation. Any attack on the RCMP is thus an attack on Canada—an attack on one of the images of Canadian identity.

The best thing for everyone, then, must surely be to make the whole unpleasant business go away. The Liberal government in Ottawa quickly set out to oblige, and the Opposition dropped the hot potato, as the Liberals knew they would have to do. But the Federal government went on to decide that the proper way to bring these illegal activities under the protection of what passes for the 'rule of law' in Canada would be to make these illegal activities 'legal'—after the fact, if need be. This would ensure that Canadian traditions and Canadian law and order are upheld. It would make it quite clear to everyone that the police are above the law in Canada.

Historically, the RCMP have always been in this extra-legal position. The RCMP is not simply a state police force, but it is also a police force organized on military lines. Thus it has no equivalent in the United States or Britain (it does in France, however). Its real equivalents in other countries are the colonial police forces of the old British Empire; in fact, it is directly modeled on one of them: the Royal Irish Constabulary.

We should not be dismayed, therefore, to recognize that, from its earliest days as the agent of the interests of Central Canada, the RCMP's conception of 'upholding the law' has always been an imperial and martial conception. The idea for such a force came to Sir John A. Macdonald, presumably in an unusually sober moment. His particularly corrupt Conservative government formed the North West Mounted Police in its own mirror-image in 1873, in the image of 'law and order for everyone else.' The English-dominated force then marched off into the sunset to bring civilization to the Canadian prairies, taking charge of dealing with all kinds of matters: from insurrection to railroad workers' strikes, from murder to playing billiards on Sundays, from control over the native Canadians and the British and French Métis, to the regulation of liquor, gambling, and blasphemy.

Item 5: Police Morality

New [police] recruits are better trained and better educated, but they are still governed by old ideologies. They are especially puzzled by what they regard as Canada's double standard on police morality: it's okay to beat and harass—it's even expected. But woe unto the constable who gets caught. . . .

—*Maclean's Magazine:* Edition of October 2, 1978 (Report by Michael Posner)

The force did have some teething troubles, however, as the Browns point out in their *Unauthorized History of the RCMP* (1973)[2]. Poor living conditions and the tyranny of senior officers led to a considerable number of desertions. Prostitution was rampant around the police forts; and the sexual exploitation of Indian women by both officers and men was accompanied by spreading venereal disease. Alcoholism and dissension between officers and men plagued the force. There were persistent charges against senior officers of corruption and mistreatment; and the practice whereby police officers served as magistrates was not stopped until the mid-1880s, after protests from the residents of the territory.

Both the power of our state police and our possible future as a police

---

[2]All references mentioned or quoted in the text and identified by author (and/or title) and date (in parentheses) can be found listed alphabetically in the 'Readings and References' at the end of this book. Members of the RCMP have fewer legal protections individually than other residents of Canada. Offences against regulations are handled by internal tribunals not subject to civilian courts. An RCMP member can be imprisoned for up to 30 days without trial by order of the commissioner, for example.

state are thus undeniable parts of our nineteenth-century British heritage. In this country, we have fewer legal rights and weaker constitutional protections against the whims of the police, business interests, the judiciary, and the government than even the 'suspects' being pushed around by Kojak and Company on the American police shows which are beamed across our undefended border night after night. It has been suggested, and it may well be true, that many Canadians are under the televised impression that there are no really significant differences between the constitutional limits on the abuse of power by the police in the U.S., and the limits on the abuse of power by the police in Canada.

This is not, of course, the case. There are indeed constitutional limits on the power of the police in the United States, and even on that of the Central Intelligence Agency (Item 63). There are also constitutional limits on the government of the United States, including its Chief Executive, as Richard Nixon, for one, found out. In contrast, there are almost *no* limits on the power of the Prime Minister and Parliament in Canada. And the power of the House of Commons to make and break the law is transmitted to the police and the courts in such a way that when the police *do* break the law, and are caught breaking the law, the courts will not in general rise to our protection, on constitutional grounds, against such abuses of the rights of the people as we ordinarily understand them in what is supposed to be a democracy.

Consider, for example, the actual results of illegal search and seizure by the police in Canada at present. The following quotation comes from *Civil Rights in Canada*, by Michael Bolton, a Vancouver lawyer (pp. 113-14):

> You can be convicted on illegally obtained evidence. Even if the police grossly misconduct themselves (for example, by beating you to effect a search), you are not entitled to an acquittal if you are charged as a result of something found during the search. If the evidence is relevant to the charge against you, it is admissible. This runs against the trend of American law, where the court tends to require observance of due process during all stages of your case, including arrest and search.
>
> Canadian law in this respect is somewhat hypocritical. . . . Police won't stop using illegal methods if they can use the evidence against you in court. It seems pathetic that the criminal courts, which should be the guardians of due process, allow the police to bring illegally obtained evidence before them. The question could be asked, 'Why has no Canadian court applied our

Bill of Rights to exclude evidence obtained as the result of an illegal arrest or search?'

It would of course be naive to expect true justice from any government in the world today, just as it would be to expect public benefits and public responsibility from the massive corporations that now rule the planet. Nevertheless, many of us are still under the impression that Canada is a democracy; and it is always important to every citizen and resident to know just where the law begins, just where it ends, and just where arbitrary and discriminatory 'law-and-order' enforcement takes over. In Canada, however, we no longer know exactly where these boundaries are (if indeed we ever did); and we are hearing too many threats from Ottawa and elsewhere these days for any of us to feel secure about any of the democratic freedoms we may have once thought we had.

Item 6: Justice 1978

Public order in Canada, says Mr. [Otto] Lang [justice minister and attorney-general of Canada], is not founded on the principle that the law carried sanctions tough enough to compel obedience. Rather it is based on the expectation that people will willingly be law-abiding. . . .

But if that principle of willing obedience deteriorates, then, says Mr. Lang, 'we have gradually to toughen things, perhaps give up some of our civil liberties' [sic].

What it means for the moment is that 'we're not easily equipped to deal with organized breaches of the law and a sudden change in attitude by a significant number of people from the basic principle that the people are going to obey the law . . . .'

'We passed a law outlawing the [postal] strike [of October, 1978],

and with certain clauses in it for penalties a little stronger than some of the laws we used to pass a few years ago, but not nearly so strong as we would pass if we wanted to move another notch in the direction of high-powered enforcement . . . .'

'. . .Obviously if the actions of individuals lead you to doubt. . . willing compliance, then the question comes: Are the sanctions adequate? . . . .'

'I hesitate to elaborate very much on the options. The only one I feel I can safely elaborate on is the one that we placed in the Great Lakes shipping bill which we dealt with Monday [October 23] where we included what you might call a quasi-automatic injunction provision. . .so that by legislating the specifics of obtaining [court] injunctions we eliminate a whole range of technical [sic] defences which civil liberties ordinarily provide for the accused. And that simplifies things.

'Now that doesn't solve some of our practical problems of summoning or arresting, and if we arrest—jail—and if we're going to arrest—are there enough police . . . . '

—Michael Valpy: Interview with Justice Minister Lang. *Vancouver Sun*, October 25, 1978

A Note to Chapter One

THE RIGHT TO PRIVACY

Consider the reported age-groupings in the following Gallup Poll, released August 29, 1978:

Question: Do you, or do you not think the Royal Canadian Mounted Police should be *legally* allowed to open mail if they have *strong suspicions* that it may contain information or material dangerous to Canadian security? [emphasis added].

	Yes	*No*	*Don't Know*
National	67%	29%	4%
18 to 29 years	59%	37%	4%
30 to 49 years	64%	32%	4%
50 years and over	78%	18%	3%

Note the use of the expressions italicized in the question. 'Strong suspicions', for example: Did you ever meet a policeman who couldn't produce a 'strong suspicion' about practically anything at the drop of a billy club? (The RCMP has actually been opening our mail for some 40 years.)

The word 'legal' in the question obviously skews the answers towards favoring increased State interference in our private affairs. What, if anything, does it actually mean? Under our British form of government, 'legal' ordinarily means whatever the Executive of the Majority Party wants it to mean. (When the Russians behave like this, we call it totalitarian.)

A comparison with the United States: Given the strong and assertive sense of individual constitutional rights and protections which one meets with in people from many different walks of life in that country (you will hear it even in gangster movies of the 1930s), this kind of question about the due processes of law and the right to individual privacy could hardly be (publicly) asked there. In contrast, the Government of Canada may well be treating the unreliable information of this poll as if it were a popular referendum in favor of the police state.

Item 7: Frontier Justice

To win a conviction against Paul Rose, for instance, special prosecutor Jacques Ducros had to resort on March 12, 1971, to this novel argument—that the accused had not 'supplied any evidence to back up his denial' that he murdered [Quebec minister, Pierre] Laporte! We know today that Paul Rose was not in St. Hubert on October 17, 1970 [the day of the murder]. The same argument was used by the prosecution at the trials of Francis Simard and Bernard Lortie.

In flagrant violation of the tenets of Canadian criminal law, it was in that case not up to the prosecution to prove beyond a reasonable doubt that the accused were guilty. Instead, the accused were expected to prove their innocence. . .without counsel and, in Paul Rose's case, *in absentia!*

—Pierre Vallières: *The Assassination of Pierre Laporte: Behind the October '70 Scenario* (1977)

The following five news items are also intructive:

The names of thousands of B.C. residents are listed in a secret government file which brands them as drug users, even if they have not been convicted of drug offences, the privacy coordinator [sic] for the federal health and welfare department said today.

The files contain the names of more than 200,000 known and suspected drug users across Canada. . . .

People are refused permission to check if their names have been mistakenly included on the list, because the file is kept from the public. . . (*Vancouver Sun,* July 17, 1978).

Teachers found guilty of marijuana offences in future will have their teaching certificates revoked, [provincial] Education Minister Pat McGeer said today...(*Vancouver Sun,* August 31, 1978).

The Canadian Bar Association today passed a resolution recommending decriminalization of marijuana for personal adult use....

[The proposer of the resolution, Ted] Seifred said the Canadian Bar Association is the last major body of lawyers or doctors in North America that had not yet recommended decriminalization.

He quoted federal figures saying that 2,240 individuals went to jail last year for simple possession of marijuana... (*Vancouver Sun,* August 31, 1978).

By 1985, . . . the storage and handling of Canadian [personal and business] data in American data banks by credit companies, insurance firms and branch plants of U.S. multinational parents [could cost Canadians] 2300 jobs [in the information sector]. And that's just the tip of the iceberg.

The ability—and the right—to run our own country is being eroded because a good deal of the information we need to do it is hidden away in foreign data vaults, controlled by managers who think, understandably, of their [own] country first.

[The fundamental issues—national sovereignty and the national economy—may be more important than the privacy issues, says Dr. Peter Robinson of the federal Department of Communications.]

. . .The question is what to do. We could enforce regulations against data export as the Swedes and the Germans are proposing to do—and as Ontario already does [for] medical information.

But the Americans are firmly opposed to this, calling it censorship and insisting on a free flow of information [sic], even threatening reprisals, such as dumping American information, via satellite, into Canada at low rates... (*Toronto Star,* March 10-11, 1979 [Report by Val Sears]).

...A Gallup [pre-election] poll released [February 16, 1980] seemed to show the Liberals at 48 per cent [of the popular vote], the Tories at 28 and the NDP at 23. CTV, in a poll released the same day, seemed to show Liberals 43, Tories 33 and NDP 22. In fact, both polls had distributed the undecided vote....The real [unreleased] result for Gallup was Liberal 43, Tory 25, NDP 20 and *undecided 11.* For CTV, it was [really] Liberal 26, Tory 20, NDP 13 and *undecided 40. (Vancouver Sun,* February 18, 1980; emphasis added).

CHAPTER TWO

Divide and Rule

With most of its population strung out like a necklace of large and small beads along the 49th parallel, Canada is often said to be 'divided from itself' by the combined effects of geography and what is vaguely labeled 'culture' (i.e. the French Canadians). But with radio, television, and easier air travel, geography is less significant in this century than it used to be; and 'culture' is still a smokescreen for the exploitation of the Québécois. Geography and 'culture' are not the primary reasons for the Canadian brand of 'separate and unequal' citizenship: the various *de facto* separatisms which presently divide our people from each other on the basis of language, region, age, religion, national origin—and class, race, and sex. The primary sources of the 'Divide' in Canada, as elsewhere, stem from the nature of the Rule.

Our country is so superficially similar to the United States that even we Canadians are inclined to get confused. If you've seen Canada at the movies, in fact, it probably *was* the United States: America and Americans in fancy dress and imaginary Canadian history. This confusion is a source of anger and annoyance for many Canadians, but not because Americans are American. The American people are not our enemies, not even in their patronizing ignorance about Canada and Canadians; and the same should be said for the British and the French. The confusion makes us angry because Canada is now the richest single colony of the United States; and because we who are colonized, like those in 'the other America,' i.e. Central and South America, have an intense and pardonable dislike of being confused with our colonizers—be they British, American, or French.

Within the colony itself, our colonizers and their collaborators have lived so apparently secure in their privileges for so long that they get away with personal, political and economic behavior towards Canadians which is cynical, ruthless, and malicious, and often vindictive as well. Along with their political representatives and their other friends and relations, the foreign and domestic business establishment in Canada continues to manage this colony as if we Canadians were orphans in their workhouse, as if we owed them something for the way they exploit us and our country.

The dominant manner of political communication between the Ruling Party and the people of Canada has been browbeating, manipulation, and ill-concealed contempt. The dominant mode of political action by that party has been bullying, provocation, and intimidation. And at the same time Canadian politicians subsidize and protect the operations of foreign capital with public money in what surely has to be the most generous system of welfare for the rich and the very rich in any semi-industrialized country on this planet.

Item 8: Multinational Waste and Inefficiency

Inadequate reforestation is costing B.C. at least 17,000 jobs in the forest and related industries, International Woodworkers of America regional president Jack Munro claimed Tuesday.

In a sombre message to employers at the Truck Loggers Association annual convention, Munro warned that current Canadian forest renewal policy is leading to an alarming loss of wood supplies and jobs, and is harming economic growth....

[According to the president of the B.C. Truck Loggers Association, Dave O'Connor,] B.C. has lost 12,000 jobs because 10 big forest companies control the lion's share of coastal tree farm licences and cutting quotas....

He said the B.C. economy is consistently shortchanged by large multinationals who hold a 'cruel monopoly' of public timber, yet renege on the 'windfall' awarded by the provincial government by consistently failing to harvest their full allowable cuts.

He said undercutting averages more than 10 per cent of the annual allowable cut issued on public lands, with one big company failing to harvest 33 per cent of its tree farm licence and another as much as 74 per cent of its quota in a public sustained [and paid for] yield unit.

[Apart from lost production] he added, the undercutting represents a direct loss of $38 million a year in government revenue....

O'Connor...challenged the government to...correct what he called a double standard that allows 'giveaways' and lax rules for inefficient and wasteful multinationals...while [government] policies undermine the efforts of smaller companies, who are often less wasteful and more efficient than their big competitors....

Present and past policies, he said, have allowed multinationals to cream off the easiest harvested trees, waste good peeler and sawlogs by converting them to pulp and neglect modernization of plants and equipment while profits 'properly belonging to B.C.' are used to 'sustain technology and efficiency else-where.'

— *Vancouver Express:* Edition of January 17, 1979

Riches (money) is not the same as wealth (resources, people). In Canada, however, foreign business interests control most of our wealth, and thus our riches. They leave some of this money lying around for the Canadian capitalist establishment to stash in the coffers of their banks and to lend out as mortgages or their equivalents. Other Canadian capitalists are allowed to play monopoly capital in their offices by building pyramids, mostly out of paper corporations. These activities produce nothing except more paper, including paper money. The real wealth of Canada is mostly 'hands off' to Canadians. In the resource industries, in particular, Canadian workers are obliged to use their creative capacities in the process of turning raw materials into wealth— but wealth that is being shipped out of the country to subsidize the operations of business in other countries.

Item 9: Plus ça change...

By about 1857 or a little later the Bank of Montreal was larger than any American bank and probably the largest and most powerful transactor in the New York money market, where it maintained and employed immense sums. This raised the criticism that the bank, by taking Canada's precious funds abroad to deal with foreigners in Wall Street, was neglecting the domestic borrowers and the Provinces' interest. It was sacrificing Canada to the States. Canadian business and farming struggled as best it could with insufficient credit, America prospered and Canadian bankers, so far from redressing the balance, worsened it.

— Bray Hammond: 'Banking in Canada before Confederation,' quoted in: *Canada: Imperialist Power or Economic Colony? (1977)*

For foreign industrial capital and for domestic capital (largely rented capital, finance and merchant capital), most of our governments play the traditional colonial role of puppets. For most of us within the colony, however, these same governments may appear to be the puppeteers. In general, Canadian and provincial governments toil in the long tradition of speaking primarily for foreign capital, not for the people they are supposed to represent and to whom they are supposed to be responsible. Unfortunately for us, these business and government interests have had a lot of practice in pulling Canadian strings.

Recently, for example, with elections coming up, we saw the old-fashioned Canadian practice of openly bribing the electorate with their own money. Polls have told the ruling Liberal Party that more women support them than men. So they have offered Canadian mothers a couple of hundred dollars each, the money being called a children's 'allowance' and paid directly to the women who qualify. Also in 1979, the Socred dynasty 'gave' us the B.C. Resources Investment Corporation, which the people of B.C. already owned. At our own expense, mostly in commissions to financial institutions, we each received five 'free' shares (with no vote). Capitalist interests now own millions of voting shares.

Many of the day-to-day manipulations of Canadians by business and by government are much cruder, however, and much more ugly. Most politicians and businessmen in this country are so habituated to using racism, for example, conscious and unconscious, as a way of keeping us divided from each other, that they can use racism as a pattern or a model to manipulate our alienation in many other matters. Whether consciously or not, government and business in Canada follow policies, transmit attitudes, and encourage behavior having the effect of exploiting the bigotry taught in school and elsewhere; and they turn this violence against any group they decide to make into official victims at any time.

Of course, you will also find these attitudes, and the accompanying behavior, being created and exploited by the dominant groups in many other countries. But, given the necessity for the rulers of a colony to create scapegoats as targets for the anger and frustration of the colonized, the divide-and-rule tactics of bigotry and elitism are even more effective weapons of social control than they are in the nations of the colonizers.

The English-language media I am familiar with compound these problems. Some of them simply open their doors, their pages, and their airwaves to local and central-Canadian bigots, for example. Most of them show little understanding of the many subtle, and some not so subtle, ways in which generation after generation of Canadian children are instructed and trained to use socially-defined scapegoats as outlets for their legitimate anger and confusion. It is only by exception that the English-language media ever try to grapple with the real sources of bigotry in Canada, and when they do, the results very often reinforce the very attitudes and inequities that English-language commentators are trying to explain or to combat.

Item 10: Patterns

'Sure, we're a colony. The federal government is just a system of baloney controlled by New York. It does what the Jewish community in New York wants it to do. They're the biggest source of our economic problems.'

—A young British Columbian businessman in 1978

'Bolshevism,' wrote the editor of the *Canadian Annual Review* in 1918, 'had a basis wherever Russians and Jews and other foreigners gathered together.'

— James Eayrs: *In Defence of Canada* (1964)

Most of the English-language news media, and especially the television news, seem to be more obviously hostages to other people's fortunes in Canada than in any other country I know. Domestic and international news in Canada is not simply 'sanitized' in flagrantly obvious ways, but it is also presented to the public in such a tedious manner that one might suspect the news media of a conspiracy to bore us all to death. This Canadian tradition seems very effective, and certainly useful to our colonizers, since it manages to convince many of us that what is really happening in the country is as tedious and uninteresting as the media manage to make it appear.

As for Canadian television in general, both the government-controlled Canadian Broadcasting Corporation (English language) and the non-government network, CTV, generally seem to be comfortably following the present Party Line on so-called Canadian unity—anti-Quebec, anti-female, anti-labor, and anti-Canadian—no matter what.

Item 11: Business Rights

Years ago, when rulers could shoot the messenger, bearing bad news was risky. Today, with the media as messenger, there's safe distance between unwelcome words and the boss man's ear. However, an angry business

group which combusted [in the spring of 1977] after smouldering individually for several years, is about to attack the most visible of modern messengers, the CBC.

Twenty-two firms and seven national associations will air their own suppressed story: CBC public affairs coverage of business is biased and unfair. The charge...is led by Kenneth Barnes, director of corporate affairs at Redpath Industries Ltd. Membership in the recently formed committee* grew by word of mouth as it became clear that producers, researchers and programmers of such shows as *Marketplace, Ombudsman, the fifth estate,* and *Fortunes* had roused the ire of business who's who.

Last week, the committee put the final touches on a 15-page brief that bursts with criticism and demands change. [News coverage, as distinct from 'public affairs coverage,' is praised in the brief.]

...Specific complaints range from allegedly biased coverage by *the fifth estate* of Noranda Mines' annual meeting when Chilean investment was discussed, to claimed disregard for fact by *Ombudsman* about a Texaco Canada distributor's dismissal....

Maclean's Magazine: Edition of October 2, 1978 (Report by Roderick McQueen)

*The Ad Hoc Committee for Improved Business Reporting includes: Bell Canada; Burns Foods; Canadian Imperial Bank of Commerce; Canadian Industries Limited; CNR; Canadian Pacific; Domtar; General Foods; Imasco; Inco; John Labatt; McCain Foods; MacDonald Tobacco; Noranda; Price; Redpath; Royal Bank; Seagram; Texaco; Toronto Dominion Bank; Warner-Lambert; Association of Canadian Advertisers; Institute of Canadian Advertising; Canadian Bankers' Association; Canadian Chamber of Commerce; Grocery Products Manufacturers of Canada; Insurers Advisory Organization; Retail Council of Canada.

In spite of their usually staunch defense of the status quo, however, even the media are in trouble in Canada today. Although one would hardly characterize the press of any capitalist country as 'free', both 'free speech' and the 'freedom of the press' are under new attack from many quarters. The timid and colonial 'freedom of the press' in Canada is under attack by police raids, by demands for newsroom film and videotapes to use against Canadian groups on trial, by intimidation from Crown prosecutors, by government and police investigations, by heavy-handed political interference, by business groups (Item 11), and by libel actions. (In a case downplayed or ignored by the Toronto media, Ian Adams faces a $2.2 million suit over his 1977 novel, *S, Portrait of a Spy,* depicting a 'Canadian Philby' directing RCMP counter-espionage. See *Books in Canada,* January 1980.)

Given the government's powers in Canada, it was not surprising to hear the Liberal government deliver a monologue of clichés about the importance of the 'freedom of the press' in almost the same breath with which it promised to prosecute a Toronto newspaper under the extra-legal rules of the Official Secrets Act. (The *Toronto Sun* was accused of 'revealing national security information' related to the North American politics of our latest 'Red spy scare'—even though the information was already an open secret.) We might reasonably have expected to see every newspaper in the country rising to its own self-defense by publishing the same material on its front page, thus challenging the government to take them all to court in secret. They didn't. Divide and rule.

Rule of Law

An example of the federal government's violating our rights is the recent secret trial of NATO consultant Peter Treu under the same Act. The 1939 Act denies the presumption of innocence and replaces evidence by 'suspicion.' On a prosecution under Section 3(2),

> it shall not be necessary to show that the accused person was guilty of any particular act tending to show a purpose prejudicial to the safety or interests of the State, *and,* notwithstanding that no such act is proved against him, he may be convicted. . . .
> (3). . .the fact that [the accused] has been in communication with, or attempted to communicate with, an agent of a foreign power. . .shall be evidence that he has for a purpose prejudicial to the safety or interests of the state, obtained information which is calculated to be or might be or is intended to be directly or indirectly useful to a foreign power. . . .
> Section 4. . .The expression 'an agent of a foreign power' includes any person who is or has been or is reasonably suspected of being or having been employed by a foreign power either within or without Canada, prejudicial to the safety or interests of the State. . . . [From William Reuben, *The Atom Spy Hoax,* New York: Action Books, 1955, p. 39.]

This dangerously vague piece of legislation is 'shotgun' legislation. The government simply points this kind of law in the general direction of the target and then starts blazing away whenever it feels like it. Like the War Measures Act, this kind of law can easily be invoked to break up any group the government disapproves of. It is legislation in the Canadian tradition of 'If you're a suspect, you must be guilty—or else you wouldn't have done what you did to get yourself arrested.'

Canada has never had a strong tradition of rising to the support of the beleaguered individual. The more the laws are vaguely worded and arbitrarily enforced, the less most people in Canada want to be associated with any form of protest against them—for fear that we may be next in line for discriminatory treatment. And yet we are told by the reigning Liberal government—true to its ten years of debasing the language of Canadian politics—that Canada is a country of the 'rule of law.'

Considering that this was said at the very time that the federal government was engaged in its Star Chamber activities against the NATO consultant, one can hardly fail to notice here the traditional Canadian connection between our lawgivers' contempt for the rights of the individual and their contempt for the principles of the rule of law, the principles which, by protecting everyone collectively, also protect every one of us individually.

To start with, a country that permits secret trials is not a country of the rule of law. One basic tenet of this democratic principle is that no one can set themselves above the law, except under the gravest of emergencies. (The rule of law was the major issue in the impeachment investigation of Richard Nixon.) A second tenet, the one principally in question here, is that justice will not only be done, but it will also be *seen* to be done—by means of public trials.

The rule of law also implies the protection of the citizenry against the government and the police by means of the *due processes of law.* Due process reduces the opportunity for executive agents to use the law as a means of dividing and ruling the populace, because it requires that everyone shall be treated equally before the law. In its modern sense, due process protects against entrapment by police officers and *agents provocateurs.* It provides for speedy trials, so as to make it difficult for the police to use their powers of arrest as a means of illegal 'preventitive detention.' It includes not simply the right to talk to counsel, but to be represented by counsel, free of charge if need be, from the moment of interrogation and/or arrest. It provides protection from willing or unwilling self-incrimination. The principle of due process refuses to allow as evidence any material or information procured illegally, such as by illegal wiretaps, searches, or break-ins. It rules against the 'fishing expeditions' and police harassment that are presently condoned by Canadian courts. Also prohibited as evidence is information produced by threats or intimidation or by physical or psychological manipulation or brutality—and so on.

Due process is also one of the principal protections of minority rights against abuses by the majority.

Item 12: Little Protection Against the Law

...The Supreme Court of Canada, unlike [the American], exercises considerable restraint in charting its own course and seems . . .reluctant to undertake a significantly lawmaking role. This is evident, for example, in the. . . rules [allowing] illegally obtained evidence [in court]. It seems unlikely. . . that the court can necessarily be counted on to overrule federal legislation that contravenes civil rights. . . In terms of judicial protection of civil rights and judicial development of the civil rights contained in the Bill of Rights, the future looks a bit grim.

—Michael Bolton: *Civil Rights in Canada* (1976)

Obviously, if every one of us felt ourselves to be protected by the traditions of due process whenever we faced a policeman, a judge, a bureaucrat, an income tax agent, and so on, we would more easily recognize that the ultimate source of our protection against the law lies in our *collective* determination to maintain our securities against it—rather than in our individual hope that in this or that instance we may perhaps be let off more lightly if we simply play along. And if we truly felt our protections to be collectively gained and sustained, then we would be much less likely to turn a blind eye to an injustice suffered by another individual.

In the Canada I know, however, we do not very often handle our relation to the law in this way. The prevailing attitude seems to be that if X is getting shafted, then that is our protection. For if they are busy shafting X, they are probably too busy to be shafting me. This, too, is divide and rule, and it may well take a generation before we can fully rid ourselves as a people of the self-administered oppression that our hidden assumptions of guilt and our (legitimate) fears of retaliation have conditioned in us.

In the economic sphere, divide and rule keeps wages down and profits up. The more that worker is pitted against worker, union against union, man against woman, white against non-white, and jobseeker against jobseeker, then the worse overall working conditions and wages will inevitably be. Divide and rule is management's one great secret weapon—it must be secret since it continues to work so well. By playing with rewards and punishments in the workplace, the managers play with people's lives and with people's conceptions of themselves. In times of high unemployment, when competition for jobs and promotions is the fiercest, the employers of Canadians gain in strength and arrogance. As we all know, 1978 produced at least one million Canadian unemployed, the highest number in our history (an official, and therefore conservative, rate of 8.6 per cent). The depression and the inflation weaken the position of every working person in the country. As a result, business and government in Canada have been able to get away with much more than usual, whether in making higher profits, manipulating prices, crushing strikes, controlling wage increases, or in paying even less attention than they normally do to the people—workers, consumers, taxpayers, voters—from whom they derive their political and economic power.

As hard times increase and natural resources decrease, the stakes simply get bigger and bigger. Business plays economic region off against economic region; the federal government plays province off against province; provincial governments use the help of big corporations to play small-business and professional people off against working people. When unemployment ranges across the country from about 5 per cent in Alberta to 30 per cent in some areas of the Maritime provinces, and when the rate of unemployment amongst young people (18-24 years old) is generally about 15 per cent, Canada's future as an industrialized country is in peril. The federal government reacts characteristically. As unemployment rises, this wasteful and inefficient monster tries to save money by cutting back on unemployment 'benefits.' And as inflation reduces real wages month by month, the various governments use every means possible to keep wage increases below 9 per cent, at a time when the price of basic foodstuffs is shooting up by at least 15 per cent a year. To the employed the message is that you must pay for inflation generated by business and government out of your own pocket. To the unemployed the message is that unemployment is your own fault. And as the right and the center seek out scapegoats, we hear the usual attacks on welfare recipients—most of whom are children.

Item 13: Wages, Price, and Profit

Consumer Affairs Minister Warren Allmand told reporters Friday he doesn't know what to do about the $395 million profit racked up by Bell Canada last year [a 37 per cent increase from the $288 million profit in 1977].

But Finance Minister Jean Chrétien, meeting businessmen the same day, told them to hold the line on pay increases to their employees.

Allmand was asked in the Commons by Derek Blackburn (NDP-Brant) to examine why after-tax industrial profits in the third quarter of 1978 were 32 per cent higher than a year earlier. . . .

The Ontario MP noted that Bell was awarded a large rate increase by the Canadian Radio-Television and Telecommunications Commission and suggested that the cabinet should consider rolling it back.

Allmand replied: 'The government is concerned by these in-creases but as far as I know there is no power to roll back the increase. But I'll look into it.'

Outside the Commons he said he is not certain [that the Consumer Affairs Department] has the resources to examine business profits.

But about those wage increases!. . .

Other cabinet ministers have expressed concern about wages going up faster than the cost of living [sic].

—*Vancouver Express:* Edition of January 29, 1979

Divide and rule also penetrates the ecological sphere of life in Canada. Many Canadians who *are* at work are threatened every day by the biological dangers of close-range industrial pollution. (These contaminants include the heavy metals, such as lead and mercury; asbestos fibers; numerous particulates, such as stone dust and coal dust; petrochemical compounds; oxides of sulfur; the highly toxic PCBs used in printing inks, tires, and transformers; and so on.) Others are threatened by the continued pesticide wars against our forests and our farmlands and the herbicide attacks on plant growth in our inland lakes.

Most of us know and hear little about these matters. The swashbuckling efforts of the Greenpeace Foundation against Russian and Japanese whalers make fancy headlines. But the tedious and undramatic business of identifying the almost innumerable toxins that threaten Canadian workers, not immediately, but over periods of 10 to 40 years, receives about as much attention from the governments, the universities, and the news media in Canada as black-lung disease did in American coal mines in the 1950s. Safe levels of exposure (if indeed any level of day-by-day exposure to industrial and agricultural poisons is safe) have yet to be calculated; and protections against these toxins have yet to be devised.

Here also, in matters of life and death, both government and business divide and rule Canadians. At one level, they encourage class conflict between the relatively privileged Canadians concerned about 'environmental' matters and the working Canadians who are told that 'if the environmentalists have their way,' Canadian jobs will disappear. (There is also no rational economic reason for this to happen. Pollution control and protection of lands, streams, and forests can easily be financed out of corporate profits, as indeed they have been since the first modern 'environmental crisis,' the coal-powered industrial revolution of the 1800s.)

At another level, the indifference of governments and the rapacity of corporations combine to divide workers from each other, and people from themselves, again on the matter of toxic wastes. In many towns all

---

Item 14: 'It's Enough to Make You Sick—or Dead'

At two sites owned by a waste-disposal firm called Tri-Chem Refineries in Delta, B.C., south of Vancouver, hundreds of battered, rusted 45-gallon drums containing 140,000 gallons of highly volatile and toxic industrial wastes such as paint solvents, toluene, sodium cyanide, hydrochloric acid and mercury have been left unguarded since the closing down of Tri-Chem in July [1978]. Last month, Delta authorities confirmed several of the drums were leaking. . .

Chilling as that may sound, the Delta situation...is actually cause for ironic relief—at least [this is a known location] of potential environmental or public health calamities. What worries B.C. environmentalists far more is this: since Tri-Chem was the only facility in the province which would accept hazardous chemicals for disposal, where are the waste-haulers depositing their morbid loads now?...

[In many parts of Canada] government and industry people share the conviction that toxic wastes are being sloughed off into fields, ditches, streams, swamps, unapproved landfill sites, and even municipal sewer systems...

Maclean's Magazine: Edition of October 2, 1978 (Report by Judy Dobbie)

---

over the country, but especially in the most biologically dangerous industries—mining, smelting, pulp and paper, petrochemicals, for instance—workers and their families are faced with the 'choice' between absorbing the pollution into their bodies or finding their wage earners out of work.

If by 'the environment,' we mean 'the natural environment out there,' these problems are not environmental ones. The issue of pollution and our future is not that of 'protecting the environment' as such. (Nature will survive no matter what society does, but society cannot survive the

---

Item 15: The Old School Tie

Overseas

Canadian Banking
Where skill always meets opportunity

A select number of people are needed for employment opportunities with Bank of Montreal. The qualifications needed are a proven track record in the banking community and a desire to apply your acquired skills within a Bank that's noted for its aggressive, ground-breaking performance in Canadian banking.

There are three distinct programs available for the right people within our British Columbia or Alberta branch network. Each is an intensive training and self-development program which, within twelve months, will lead to one of the following managerial positions.

Branch Managers
You'll be developing the loan service and deposit business of your branch, commensurate with divisional growth and profit objectives. You'll be actively managing and building up a consumer and/or commercial loan portfolio, as well as assuming full responsibility for profitably increasing the customer deposit business of your branch. For this program not only will you have substantial lending experience, but also well developed supervisory and interpersonal skills.

Account Managers
Under the direction of your Branch Manager, you'll be held accountable for profitable expansion of commercial lending and deposit business. It's a job that demands strong negotiating skills, financial analytic ability and previous experience in assessing credit requests from commercial clients.

Branch Administration Managers
There's not a job with Bank of Montreal that doesn't require people skills, but the Branch Administration Managers are the people who will be applying this valuable talent most often to branch staff and customers alike. A minimum of five years banking experience should give you the thorough knowledge of banking procedures and the supervisory ability to plan, direct and control all the non-lending operations in your branch that's necessary for entry into this program.

For people with more extensive banking experience, Bank of Montreal has a selected number of senior positions available in the above areas.

Bank of Montreal knows the value of people who can make things happen. If you know you can, we can do a lot to make things happen for you. We'll be in the UK to talk about salaries, benefits, relocation allowances and much more. Just send us a fully comprehensive letter about yourself and your experience, along with a telephone number, addressed to: Greg Wells, Recruitment Co-Ordinator, c/o Personnel Manager, Bank of Montreal, 246 Bishopsgate, London, EC2M 4PA.

The First Canadian Bank
Bank of Montreal

poisoning of our living environment.) The 'environment' we should be protecting is not 'out there' at all, for this 'environment' is ourselves and our children. We human beings form part of the natural environment of capitalist industry. Like other organisms affected by the deadly disorders industry discharges all around us, we ourselves, as organisms, are simply one more endangered species which nature can very well do without.

Capitalism thus forces us to pit our social being against our biological being—the ultimate in divide and rule.

A Note to Chapter Two

THE BOYS IN THE BANKS

The advertisement reproduced as Item 15 was brought to our attention by Mr. T.E. Hooley, in a letter to the *Vancouver Sun* (September 10, 1978). He writes:

Is it any wonder that Canada boasts the highest unemployment rate in the Western world when even trainees can be recruited overseas with the apparent blessing of our department of employment and immigration?

I refer in particular to an impressive Bank of Montreal advertisement appearing in the London Daily Telegraph (Aug. 9), and outlining employment opportunities in the British Columbia and Alberta branches.

Three distinct training programs leading to junior management positions within 12 months were described.

Must we really accept that no suitable candidates can be found within the Canadian banking community? If so, this is a sad indictment of the banks' initial selection and hiring procedures and their failure to provide effective career development programs thereafter. Or could it be that overseas recruiting junkets have now become an institutionalized 'perk,' with appropriate rubber stamping provided by our ever-compliant immigration officials?

Whatever the explanation may be, the losers in this irresponsible game are easy to identify.

First, there are the passed-over employees who would otherwise have been promoted and, of course, their equally frozen juniors on the promotion ladder.

Second, would-be new entrants—Canadian high school and university graduates—now condemned to the ranks of the unemployed.

Finally, the public who, in the role of consumers, taxpayers, and citizens, must ultimately pay for this selfish and short-sighted policy.

This kind of policy is part of what makes Canada, like most colonies, a low-mobility society (compare Item 47). Moreover, not only do the emigrants begin their life in the new country with a primary loyalty to the company that hired them, but (as the company also knows) many British immigrants to Canada make excellent colonial agents to be used, with little awareness on their part, in keeping other people 'in their place.'

Item 16: More of the Same

MacMillan-Bloedel Ltd. . . . announced in a preliminary report [February 1, 1979] that it had record earnings of $100.9 million or $4.50 a share for 1978, up 66 per cent from [1977]. . . .

B.C.'s second largest forest company, B.C. Forest Products Ltd., also reported record earnings for 1978. . .[saying that] its earnings almost doubled to $69 million, or $4.53 a share. . . .*

. . .New Democratic Party leader, Ed Broadbent. . .asked what the [federal] government plans to do to head off an anticipated 20 per cent increase in lumber prices this year.

The NDP leader said lumber prices increased 40 per cent [in 1978] and 20 per cent [in 1977].

. . .A $235 million national development policy to assist modernization of Canada's forest products operations—including many in British Columbia—was announced [February 1] by Robert Andras, president of the Board of Economic Development Ministers. . . .

Vancouver Express: Edition of February 2, 1979

*MacMillan-Bloedel net profits for 1979 were $154.9 million, up 56% over 1978. BCFP also reported record profits: $96.7 million, up 40% over 1978.

CHAPTER THREE

Colonization

Ever since the briefly liberal days of civil rights in the United States (ending in about 1969), most of us have found ourselves as spectators of revelation upon revelation of the escalating violence of our civilization in this century. Some of it we have seen and experienced personally; most of it we see on television. We have watched the violence of the world economic system being directed at group after group on this tiny planet—violence physical, logical,[1] and psychological; violence verbal and non-verbal; violence sexual, political, ecological, and social. Relatively little of this violence, however, is aimed at male WASPs like me.

As a result, like other white males in the teaching profession, I have found myself involved again and again in an unavoidably patronizing position. As a member of the dominant race and the dominant sex, I find myself in the patronizing paradox of talking about the oppressed and exploited situation of people whom I do not in any direct way represent.

There was a time, of course, when—true to the teachings of the dominant value system—I did not perceive that oppression is systematic in our society. I thought it was personally aimed at me. With the obvious exceptions, I considered myself to be 'just as oppressed as everyone else.' Seven years of Basic Training in the complicated brutalities of an English charity school tended to convince me of this. Fortunately for me, experience taught me better.

In September, 1965, the family and I moved to Baltimore, where I had been accepted into graduate school at Johns Hopkins University. This unexpected adventure had been made possible by a fellowship from the H.R. MacMillan Family Funds of the Vancouver Foundation.

Patricia Anderson and I had met each other in 1956, when we worked at Northern Magneto and Electric in Prince George, B.C. Her family had moved there from Saskatchewan. We were married in Nanaimo, on

---

[1]For an analysis of the use of a certain kind of logic as an instrument of violence against people, especially women and children, see the article by Wilden and Wilson: "The Double Bind: Logic, Magic, and Economics" (1976). This is a development and an extension of the discovery of the double bind by Gregory Bateson and his colleagues in the mid-fifties. The article also summarizes major theoretical aspects of the perspective on which this book is based.

Vancouver Island. She was seventeen; I was twenty. When we moved to the Eastern U.S., Mark Wilden was seven, Paul Wilden was five.

Like many small-town Canadians, especially out West and especially those on low incomes, we had an entirely imaginary picture of the United States. This was a picture derived mainly from *Father Knows Best, I Love Lucy, December Bride,* and *Dragnet,* with a camping trip to Oregon thrown in besides. (Moreover, practically all we knew about Middle-Eastern Canada—Ontario and Quebec—was ice hockey.) Our imaginary picture of the U.S. included a confused dislike of the American[2] war in Vietnam and its recent escalation by Lyndon Johnson; immense excitement and concern about the new opportunities being offered by Johns Hopkins, some forty miles from Washington, D.C. (and thus below the Mason-Dixon Line, i.e. in the South); and a hazy image of the activities of an American identified on television as a 'colored troublemaker': Malcolm X. Malcolm X had been assassinated by someone's hit men on February 21, 1965.

We arrived at the railroad station in Baltimore, Maryland, in the middle of a heat-wave. This kind of weather meant that practically everyone who was not working, who was out of work, and who lacked an air-conditioner, was out on the street. As the taxi took us northwards toward the university, we passed block after block of three-story 'row houses,' the like of which I had not seen since childhood in London, England. Their front doors opened directly onto the sidewalk; and there were many people on their doorsteps, just sitting around in the stifling heat. Others were congregated near little stores at street corners that had apparently not been visited by city street-cleaning equipment in recent memory. Newspapers, bits of cardboard boxes, candy wrappers, and plain old city dirt stirred idly in the slipstream of the passing cars, all of which seemed hell bent on going anywhere else but *here.*

This was part of Baltimore's east-side city ghetto. Everyone on the street was black—including scores of men whom one would ordinarily have expected to be fully and regularly employed. We had never seen anything like this before. It made no sense to us that these American streets were so far from being 'paved with gold.' This numbing 'culture shock' was the beginning of our real political education, and we have never forgotten our amazement that this too, this devastated community, was America—America the beautiful.

[2]With India and Poland, Canada was a member of the International Control Commission set up to supervise the military truce after the Viet Minh had defeated the French at Dien Bien Phu in 1954. In 1965, I had just found out that Ottawa had collaborated completely in the American escalation of the war.

A short time later, I went to see D.W. Griffith's tour de force and lionization of the Ku Klux Klan, *Birth of a Nation* (1915)—and discovered during reel-changes that the man I was sitting next to was Jewish. Second shock: I couldn't recall having met anyone who was Jewish since elementary school near Golders Green in London—and one of Griffith's main targets in the film, beside the blacks, intended or not, was obviously the Jews.

Shortly afterwards, I bought a secondhand car and took it out on the Baltimore Beltway to try it out. Third shock: not being used to congested freeway driving, I fouled up and got cut off by a much more ancient car than mine, a car full of 'negroes'. . . . The word appeared in my consciousness, as if by an equal and opposite reaction: 'Damn nig. . . !'

That week I recognized for the first time in my life that, although I felt personally 'liberal' in some vague way, this was the 'liberalism' of ignorance. In England and in B.C., I had been raised as a bigot, that is to say, I had been raised in a systematically racist and anti-Semitic way. (Recognition of sexism came considerably later.) And just like the white Americans driving hastily through the black ghettoes in Baltimore, I had repeatedly driven just as quickly past the Indian 'reservation' outside the city of Duncan on Vancouver Island, also without giving it a second thought.

I don't remember ever having consciously given my personal consent to the latent bigotry I had been trained in.

I began to realize in Baltimore that conscious consent and personal views have nothing essential to do with bigoted attitudes and bigoted behavior, behavior consciously and unconsciously disseminated, and unconsciously learned.

Fourth shock: In early 1966, a friend in Canada sent me a copy of a bestselling Canadian book. It had been written to capitalize on what the book called 'the Quebec problem.' Strange, how similar that expression was to 'the Negro problem'—actually 'the White problem'—that American whites talked about in Baltimore. The book was called *The Squeaking Wheel,* written by two English-speaking Montrealers. One was a doctor who clearly dabbled in psychology and who seemed moderately expert in making socioeconomic and historical problems appear to be personal and psychological problems. The other was an advertising executive who was clearly proud of his skill in selling people a bill of goods; and one who had apparently developed considerable expertise in attacking French Canada, French Canadians, prairie people, people from small towns, women of all nations, and the working class (amongst others) in many subtle and some not so subtle ways.

At the same time, the two authors tried to disclaim responsibility for what they were actually saying, usually through psychological denials[3] or by putting the basic messages of the book into other people's mouths. A slick and artful dodge, carried out with a brand of supercilious contempt that must surely have been learned from the English. The English 'upper' classes have long specialized in this particular way of communicating insults to those they believe to be their inferiors.

> 'Will it never end?' asks the newspaper reader in Hairy Armpit, Saskatchewan.

Then comes the stinger:

> 'Why does the United States have its negroes, and why does Quebec have its French-Canadians?' goes a current witticism.
> 'Because the United States had first choice,' is the answer.

I still remember vividly my reaction to this book and to this English 'joke,' because this was the fourth major aspect of a *pattern* that even a few months of living, teaching, and studying in Baltimore was enabling me to recognize. With the help, in particular, of Jean-Paul Sartre's remarkable analysis of the psychology of hatred, *Anti-Semite and Jew,* written in 1946, I had begun to recognize that racism and other forms of bigotry all tend to depend on the same kind of lies, on the same kind of misrepresentations, on the same kind of vicious humor, on the same half-truths, and on the same sniggering alliances with those one is sharing one's bigotry with. Different forms of bigotry also share the same fear of the 'other' who is being attacked, notably the fear that *they* (blacks, women, Indians, Jews, Chicanos, Orientals...the workers ...or French-Canadians) *are trying to take over.* In other words, I

---

[3]Psychological 'denial' (*Verneinung*) was the name given by Freud to the process whereby one inserts a 'not' into a statement that without the 'not' is actually true, usually in order to avoid facing up to what is really being said. For example: 'That man in my dream is *not* my father' (the repressed message remains repressed). Other forms, with different messages, would be: 'That man in my dream is not my *father*; or 'That *man* in my dream is not my father'; and so on. Consider here the possible significations of the phrase: 'I'm not American.'

According to Freud, the repeated use of 'denial' to hide the truth is character-istic of what he called 'neurosis.' In contrast, the repeated use of 'projection' or 'rejection'—e.g. putting our own messages into other people's mouths—is characteristic of 'schizophrenia.' *The Squeaking Wheel* repeatedly uses all three.

recognized that bigotry tends to have the same *structure,* and often the same content, no matter where and how one finds it.

Item 17: Imperial Unity in the South African War

...The Boers had heard of the Canadians, and [during 1899] a rumour had gone abroad through South Africa that they were half savage and scalped their enemies. . . .

...Hamilton of the *Globe*... thus describes [the Boer prisoners:] 'Slouching, round-shouldered, matted of beard and hair, beastly dull, and brutal as to eye.' They seemed less than human in their animal grossness, rags and filth.

—T.G. Marquis: *Canada's Sons on Kopje and Veldt* (1900)*

Canada sent a total of 7368 officers and men to fight the Boer Republics (1899-1902).

From this small beginning, I eventually made a series of connections somewhat like the following: (1) If bigotry displays patterns that are relatively independent of time and place, then bigotry is also relatively independent of any particular person. (2) The individual bigot is in effect allowing these patterns to *speak themselves* through him or through her. (3) Bigotry is a violent and oppressive attack on people who are also under other kinds of attack every day by an oppressive society. (4) It seems likely, then, that, just like the sources of bigotry in society (not 'in the mind'), the sources of oppression are not themselves significantly personal or individual. (5) Presumably, then, oppression has generalized social and economic patterns also, patterns which communicate themselves through individual oppressors.

Three questions followed from this reasoning: (1) If oppression is systematic, what are its patterns? (2) Where do we fit into these patterns? (3) Why?

And that, as best I can recall, is pretty much how and where all this began.

In the University

Between the racism and the pseudo-aristocratic elitism of Johns Hopkins University, the 'repressive tolerance' of the University of California at San Diego, and what Scott Symons has called our Aztec gas station on Burnaby Mountain, my feelings about the university system have undergone some changes since the 1960s.[4]

But a colony desperately needs its universities and schools in its struggle for independence. It needs the best schools providing the best education to all of its people, because the schools are one of the places where resistance to domination both can and must begin.

However, when the universities who train professional elites are themselves an instrument of this domination, as they are in colonies, this task is not an easy one. Such universities are corrupted by collaboration with the colonizing powers and they are too comfortable to care very much about reforms.

The hidden subject in these schools is not simply oppression, as it is in the schools of the colonizing nations, it is colonial oppression as well. And since the colonization of an entire people cannot be maintained without constant resort to naked power and violence, a colonized and colonizing university will tap the same sources of authoritarian control over the generations who pass through it. Depending on the university's flexibility, there will be a range of exceptions to the general rule; but the basic hierarchies of top-down power will not necessarily be changed— except in the sense that the upper-class schools for young Canadian ladies and gentlemen will be much more discreet about the use and the abuse of power than other schools.

Colonial attitudes are bigoted attitudes. Colonial universities are bigoted places. It is true of course that British, American, and French universities are also bigoted in many different ways—against whoever they define as 'everyone else,' for example. They serve and preserve these attitudes because they too are instruments of domination. But oppression under capitalism has many distinct levels. Whatever patterns of oppression you may find operating in a French university, you will also find them operating in a colonial university—with this difference, that the colonial university will include a level of oppression which is not part of the universities of nation states, i.e. colonialism in the strict sense.

The British, for example, are not prejudiced against 'the British'; the Americans are not prejudiced against 'the Americans.' But the

[4]Johns Hopkins is on the north edge of the east-side ghetto. The medical school and hospital (organized by the Canadian physician, Sir William Osler) are right in the middle of it. In the mid-sixties, the hospital was implicated in demolishing the black community living in the decaying tenements encircling it. The white and middle-class residents and interns at the hospital lived nearby in a square block of suburban-style townhouses surrounded by a chain-link fence.

universities in Canada are profoundly prejudiced against those they call 'the Canadians' (of whatever origin)—just as our foreign and domestic capitalists are.

In spite of all this, however, and given the lack of alternatives, some education also takes place; and many faculty members are dedicated teachers.

For a while, it even appeared that academia was going to break the traditional strangleholds on creativity in education, and open its doors

---

Item 18: As They See Us

1889: But not rotten to the core, I hope

Canada is like an apple just beyond reach. We may strive to grasp it, but the bough recedes from hold just in proportion to our effort to catch it. Let it alone, and in due time it will fall into our hands.

> —*James G. Blaine,*
> *Secretary of State*

All there

Canada is absolutely vital to this country. There is no nation in the world that can compare with Canada as a safe, reliable supply of needed resources. Political stability is there, the resources are there, the friendship is there, and the need for American dollars is there. It's all there.

> —*Research assistant, oil*
> *company, New York City*

Just take it

I think if we need it and they won't give it to us, we should just take it.

> —*National Guardsman,*
> *Freemont, Ohio*

Cautionary note

If the Canadians turn over their resources to us after the way the big corporations have screwed around the resources of this country, well, they're just crazy, is all I can say.

> —*Student, University of*
> *Arizona, Tucson*

Too damn soft

How come they put up the [price of] oil, for Christ's sake? We did enough for Canada, two world wars and Vietnam and then they join the Arabs. Ask me, we're too damn soft on them, we don't have to take that crap from any place like Canada.

> *Gas Station Attendant,*
> *Homestead, Florida*

> —Walter Stewart: *As They*
> *See Us* (1977)

to its real context, to the people who actually pay for it.

But just as economic hard times obliged the ordinary media to cut back on their excursions in social realities, so also did the same economic retrenchment force academia to get back to business as usual. The ordinary media cut back on their most recent forms of investigatory journalism and 'progressive' documentaries. They returned to the production of nostalgic, sexist, religious, and otherwordly fantasies more suited for times of economic depression (as witness the renewed and malignant violence of the Canadian and American television networks against the rights and the persons of women, including the so-called 'soft porn').

The ongoing economic crisis of modern capitalism similarly obliged academia to turn back in on itself, and to concentrate on the production and the reproduction of a more limited and more saleable kind of knowledge— and at lower costs in time and money per student-hour.

Governmental economic coercion from outside, and escalating loads of busywork on the inside, are now closing the doors of many Canadian universities to most of the students who also have to work for a living outside the campus in order to continue in school. Because these impediments to education are primarily articulated on class lines, the critical analysis of class relationships continues to remain the one subject which is the most foreign to the dominant concerns of academia.

Not that class relationships are not brought up in numerous university courses. But they are brought into the classrooms in ways that have the effect, in most cases, of reinforcing the very class-elitism and the very anti-labor attitudes that academics concerned for the 'quest for truth' ought to be questioning and investigating. 'Love it or leave it,' as reactionary Americans used to say? 'Like it or lump it' is I believe the dominant Canadian equivalent.

Restriction of Alternatives

Both by what academia does, and more importantly, by what it does not do, it contributes to oppression, colonial and otherwise.

For example, the permissible range of topics enforced in universities in Canada is much more restricted politically than it is in the universities of our colonizers. Oppression takes many different forms; but one of its forms shares at least one central characteristic: the limitation, by the oppressors, of the alternatives in life available to the oppressed. These limits are represented in our universities by the dominant 'idea-managers.' This academic caste seeks to restrict the established university curriculum to the study of 'civilized' subjects—the more removed from reality or from Canada the better.

Within the 'educational' system of the universities, the students as a whole are in the position of the oppressed. As elsewhere, the manifestation of this oppression in the individual case depends largely on the class, race and sex of the student. But the academic system serves elites, rather than people. Hence, the class of the student, being so similar to the class of everyone else in the 'educational' sphere, becomes much less important, as far as oppression in school is concerned, than the student's race and sex.

Universities as a whole are 'middle class' only in the sense that 'middle class' refers to the social and economic class in society without consciousness of class. In contrast, the representatives of the 'upper class' in our universities know class oppression only too well, since they use it all the time.

They call it 'standards.'

The managers of the corporation call it money.

The faculty call it 'intelligence.'

Item 19: One Heritage of the British Tradition

It seems...to have been considered the policy of the British Government to govern its colonies by means of division, and to break them down as much as possible into petty isolated communities, incapable of combination, and possessing no sufficient strength for individual resistance to the Empire. Indication of such designs are to be found in many of the acts of the British Government with respect to its North American Colonies....

—Lord Durham: *Lord Durham's Report* (1839)

In other contexts, oppression in the university is measured by 'track records'—often equivalent to the coefficient of slavery in academia: the relative number of graduate students and junior faculty toiling in the shadow of a slavedriver or an academic dynasty.

Consider the position of students in Canada in more detail. Many of them are struggling along with very little ready money, and often working at part-time jobs to make ends meet. It is understandable if many of them confuse their own position with the institution of poverty in our society (institutionalized poverty being one of the inventions of 'civilized society,' i.e. class society). It is also understandable, if regrettable, why so many of the students perceive working people in day-in-day-out, repetitive, and truly alienating jobs to be better off than the students are. It is even understandable why so many students consciously and unconsciously consider themselves to be 'genetically superior' to working people.

After all, this is what many of the faculty believe. Such beliefs may quite possibly slip into their teaching—which is not to say that this behavior is necessarily intentional (cf. Chapter Four).

Many students treat the 'support staff'—i.e. those who actually keep the university going, most of whom are women—in supercilious and elitist ways. So do many faculty members and administrators. But the students themselves are often treated in coercive and unprofessional ways by faculty members and others—and the whole tissue of contradiction, confrontation, and conflict goes on reproducing itself year by year.

There are many reasons for such attitudes and behavior, as the offenders know better than anyone else. Two basic reasons behind these abuses of privilege should be mentioned.

In the first place, the social and economic politics of 'success' has induced many students, faculty members, and administrators to confuse their behavior with intelligence. They have been induced to confuse the training in 'success' provided to them by their class background with a supposedly 'innate' quality defined as 'intelligence' by the class structure.[5]

Secondly, most people in academia have been brought up to believe that real poverty and real class relationships are simply or basically a matter of individuals and/or dollars and cents. And students, faculty members, and administrators who have spent a few months or a few years in 'ordinary' jobs quite often believe that they have actually had 'working class' experience. (In the sixties, one of the Chancellors in the University of California system used to refer to his months as a garbageman with great pride.)

Fortunately, we do not have to go into the complicated relationships between labor and capital—and between the different kinds of labor—in order to deal with these kinds of misunderstandings. In

[5]There is also a more liberal version of this confusion. This is the position taken by those who also believe in the same so-called intelligence, but who try to take 'environment,' as well as genetic make-up, into account. They do this in the individual sense most often, however, rather than in the collective sense of the social environment defined by class, race, and sex, i.e. by privileged WASP males.

general they stem from the failure to recognize that class relationships are collective and systematic, not individual; and from the failure to recognize that the basic distinctions between the classes are defined by *available alternatives.*The same is also true, in a different way, of the social and economic hierarchies based on race and sex.

It ought to be obvious from the fact that all of us in academia could have in principle chosen *not* to enter university, that we have been provided with choices between alternatives (and with the training to make use of them) which are not actually available to most of the population—94% in the early 1960s, 87% in 1976, 88% in 1979, according to the *Toronto Sun.* These are alternatives that are almost never available to members of specific social groups, such as the original inhabitants.

In society as presently organized, the interwoven hierarchies of class, race, and sex thus restrict the alternatives in life that are actually available to most members of the 'lower' classes, the 'lower' races, and the 'lower' sex. A few tokens get through these barriers, of course, but not enough to make much significant difference—and too many of them go straight over to the colonizers on their way.

As for the question of 'working-class experience,' here again it is a question of alternatives. It should be obvious, one would think, that a job on a factory production line, for example, or on an office production line, or on a family production line, can never really be a working-class or equivalent experience unless that kind of job and the limited future it offers are all that you can reasonably expect out of life.

Undoubtedly the most unpleasant aspects of the class elitism of academia are the social attitudes it accepts as 'normal.' The laboring population is rarely given credit and recognition for the alienating work they do, the labor that supports the country as a whole. The laboring population, and especially the unionized, are more often than not regarded by the privileged as 'lazy,' 'overpaid,' 'inferior,' and 'greedy.'

Because of their class background, many students and faculty members share this inhuman and self-serving attitude. Many of the faculty members who ought to be doing something about it because their responsibility to the students and the taxpayers requires it, are too ignorant, too tranquilized, or too lazy to do so. Again, the students' attitudes are more understandable. Within the university system, they ordinarily experience such coercion, manipulation, and discrimination that it is hardly surprising—given the way one form of violence maintains and generates other kinds—that so many of them harbor the oppressive (and self-oppressive) feelings about class, race, and sex that they do.

However, there is change afoot. In Canada, we are presently faced with an increasing 'proletarianization' of the students. The jobs they were promised by society if they went on in school are now getting harder and harder to find. In consequence, as already noted, the universities are returning to policies designed to keep the universities as a haven for the even more privileged. The results of this economic retrenchment and of these even more exclusionary policies—besides the increasing numbers of university and high-school graduates whose legitimate aspirations are not being met—can probably be counted on to produce a Canada of the 1980s that will be an even more angry place than the Canada of the 1970s.

Item 20: Foreign Investment: Favoring the Already Privileged

The 'common sense' of Canadians (and the dominant ideology) would tell them that foreign direct investment means greater investment in their economy, more jobs and better ones, more affluence, and, however vaguely, 'progress.' On the contrary, the 'uncommon' reality is that after a brief period of growth, foreign direct investment means that more capital flows *out* of than into the economy; that there are fewer jobs in the capital-intensive branch plants than in Canadian-controlled firms; that there are few jobs in branch plants requiring highly trained manpower because much of the research and development is done in the country of the parent; and finally, that the 'affluence' and 'progress' created by these developments are deceptive, favouring the already privileged.

—Wallace Clement: *Continental Corporate Power* (1977)

Capital may be brought into any country, but under an arbitrary, imprudent, and irresponsible government it will be impossible to retain a large share of it.

—William Lyon Mackenzie: *Seventh Report on Grievances* (1835)

Colonial Inferiority

If we recognize that oppression and exploitation in the hierarchies of class, race, and sex can be most readily defined as various levels of restricted alternatives, it follows that the same kind of structures will be found in a country colonized by foreign powers. But in a colony, there will also be a restriction of alternatives in life for *all* of the colonized in the country, except for the richest and the most privileged. Colonial oppression is an extra level of exploitation in the system.

It also follows that the more alternatives an individual is provided with and/or earns in this system of oppression, the less likely it is that the individual in question will be conscious of the restrictions placed on the lives of other groups of people (minus the tokens) in society. And most of the privileged will have been taught to believe that these restrictions on other groups are justified—because the people 'aren't working hard enough, or 'lack initiative,' for instance.

Always and everywhere, a colonized people is defined by the colonizers as an 'inferior' people. The dominant teachers and commentators in the media of the colony accept that absurdity as a fact, and proceed to propagate it—complete with the cynicism, the apathy, and the defeatism that infects most of the English-language media in Canada—inside and outside the schools, inside and outside the dominant political parties, inside and outside business in Canada, practically everywhere you look. (I cannot of course speak for Quebec.) Whether we like it or not, we know only too well that we are regarded as not being quite as good at anything we do as the British, the Americans, or the French...or the Chinese, the Germans, the Japanese, or indeed practically any one of the non-colonized (or no-longer-colonized) nations represented amongst our diverse population.

Item 21: Defeatism

In our literature, heroic action remains possible but becomes so deeply tinged with futility that withdrawal becomes a more characteristic response than commitment. The representative images are those of denial and defeat rather than fulfilment and victory.

—Robert McDougall:
In: *Contexts of Canadian Criticism* (1971)

When the realities of colonization are translated by those who ought to know better into the politics of apathy, defeatism, and inferiority—'Canadian' apathy, 'Canadian' defeatism, 'Canadian' inferiority—and when the people of the colony are fed a rarely interrupted diet of this ideological trash, then the people of the colony are going to end up believing it to be true.

As we know from the experience of other colonized groups—Jamaicans, Algerians, women, for example—when a people are repeatedly and consistently implied to be inferior, *then they will learn to act inferior as well.*

The blacks in the United States began to demolish this 'inferiority' imposed on the colonized by the colonizer with the slogan of the 1960s: 'Black is beautiful.' The Algerians did so by fighting the French to a barely concealed national defeat. Women now have an entire and expanding literature attacking and refuting the male myths of their supposed 'inferiority.' And we Canadians are already off along the same troublesome but liberating road—liberating because it points to the only way out, troublesome because if we want our liberation to be real, rather than imaginary, then we have to recognize just what it is we are trying to be liberated from.

CHAPTER FOUR

The Old Question,
But Not the Old Answers

Since our governments still call themselves 'democratic,' we may find there the beginnings of a ground to stand on and from which to defend ourselves and each other. We can begin by standing firm on the question of our civil liberties and our democratic rights. This is already happening, in any case. As we can see from the new kinds of books and histories being published in Canada in the 1970s, as well as from the various groups and protests springing up in different parts of Canada even in the past year or so, many Canadians are already agreed on the question of making democracy safe for the citizens and residents of Canada.

Of course, our problems in this country go far beyond the relatively simple question of democracy. Few people would suggest that introducing democratic government to Canada—and insisting that executive groups at all levels be *representative* of the grass roots from whom they derive their power, and fully *responsible* to them—will solve the very serious difficulties we now face. Democracy alone cannot solve the problems of our economic exploitation, the destruction of our natural environment, the theft of our national resources (including our sources of energy), our perennial unemployment, inflation, confiscatory interest rates, the constant attacks on Canadian labor, the regressive taxation, the racism, the sexism, and the growing and ever more concentrated power of business in Canada.

But trying to solve huge problems all at once is not the point of our coming together to demand our rights as persons under the traditions of capitalist democracy. One point of the demand for democratic rights is that if we succeed, we may just be able to live a little more securely than we have been; and that alone is reason enough. And just because we choose to make a beginning there does not mean that this is where the process will end.

There is a much deeper and more important reason for making such a stand. Practically by definition, colonized peoples are inexperienced peoples. Colonization ensures that they are misinformed about each other and about the rest of the world. As a diverse and still relatively insulated people, we Canadians are inexperienced in working together, in learning from each other, in understanding the deeper social and economic issues which would unite us once we realized that they involve our common fate. We are too used to the anti-Canadian tradition of divide-and-rule in this country—but the only people who can do anything to change that situation are Canadians concerned with the long-range survival of Canada and its people.

We are not talking about a 'one-time' solution to a 'one-time' problem. Not at all. We are talking about a *process,* a long process of change that no one but ourselves can set going. Part of this process involves finding out about each other, about who wants what, about which priorities different groups and different regions regard as essential, and about who can be depended on to do what in this or that particular circumstance. In other words, what happens and what does not happen in this country is going to depend on the process of our mutual political education.

Item 22: Mergers

In the United States, a merger involving corporations the size of the Hudson's Bay Co., Simpsons Ltd. or Simpsons-Sears Ltd. would probably never be allowed to occur. [Cabinet approval has been given for the merger between Simpsons and Simpsons-Sears; the controlling shareholder is the American Sears, Roebuck & Co., already the world's largest retailer.] Indeed, anti-trust legislation there has proven a strong deterrent to mergers of much smaller companies than the Canadian merchandising giants. But in Canada, anti-trust legislation (called the Combines Investigation Act) is so soft on mergers that it is widely viewed as little more than a make-work program for lawyers...Since the act was passed in 1910, just one firm has been convicted of an anti-competitive merger—and it pleaded guilty. Such major and controversial mergers as the acquisition of Dow Brewery Ltd. by Canadian Breweries Ltd., Manitoba Sugar by B.C. Sugar Refinery Ltd. and every English-language daily newspaper in New Brunswick by the K.C. Irving interests have been acquitted in the courts.

Thus it came as little surprise last week when Robert Bertrand, director of the government's combines branch, announced the government would not try to block a Bay-Simpsons merger...
—Maclean's Magazine: Edition of December 25, 1978 (Report by Ian Urquhart)

All these issues and concerns keep returning us to the major *symptom* of the real situation of Canadians in the modern world: the social, historical, and economic question of Canadian identity.

Why is This Question So Important?

Why is the question of Canadian identity of such strategic importance in Canadian political consciousness and in our political and economic future?

We all have many different and distinct identities (identities in relation to others, for identity is always a relation). In various contexts, we have many distinct *levels* of identity as well: race, class, color, creed, sex, national origin, family background, region, and birthplace—and so on. Every person is made up of this complicated network of relationships to different contexts, and many more besides. Real identities are essential to the social individuality that makes us unique persons (as distinct from the imaginary individual*ism* that makes us into alienated objects). Real identities—real relations to real contexts—are what help to define for each of us the ground of our existence in all these many contexts.

But if we are lacking the real identity which arises in the shared and collective relationship of *nationhood* (not nationalism in the sense of chauvinism and jingoism), then where on earth do we stand, as Canadians, in a world in which nations still exist as powerful collectivities? Where do we Canadians stand in a world in which most oppression and exploitation (whatever may be said about multinational corporations) still has national, as well as transnational, characteristics? Not on our own feet, that's for sure, but more than likely under someone else's.

'Nationhood' is still considered a dirty word in Canada, however, especially—and obviously—by our colonizers and by their 'Canadian' collaborators. It is a forbidden word to them because the shared sense of nationhood provides the colonized with a special kind of unity and strength, a unity with which a people can resist the divide-and-rule of the colonizing interests.

There is in the common misunderstanding of the importance of national identity a misunderstanding of the actual processes of history—as distinct from the way we might like history to be. Because Canada is a neocolony of the United States, there is no truly international relationship between the people of Canada and the people of the United States. And even if the relationship between the working classes (for example) of both countries was a relationship between the working classes of two nations, this would not make labor transnational in the continental context, as capital is, and always has been.

For as long as Canada remains a colony of the United States, then American workers, brothers and sisters of ours as they may be, are nevertheless benefiting every day from the surplus value produced by Canadian workers in the resource industries, just as they benefit from the manufacture of the goods that we, in our mercantile subordination as a colony, are obliged to import from the United States.

Item 23: Home Sweet Home

'Canadian families need almost twice the income of U.S. families to buy an equivalent home,' said James McCambly, executive-secretary of the building and construction trades department [representing 400,000 Canadian tradesmen] presenting a brief to [Federal] cabinet ministers.

McCambly said a Canadian family needs a total annual income of $29,000 to afford a house, but a family in the U.S. can buy with an income of $14,000. . . .

'In 1975, only nine per cent of Canadians could afford the average new residence, but 42 per cent of Americans could afford to buy their average new home,' he said.

— Vancouver Express: Edition of December 13, 1978

The plain fact is that 'internationalism'[1] refers to a relationship between two or more nations, each with control over its economy and its national territory. How then can such a term be applied to us, in any proper sense, when the country called Canada is not yet a nation?

There is also another problem here. Our major colonizers, the British and the Americans, are of course cultural and ideological colonizers, besides whatever else they are. This ideological colonization affects many different aspects of life in Canada, and many aspects of the ordinary spectrum of political positions and beliefs. The result is that most of the political positions taken by different groups in this country have been historically derived from the politics of colonization, the politics of colonizers, rather than from the politics of the colonized. Neither the British nor the Americans look upon Canada as the foreign country that

---

[1] On this topic, see for example the articles on 'international' unions in Canada by R.B. Morris, and by R. Howard and Jack Scott, in *Capitalism and the National Question in Canada* (1972), edited by Gary Teeple.

it is; and their attitudes to Canada and Canadians are all too often infected with an imperial paternalism, both conscious and unconscious.

The result is that we have to face these colonial attitudes almost everywhere we look, colonial attitudes that most Canadians have been brought up with for so long that we too often take them upon ourselves, as if they were our own. The internalization, by the colonized, of the attitudes of the colonizers is a complicated and contradictory process, and one that it will be necessary to return to and to analyze in more detail later on in this book. But what should be pointed out is that, in spite of all that we can and do learn from the French, American, and British political traditions, and especially from their radical traditions, we can learn very little from them about modern colonization and neocolonization as it is experienced by the colonized countries.

The politics of the colonizers are so deeply impressed upon most Canadians—and so much a part of the acceptance of the imaginary superiorities drummed into Anglo Canadians and repeatedly carried into the country by British and American immigrants—that few political positions in English-speaking Canada are immune from their unconsciously anti-Canadian ignorance. ('Ignorance, like knowledge,' observed the Swedish sociologist, Gunnar Myrdal, 'is purposefully directed.')

From this kind of ignorance there arises the inappropriate tendency to treat Canada as just another 'industrialized' and 'independent' country, rather than as the colony it actually is—a colony, moreover, which for the last twenty years at least has been progressively *de-industrialized* and *de-developed* by its colonial masters, by those whose control over industrial technology and research and development in Canada continues to increase (Items 24 and 33).[2]

---

[2]Canada has always been permitted by its colonial masters to export imperialism into other colonies (e.g. into the Caribbean and South America). Canadian and British-Canadian banks have often helped to prepare the way, and other capitalists from Canada have ridden into these countries on the coat tails of British and American imperialism. As we did for the Americans in their attempt to colonize Vietnam, Canada has often acted as the agent of imperial interests around the world. As a result, it is easy to confuse our subordinate role in these activities with 'Canadian imperialism,' so-called. The common tendency is to think that a country is *either* a colony *or* an imperialist power. If Canada is in certain ways *less* colonized than, say, Jamaica or Brazil, this does not mean that Canada is *not* colonized. The fact is that Canada is *predominantly* a colony, at the same time as Canadian businesses and governments collaborate with the dominant imperial powers in the world-wide imperial system. On this topic, see the analysis by Red Star Collective (1977).

Item 24: De-Industrialization

Over the decade [1968-1978], Canadian manufacturing has deteriorated, says the Science Council of Canada, to the verge of 'de-industrialization,' of reversion to its historical role as hewer of wood and drawer of water for the major industrial countries. 'Canada is a declining industrial power,' says Robert Scrivener, chairman of Northern Telecom,* one of the country's few success stories in the manufacturing field. 'Some observers already believe that we are only a semi-industrial power at best.'

In 1969, for example, 23.4% of Canadian jobs were in the manufacturing sector. By 1976, the proportion had declined to 20.6% and the trend is continuing....

Structural change [to deal with the long-term problems of Canadian industry] means rationalization of industry to cut out nonprofitable firms and sectors, new curbs on foreign investment and stimulation of Canadian ownership, promotion of domestic research and development rather than importation of foreign technology, revamped competition legislation to punish price fixers but reward efficiency, and a modern approach to industrial relations in place of the present adversary system....

—*Maclean's Magazine:* Edition of April 3, 1978 (Report by Ian Urquhart)

'Northern Telecom, the only Canadian company manufacturing telephones for Bell Canada, sells the same phones for less in the U.S. It comes down, says the company, to "what Americans are willing to pay and what Canadians are willing to pay." Hmm....' (Roderick McQueen: 'The great Canadian take-over binge: someday soon this will all be theirs.' *Maclean's Magazine*, January 22, 1979).

The struggles of the Canadian working class, for example, cannot fully be analyzed or understood solely from a perspective which is derived from the struggles of the working classes in the countries of the imperial powers. The same applies to the situation of the native Canadians, colonized by the colonized; as also to the situation of the Québécois, as also to the situation of women in Canada. By the same token, the dominant class in Canada, allied as it is with enormously powerful foreign interests, has to be understood and treated differently from the way in which its apparent counterparts would be in Britain or the United States (or France, for that matter).

A significant part of politics in Canada thus still exists in a subordinate relationship to politics in Britain and in the United States. This is a colonial relationship; and it will remain as one just so long as we fail to treat the Canadian reality and the dominant Canadian consciousness as a colonized reality and as a colonized consciousness.

Intentions and Effects

There are two interrelated problems within this problem. One involves the question of conscious intention, and specifically 'good intentions.' The second requires us to consider just how much we can depend on advice and help from the persons, the actions, and the writings of people who were brought up as citizens of the imperial powers (the dominant Others), rather than as the colonial subjects of those powers.

To deal first with the question of intent. Colonial attitudes on the part of Anglo Saxons and others in Canada are not necessarily consciously maintained or intentionally expressed. A sole or primary concern for (conscious) intentions, good, bad, and indifferent, is not usefully relevant to a critical understanding of society, and much less to an understanding of colonization. As the Chinese have long said, it is not intentions, but *effects* that count. Allowing for the legal concept of premeditated crime, it is effects and behavior that have to be understood. Who can seriously doubt, for example, that as far as many Germans and non-Germans were concerned in 1933-45, Hitler was guided by the best of intentions? (And who can prove otherwise?)

One of the great fables of the British tradition, for example— especially once it became too obviously self-serving to praise the 'civilizing' mission of British imperialism—is that the English 'muddled' their way into colonialism, that the English never intended to embark on the economic and military conquests—including the subjugation of the Celtic inhabitants of the British Isles, notably the Irish, the Welsh, the Cornish, and the Scots—which eventually produced the British (i.e. the English) Empire.

Perhaps this typically psychological excuse of 'we didn't mean to do it' makes its inventors feel better, who knows? But it doesn't help the colonies one bit, the colonies who were—and still are—on the receiving end of the effects—no more than does the dominant American fable, the fable that the kind-hearted, fair-minded, and generous United States is an anti-colonial power whose repeated interferences or worse in everyone else's affairs is intended to provide the world with 'democracy,' 'self-determination,' and 'human rights.'

This brings us to the second problem. In terms of the understanding of colonization, the critique of the jesuitical excuse of 'good intentions' has an intimate connection with the dangers that arise when people brought up in the dominant country or group set out to help people in the colonized country or group.

I learned to make the crucial distinction between intentions and effects the hard way—I hope that this is not the only way in which it is usually learned. I recall how so many well-meaning whites, including myself, had to learn during the peak of the civil-rights movement in the 1960s in the United States that we had no business getting ourselves mixed up in 'leading roles' in relation to black reformist and black militant groups, even when invited. Fortunately, wiser counsels prevailed, and they threw us out.

This they did, not because of who we were, but because of what we *represented*. Their action was not personal, it was political. From bitter experience, they knew only too well how it happens that, in a society where 'white is right,' the mere presence of white men and women in black groups is disruptive. The white presence in black councils re-affirms the socially defined dominance of whites in a way that becomes even more disruptive when the whites start talking as well. It gets even worse when personal relations get mixed up with political activities—as the Student Non-violent Coordinating Committee found out in the South in the earlier days of the movement.

As a result, we learned some important political lessons, besides the lesson that effects, rather than intentions, are what ultimately count. We became involved in 'supporting roles,' when asked, and learned to hold our peace when we weren't. We also learned that, in terms of racism, the constituency to which we should address ourselves is the constituency that is primarily responsible for the modern form of racism in the modern world, the constituency of whites, the constituency of which we are representative.

But the most important lesson many of us learned from our socially defined dominance as whites was that *dominant Others can never be fully trusted*. (This remains true for whatever way their dominance is defined in a particular situation. Moreover, dominant Others do not have to behave in an overtly domineering way to be oppressively dominant.) This is not because such dominant Others cannot act in the best of faith, not because they cannot provide useful experience and expertise, not because they may not be working as hard as possible to understand...but basically *because they are too damned used to being dominant.* That's a fair warning, I would think.

Common Ground

We can learn a great deal from the experience of blacks, Chicanos, and Puerto-Ricans in the United States—except that their domestic colonization is not quite the same as our colonization from outside, because those born in any of the fifty states also bear the national identity of Americans. All of us can learn from the labor movement and the women's movement—except that *national* identity is not the issue here.

Who then do we turn to in order to become aware of the crucial importance of nationhood to Canada? I suggest we turn to the peoples we have most in common with, the peoples of the third world—to their successes and their failures. To the Algerian War of Independence against the French; to China's victory over Japan; to Nicaragua; to the Vietnamese Wars of Independence against the Chinese, the French, the Japanese, the British, the French again, and eventually against the Americans and their colonial troops (e.g. the South Koreans). Whatever the failings—indeed, because of the failings—we have much to learn from them, just as we can learn from third-world countries protecting their present and their future by forming raw-materials cartels.

What we learn very quickly from the experiences of other colonized countries is that a colonized people, if they are to set out on the thorny and heady path of decolonization, have no choice whatsoever about nationhood.

A colonized people must unite on the common ground of their national identity and their national territory if they are ever to attain any significant measure of control over their own destiny.

This is in any case part of the message of the latest demand for independence and for control over resources and development from within the national territory of Canada: the Déné Declaration of 1975, reproduced as Item 25.

This declaration by the Déné Nation of the Northwest Territories was adopted by the General Assembly of the Indian Brotherhood and Métis Association of the North West Territories at Fort Simpson in July, 1975, and thence communicated to the United Nations. (These territories do not have provincial status; they are subject to the Federal government and 'Indian Affairs'; their 'government' in the territory is dominated by a white minority.) The Declaration was also published in *The Canadian Forum* (November, 1976). Perhaps needless to say, the policy of the Federal government in regard to land settlements (and the pipelines and oil exploration they are holding up) is to offer seemingly large settlements

Item 25: The Dene Declaration

We the Dene of the [North West Territories] insist on the right to be regarded by ourselves and the world as a nation.

Our struggle is for the recognition of the Dene Nation by the Government and people of Canada and the peoples and governments of the world.

As once Europe was the exclusive homeland of the European peoples, Africa the exclusive homeland of the African peoples, the New World, North and South America, was the exclusive homeland of Aboriginal peoples of the New World, the Amerindian and Inuit.

The New World like other parts of the world has suffered the experience of colonialism and imperialism. Other peoples have occupied the land—often with force—and foreign governments have imposed themselves on our people. Ancient civilizations and ways of life have been destroyed.

Colonialism and imperialism is now dead or dying. Recent years have witnessed the birth of new nations or rebirth of old nations out of the ashes of colonialism.

As Europe is the place where you will find European countries with European governments for European peoples, now also you will find in Africa and Asia the existence of African and Asian countries with African and Asian governments for the African and Asian peoples.

The African and Asian peoples—the peoples of the Third World—have fought for and won the right to self-determination, the right to recognition as distinct peoples and the recognition of themselves as nations.

But in the New World the native peoples have not fared so well. Even in countries in South America where the Native peoples are the vast majority of the population there is not one country which has an Amerindian government for the Amerindian peoples.

Nowhere in the New World have the Native peoples won the right to self-determination and the right to recognition by the world as a distinct people and as Nations.

While the Native people of Canada are a minority in their homeland, the Native people of the [North West Territories], the Dene and the Inuit, are a majority of the population of the NWT.

The Dene find themselves as part of a country. That country is Canada. But the government of Canada is not the government of the Dene. The government of the NWT is not the government of the Dene. These governments were not the choice of the Dene, these were imposed upon the Dene.

What we the Dene are struggling for is the recognition of the Dene Nation by the governments and peoples of the world.

And while there are realities we are forced to submit to, such as the existence of a country called Canada, we insist on the right to self-determination as a distinct people and the recognition of the Dene Nation.

We the Dene are part of the Fourth World. And as the peoples and Nations of the world have come to recognize the existence and rights of those peoples who make up the Third World the day must come and will come when the nations of the Fourth World will come to be recognized and respected. The challenge to the Dene and the world is to find the way for the recognition of the Dene Nation.

Our plea to the world is to help us in our struggle to find a place in the world community where we can exercise our right to self-determination as a distinct people and as a nation.

What we seek then is independence and self-determination within the country of Canada. This is what we mean when we call for a just land settlement for the Dene Nation.

---

in bits and pieces for parts and parcels in different areas—the predictable divide-and-rule.

Others also fight for popular sovereignty and self-direction in Canada. A B.C. labor leader, Jess Succamore, recently said that the support the United Steelworkers of America gave to anti-Canadian trade legislation in the state of New York is likely to contribute to unemployment in Canada. Passed by the State Assembly, the legislation prohibiting the import of foreign steel was vetoed July 13, 1979, by Governor Carey. Canadian trade officials, however, expect that the bill will be revived. Says Succamore, national secretary-treasurer of the Canadian Association of Industrial, Mechanical and Allied Workers: 'Once again, this so-called international union [the Steelworkers] has taken a position reflecting its role as an American nationalist union that treats its Canadian members in a purely colonial manner' (*Vancouver Sun,* July 30, 1979).

Such 'external' interference is serious enough. Other independent Canadian industrial unions face 'redbaiting' and anti-democratic attacks from within the labor movement in Canada itself.

PART TWO

Ideological

The Imaginary

In the 1950s, a conservative and Freudian French psychoanalyst named Jacques Lacan developed an interpretation of certain relationships concerning the 'self' and the 'other.' He based his psychoanalytical interpretation mainly on Freud's discussions of the *'ego'* (the 'I' and/or the 'me'), the *'ideal ego'* (the 'I' or 'me' of another person we may wish to emulate), and the *'body image'* (the image we have of our selves in our imaginations, as if we stood before what has been called the 'mirror of the mind').

Following in important respects the work of the leading French existentialist, Jean-Paul Sartre, and twentieth-century interpretations of the German idealist philosopher, G.W.F. Hegel, Lacan began talking about an individualistic and competitive relationship between 'self' and 'other,' a relationship he called 'Imaginary.'

I came to know about this interpretation in the mid-1960s when I translated and commented on some of Lacan's work (in *The Language of the Self,* 1968). In a later book of essays (*System and Structure,* 1972), I analyzed Lacan's individualistic and male-imperialist perspective from the standpoint of the ecology of communication in society. This critique cannot be gone into here, nor is it really necessary to do so. I mention this background for three reasons. First, Lacan deserves the credit for drawing our attention to this kind of relationship between human beings in society. Secondly, my use of the concept of Imaginary relations is not derived from the same sources as Lacan's.

Thirdly, and most importantly, although the *term* comes most immediately from a psychoanalytical perspective—a perspective which is demonstrably inadequate for the understanding of society, and one which has rarely failed to support the status quo—the *relationships* it refers to are primarily social and economic relations, rather than 'psychoanalytical' ones. Indeed, if we now look back at the social and economic analysis of capitalism in the work of Marx, for example, we find that much of his discussion of the effects of alienation under the power of modern capital is, in retrospect, a discussion of Imaginary relations (notably his analysis of what he called 'the fetishism of commodities').

The argument of the next three chapters is based on a way of perceiving and analyzing social relations which is not yet taught or discussed in very many schools. Depending on your interests, therefore, you may wish to skim through these chapters on a first reading in order to get an idea of the approach and the direction, and then pick up the rest of the argument beginning in Chapter Eight. Chapters Eight to Ten return to more of the specifics of the Canadian situation: to our hidden history and to the nature of our economy. Chapters Eleven to Thirteen analyze the dictatorial nature of government in Canada: the tyranny of the executive power in our kind of democracy. Chapter Fourteen considers the relation between our future and our past. You may then find it useful to come back and reconsider the next three chapters.[1]

---

[1]As Marcel Rioux has pertinently pointed out in his preface to the earlier and shorter version of this text, *Le Canada imaginaire,* the critique of the alienating role of the Imaginary in capitalist social relations is not to be confused with the positive function, in human affairs, of real images and real imagination.

CHAPTER FIVE

Stereotypes and Scapegoating

The analysis of Imaginary relations in Canadian society requires us to be concerned with two basic questions. One is the distinction between Imaginary relationships and real ones. This distinction exposes to analysis the real contradictions between our Imaginary view of society, at one level, and its real characteristics, at another level. The second question concerns the contradictions and inconsistencies within the Imaginary viewpoint itself. These are primarily logical contradictions and misplaced oppositions.

Especially in the colonies, the Imaginary presently dominates our understanding of social and economic relationships. This means that we do not primarily perceive and understand our relationships to the many different kinds of people in Canadian society on the basis of real images and real concepts. Rather we depend on Imaginary images and Imaginary concepts. These are in effect socially defined and accepted fantasies which are commonly assumed to be real.

In the process, society induces us to stereotype other people and to turn different groups of Canadians into scapegoats for our fears and frustrations. 'Other people' may thus be turned by dominant social and economic values into '*the others*,' that is to say, into Imaginary *others*, or stereotypes, who can conveniently be blamed for practically anything the dominant groups in Canadian society want to blame them for.

This scapegoating is always a powerful weapon of oppression and confusion in the colonies, but it is not of course confined to such countries.

The Imaginary is a weapon used in the subjugation of women, for example. One type of Imaginary image has long been used against them. Consider the Imaginary person created by Hollywood in the Marilyn Monroe of *Gentlemen Prefer Blondes* (1953), for instance. She was one of the most prominent victims of the social coercion which, beside all else, has periodically obliged women to appear in public wearing Imaginary faces.

Selves and others

Imaginary relationships imposed over real social relations are thus constructed out of images, imaginings, and fantasies—images of the 'self,' images of the 'other.' But they are ordinarily constructed in such an unrecognized or unconscious way that we are easily induced by the real social and economic alienation we experience (in many different ways) to believe these Imaginary relations to be real, and hence to go on treating them as if they actually were. Indeed, alienation as we experience it at work, in school, in the family, in personal relations, and in the madhouse is always dominated by an Imaginary interpretation of our real relations.

The dominance of the Imaginary over our actual social and economic relations in our kind of society is a collectively experienced and collectively supported system of mirages. This collective experience leads to apparently individual and apparently psychological behavior (behavior seeming to have its main source in individuals or in 'human nature'). In fact, this behavior has its primary source in social and economic relations. The reason that it may appear 'inherent' in the 'individual' is simply that this behavior is characteristic of the social and economic *system* which brings us up to behave as we actually do.

This is not to say that we all behave in precisely the same ways, because we do not. But it is to say that all of us are constrained by society to behave within certain *limits*, and that these limits or *constraints* are defined by society, not by individuals.

In other words: within the general constraints of the dominant values of our society; within the constraints of the socially and economically enforced hierarchies of class, race, and sex; and within the limits of what is believed to be 'normal' behavior in our system; we can do what these limits permit us to do (hence the diversity of individual behavior). But we cannot ordinarily do what the limits (the constraints) do *not* permit us to do, without running into social and economic and political sanctions which, at the very least, can make life extremely uncomfortable for us. (Hence the overall similarities of the *patterns* of individual behavior, the patterns which can be detected, at deeper levels, within the diversity of our individual actions.)

If the dominant values and constraints of our socioeconomic system were different, then our range and type of social behavior would be different also, and, within the biological constraints of our physical make-up, we individuals would be different too.

When our dominant social relations induce us to accept the Imaginary as the value-system which constrains the type and extent of our 'freedom of action' (relative to the social whole), the Imaginary sets the stage for specific kinds of alienated social behavior. This behavior includes the social (and ideological) processes of Imaginary projection, identification, objectification, and opposition.

Imaginary *projection* is a social and ideological process associated with paranoia (personal and/or collective feelings of persecution), as well as with stereotyping and scapegoating. Projection in this sense is the process by which we are induced, by the combination of apparent personal experience and social norms, to select a particular *other* or a group of *others* as the supposed source of the alienation we feel, and to blame these *others* for our alienated feelings. These *others* are most often groups of people who are defined by society as subordinate in the various socioeconomic hierarchies (non-whites, women, workers, children, and so on). These *others* are people who cannot possibly be responsible for our situation, and yet by Imaginary projection, we make them so. We project onto them our unrecognized desires, our unrecognized alienation, and our unrecognized behavior. This kind of projection is an act of violence against other human beings; and in consequence, it has its almost automatic complement: the fear of retaliation. Thus we make the *others* responsible for aspects of our selves and our behavior that we cannot for some reason bear to recognize; and what we fear in them is what we fear about ourselves.

Such paranoid behavior always has its source in violence. We experience our alienation by the social system as various forms of violence against our own persons. We proceed to look for someone or some group that may be 'safely' blamed, and then we project the violence we have experienced onto them. By blaming *others* in this way, we participate in the social manipulations of divide-and-rule.

Whatever our supposed intentions, most of us have been induced to believe that if only the *others* would stop doing whatever it is we have been persuaded to believe that they are doing, then our own alienation would disappear. We would at last be safe and secure in the selves that our social relations have induced us to construct. But those very selves, our Imaginary selves, are dependent for many of their characteristics on the paranoid relationship of opposition to the *others* ('I'm *not* like *them*'); and this is where Imaginary identifications come in to complement Imaginary projections.

Imaginary *identification* is the process by which we identify the image of our 'self' with the image of the *other* (positive identification); or else we identify our 'self-image' in *opposition* to the *other* (negative identification). In both cases, we are defining the *image* of the *other* (as distinct from the reality of the *other*) as essential to the image of our self.

This is true whether the *other* is viewed as positively essential to our image, or as a negative threat to that image. Both of these aspects of the social process of Imaginary identification will ordinarily turn out to involve the same practical effects, because in the Imaginary both will be operating—usually in contradictory ways—at the very same time.

(These relationships, as well as the distinction between particular others and dominant Others, are taken up in more detail in Chapters Six and Seven.)

In human terms, *objectification* is a way of closing one's 'self' off from the *other*, a way of trying to maintain a radical separation between self and *other*. It is a way of basing a social relation on the attempted denial or rejection of relationship itself. The *other* becomes the *alien,* the thing—'beyond the pale,' 'outside the Law,' 'on the wrong side of the tracks,' 'beyond freedom and dignity.' The objectification of the *other* thus serves both personally and collectively as a defense against our actual relation to the *other*; as an (illusory) protection against recognizing our collusion in the oppression of the *other*; and as a persistent reaffirmation of the 'group-self' *we,* and the individualized *'I,'* both defined in opposition to *them.*

The Imaginary *other*, the *other* we exploit and oppress actively (by what we say and do) or passively (by what we do not say and do), may also be translated by our own social and economic alienation into an Imaginary Other, into the worst image of all our strangled hopes and distorted fears (Chapter Six).

An Imaginary relationship is thus dependent on the collective and individual projection of image into image, on the identification of image with image, on the opposition of image against image, and on the objectification of images (and therefore other human beings)—and all this pathological behavior takes place as if in a single dimension, at a single level, and without a real context whose recognition would bring the whole insane business to an immediate end.

Imaginary Images

An Imaginary image is not the same as a real one. Nor does an Imaginary image have to be communicated in the visual and painted sense of the term 'image.' Imaginary images are also expressed in speech and print and tone and gesture.

Some of the commonest Imaginary images of other people are those produced by war propaganda. These include the images produced and reproduced by the warfare of the dominant groups against the subordinates under modern capitalism. Such propaganda is designed to create hatred, and thence to use this hatred as a deadly weapon against whoever has been defined as 'the enemy' in a particular situation. The dominant thus hold a pistol to the head of the *other*, for the 'final solution' to the '*other* problem' is always some form of genocide.

Apart from the stereotyping of women, peasants, and workers, probably the commonest stereotype in the Anglo-European tradition is the Imaginary image of the Jew. One version of this image is the Fagin of Dickens' *Oliver Twist* (serialized 1837-39). Along with 'lower-class' criminals and prostitutes, Fagin is described as 'the vilest evil' by Dickens. A more recent example of this image of Fagin—the alien, non-white, 'medieval Jew'—is the Fagin portrayed by Alec Guiness, wearing a grotesquely artificial nose and repeatedly slipping in and out of his 'Jewish accent,' in the film *Oliver Twist* (1948). This English film by David Lean is a stunning example of the combination of sight, sound, and sense in the *film noir*. However, one naturally wonders why Lean, a magnificent artist, should have chosen to make this particular film so soon after the Holocaust of 1933-45. I remember the effect of this film on me. I have since wondered whether Lean's choice of this image of the Jew, 'intentional' or not, had any connection with the underground warfare being waged by the Jews against the British in Palestine at that time.

Relatively more common examples of the violence of the Imaginary in Canada today—not to mention the television series 'Charlie's Angels,' 'Fantasy Island,' and their ilk—are the images of French Canada, third-world immigrants, and the native Canadians as they are projected by the media, both in and out of school, to the non-Québécois and the non-native Canadian majority. These Imaginary images (e.g. *Riel!* by the CBC and General Motors of Canada, 1979) do not originate in the media as such, however: they originate in society. The various media—in which we have to include the schools, the family, and the history books—simply use for their own and others' purposes, the *expression*, in Imaginary terms, of real social and economic conflicts.

Consider the so-called 'battle of the sexes,' for example. This 'battle' is wholly Imaginary.[1] But the domination exercised by men over women—as well as the resulting conflict—is all too real.

Similarly, the male paranoia about women is Imaginary, whereas the feeling women have that male domination is based on the wholesale persecution of their sex is supported by fact.

---

[1]The 'battle of the sexes' is Imaginary because this expression disavows the social and economic reality of male domination in our society. The implication

Racism and Responsibility

Imaginary relationships extend from images considered valid by the dominant in society as a whole to equally Imaginary images constructed by individuals on the basis of what are believed to be real personal experiences. In such relationships, the Imaginary components of the stereotype, the 'other half' of an Imaginary 'self,'[2] are commonly quite complex, and usually far more difficult to recognize and understand than the Fagin example.

If we, as individuals, have been induced by our 'socialization' into participating in the many aspects of the Imaginary—in an Imaginary world more like *Star Trek* than reality—then we will unconsciously develop a *vested interest* in protecting and reproducing these our Imaginary images of 'self' and 'other.' These socially-constructed images of ours will come to appear to us to be real relationships that we cannot afford easily to give up—for the simple reason that in accepting the social construction of an Imaginary image of the *other*, we are willy-nilly involved in accepting an equivalently Imaginary image of our *self*.

Along with its other characteristics, our Imaginary self will ordinarily be constructed out of all that we believe the *others* are *not*. The Imaginary *other* will take on the characteristics of an (absolute) *not-self*—which means that any time when we discover that we, as social beings, are very much like *it*, then we are likely to feel even more uneasy and insecure

---

behind the expression is that the two sexes are like two armies drawn up on a battlefield, each sex with a 50/50 chance of winning whatever the 'battle' is about.

The 'battle of the sexes' was of course also invented by men—and given its modern 'sociobiological' rationale—"The Female of the Species is Deadlier than the Male"—by Rudyard Kipling (born in Bombay, India in 1865, Nobel Laureate in literature in 1907, died in London, England in 1936). This is the Kipling long remembered as the apostle of the 'White Man's Burden.'

[2]Note that only in the Imaginary does the 'not-I' appear to be the 'negative' or the 'opposite' of the 'I.' In the Real, the 'not-I' cannot be the 'opposite,' the 'negative,' the 'negation,' the 'symmetrical complement,' or the 'other half' of the 'I'—no more than 'nature' can be the 'opposite' or the 'negative' of 'society.' The reason is so obvious that we rarely recognize it. It is that the 'not-I' (which is a *general* relation englobing the rest of the universe) is the *environment* of the 'I' (which is a *particular* relation)—or, in a different terminology, the 'not-I' is the ground or basis of the 'I.' As the environment of the 'I,' the 'not-I' is of a level of relation which is distinct from the level of relation of the 'I.' And the 'not' is the boundary between them.

(about our 'selfness') than we were already. The Imaginary *it* which our social relations have created in the process of providing each of us with an Imaginary identity as an individual(ist) will return to us from the *others* as what we perceive to be a threat.

Item 26: Obliterating French-Canadian Nationality

It may be said that, if the French [Canadians] are not so civilized, so energetic, or so money-making a race as that by which they are surrounded, they are an amiable, a virtuous, and a contented people, possessing all the essentials of material comfort, and not to be despised or ill-used, because they seek to enjoy what they have, without emulating the spirit of accumulation, which influences their neighbours. . . .

. . . The English have already in their hands the majority of the larger masses of property in the country; they have the decided superiority of intelligence on their side. . . .

. . . Is this French Canadian nationality one which, for the good merely of that people, we ought to strive to perpetuate, even if it were possible? I know of no national distinctions marking and continuing a more hopeless inferiority. . . . It is to elevate them from that inferiority that I desire to give to the Canadians our

English character. . . .

. . . If [the Canadians] prefer remaining stationary, the greater part of them must be labourers in the employ of English capitalists. . . . It would appear that the great mass of the French Canadians are doomed, in some measure, to occupy an inferior position, and to be dependent on the English for employment. The evils of poverty and dependence would merely be aggravated in a ten-fold degree, by a spirit of jealous and resentful nationality, which would separate the working class of the community from the possessors of wealth and the employers of labour. . . .

The only power that can be effectual at once in coercing the present disaffection, and hereafter obliterating the nationality of the French Canadians, is that of a loyal and English population. . . .

Lord Durham: *Lord Durham's Report* (1839)

The Imaginary *others* in this Imaginary opposition between 'self' and 'other' are collectively regarded by the various groups of dominant 'selves' as inferior, as alien, as evil, as 'uncivilized,' as 'genetically' or 'biologically' unequal, as dangerous to 'law and order,' as 'primitive,' as 'irrational,' as 'hysterical,' as 'promiscuous,' and so on. In this way, whole groups of people, including the female majority, are stereotyped to act as scapegoats to be blamed for personal and collective problems. Note, for example, that in ordinary speech (the 'dominant discourse' in our society), there is no *male* equivalent of the epithet 'promiscuous,' even though 'promiscuity,' as defined by our society, is a predominantly male way of behaving.

When one or many *others* are being used in this way to mask the real sources of discontent, dissatisfaction, and distress in our society, then we are not likely to recognize that when we consciously and unconsciously attack these Imaginary *others*—when we blame the victims—it is in reality the other half of our Imaginary selves we are seeing in the *others* we blame or condemn.

This divisive and destructive activity, derived from alienating 'social norms,' is nowhere more obvious than in the colonies, where one group of the colonized, e.g. the Anglicized Canadian majority, project the violence they experience onto another group, more colonized than they are, e.g. the Québécois.

We may quite sincerely believe that, in expressing our Imagined 'superiority' over the *other*, or in blaming the *other*, we are responding to real characteristics of these *others*—having failed to notice that between our 'self' and the *other*, our social and economic alienation has erected a mirror, as it were, a mirror in which it is our own Imaginary reflection that we see.

It can easily be shown, for instance, and by means of a host of examples past and present, that every stereotype of supposedly 'primitive' behavior which whites attribute collectively to non-whites, partakes in its essence of this Imaginary relation. Some of the commonest adjectives applied with a generous lack of discrimination by whites to non-whites—and by Anglos to Québécois—include their stigmatization as savage, crafty, greedy, untrustworthy, ignorant, backward, superstitious, cowardly, stupid, irrational, reactionary, lazy, given to sharp practice and to supposedly childlike emotional gratification, or to too much or to too little concern for their own kind—not to mention racist[3] and violent. They also work like hell when driven.

---

[3] To attempt to correct a rather common misunderstanding of the term 'racist,' we should note that under white domination (i.e. foreign and domestic colonialism articulated in terms of race), all racism is white racism, no matter who actually expresses it. Similarly with sexism. Under male domination (e.g. slavery in the home and over the office copying machines and coffee pots, sexual

To make matters worse, some groups already defined by society as *others* will use the very same terms to attack other groups of *others*.

Yet every one of these characterizations is in reality an accurate description, not of the *others*, but of the ordinary pathologies of the collective behavior of WASPs and WASP males towards those they believe to be—or want to make—inferior (Irish or Portuguese Catholics, for example). This white collectivity includes people who actually teach, encourage, and perpetrate violence, physical and otherwise, against those defined as the *others*; people who condone such activities; and people whose ignorance of the reality, or whose refusal to recognize it and its daily violence, can not excuse them of responsibility for it, in both word and deed.

Whites have had plenty of practice in such matters. After all, practically every one of the characterizations mentioned—as well as the statement that 'they breed like rabbits'—was commonly applied to the laboring poor in England throughout the nineteenth century by the upper and middle classes, but especially by the upper class, the one that believes in 'merit' supposedly attained by 'good breeding' (the 'eugenics' that they have traditionally applied to cattle, horses, and dogs). Their descendants still do the same in one way or another—as their equivalents in North America also do for those they call the 'masses,' the 'rednecks,' the 'white trash,' the unemployed, the 'welfare bums,' the workers. . . .

So widespread and interconnected are these attitudes and behaviors that one may well wonder where individual responsibility fits into the system.

The 'equal' and 'individual' responsibility invented by the capitalist revolution on its way through the seventeenth century is mostly Imaginary. In contrast, real responsibility is not an 'absolute' or 'innate' or 'individual' or 'either/or' characteristic of members of our society. Responsibility is a function of the *relative power to be responsible* in a given social and historical context. In societies such as ours, where relative power is distributed in a hierarchical fashion at various levels, relative responsibilities will be similarly distributed.

---

commoditization, objectification of the person, the exploitation of women's emotions in the name of 'love', and economic discrimination against women), all sexism is male sexism. It is the *coding* of racist values by whites, and the *coding* of sexist values by men, that makes the definitions just given valid in our kind of society. Moreover, the white expression 'black racism,' and the male expression 'female sexism,' are in reality prime examples of Imaginary projections of the actual values of the dominant onto the supposed values of the (socioeconomically) subordinate.

For example, a man at work cannot be held responsible for his exploitation on the job, for it is not within his individual power to change it. But if he brings the resulting alienation home and turns it into oppression in the family, then he is fully responsible for what he does at the family level. He is responsible because in a male-dominated society, the male is given power over wife and children. At another level, the mother is not responsible for male domination. But if she, in turn, converts this alienation into oppression of the children, then she is responsible, within the family, in so far as she, being an adult, has the power not to act in such a way. (No adult is entirely powerless in our society.) Similarly, also, with an older child who takes out on brothers and sisters the (verbal and non-verbal) violence of parents and/or teachers.

Subjects and Objects

As we become aware of the role of the Imaginary in capitalist social and economic relationships—relationships in which the dominant use Imaginary excuses to explain away real oppressions—we are faced with understanding how such mirror-like relations become socially and economically articulated as Imaginary *symmetries*[4] between the dominant and the subordinate in modern society.

A dominant-subordinate relationship is a hierarchical relationship of *levels* (levels of oppression, levels of exploitation, and so on). Such relations cannot be properly understood unless the mode of explanation one uses itself includes explicit ways of talking about the various levels of relationship which actually occur in real socioeconomic hierarchies. This is the mode of explanation being employed throughout this book.

In contrast, relationships of symmetry are very much like the relation between ourselves and our images as reflected in a mirror. There are of course differences between the self and its mirror-image, but the reflection of the 'body-image' in the mirror does not involve differences or distinctions in levels. Reflections are symmetries in which there is but a single level.

The Imaginary involves much more than a simple visual relationship,

---

[4]In the Imaginary, social action and reaction appear to be equal and opposite, as if governed by the symmetry of Newtonian mechanics. In our society, the Imaginary does indeed have these mechanistic characteristics, whereas in a different socioeconomic system it would not. In our society, the Imaginary is a mechanistic, atomistic, single-level, and closed value-system—but one that is imposed on a communicational, multi-level, and open-system (social) reality.

but the metaphor of the mirror-image is a useful one to employ in explaining it. The metaphor of the (single-level) reflection or (symmetrical) image emphasizes that so long as we are perceiving and experiencing the real context of our lives in an Imaginary way, then the real relations of 'self' and 'other,' and the real levels of relationship between people in an oppressive society, become practically impossible to sort out. Not only do we commonly fail to perceive and understand the levels of relationship in which we ourselves are actually involved, but when the Imaginary is dominant in our perceptions, we have no reliable way (no point of reference in the real context) which enables us to tell the difference between what we perceive (and do and say) and what we think we are perceiving (and doing and saying).

In the world of the Imaginary as it now dominates our understanding and our immediate behavior in this society, actual social and contextual relationships between people become individualized and atomized. The real relationship of communication between you and me (for instance) is often represented in the Imaginary as a relationship between two 'independent' atoms floating about in a social void—instead of as a relationship between two communicators dependent on a real social and historical *context* which makes our actual relationship possible. In the Imaginary, in other words, the social relation between us, full as it actually is with all kinds of information (the context of the Real), is represented as an empty space between us, an empty space just like the space that appears at first sight to exist between an object and its image in a mirror.

The Imaginary 'flattens out' and obscures the real contexts of relations between people (which are always relations of communication). As a result, many important social relations are *represented* in the Imaginary as being relations between subjects and objects. In the Imaginary, there is only one subject in the world—you (or me!)—and in this *'either/or'* relationship in the Imaginary, everyone else is simply an object floating around in your 'field of view' (or mine).

And one of these objects in the Imaginary is of course the distorted image of our own reflection in the mirror in the morning.

The Real, however, is inhabited by persons, not by people defined as subjects and objects. But every form of social and economic oppression and exploitation depends at some or several levels on objectification. The exploited person is treated as the equivalent of an object, as a thing, or as an organism considered to be a thing.

Symmetrization and Inversion

There are four basic Imaginary interpretations of inequity and inequality in modern society: the fascist, the pseudo-democratic, the liberal-idealist, and the utterly paranoid.

The fascist version recognizes that inequalities exist, but ascribes their sources to supposedly biological factors outside society as such. This is the pseudo-genetic or 'socio-biological' justification of oppression, the 'causes' of which will be said to be 'lack of ambition,' 'constitutional laziness,' 'lack of physical strength,' or 'being Canadian,' and so on.

The pseudo-democratic version of this Imaginary interpretation implies that while individual inequities and inequalities exist, collective oppression and exploitation do not. Like the fascists, the pseudo-democrats believe that 'equal opportunity' (to compete) exists. Thus, they help to maintain real oppressions.

The liberal-idealists recognize that there is '*unequal* opportunity' (to compete) in our society, but also believe that if we could just get the system working properly (without changing it significantly), then all would be well. Since they do not recognize that competition between people as it is required under capitalism is an inherently oppressive relation, nor pay much attention to what it is that people are obliged to compete for, the liberal-idealists also contribute to the maintenance of oppression.

The utterly paranoid take practically any political position you can name, including the three just outlined. They depend on various and shifting definitions of the Imaginary *others* who they believe to be the source of the persecution they experience. In general, these unfortunately misguided people believe that they are threatened by those below them on the various social scales. Their paranoia has real sources in the oppression and alienation they experience, but they fail to recognize these sources for what they are. Thus they commonly interpret their real oppression by dominating Others (e.g. business) as if it were an attack on their freedom and security by various Imaginary *others* (e.g. labor). In doing so, they come to believe that these *others* are threats from above them in the hierarchies of power. The Imaginary *others* are thus converted ideologically into Imaginary Others (Chapter Six).

When these and other Imaginary interpretations are imposed over our real social and economic relations—when they mediate those relations—the consequence is a denial, a repression, or a rejection of the actual social reality we experience.

In this way, real socioeconomic hierarchies between people and groups (levels of relation, levels of power) become ideologically deprived of the political, economic, and historical context which would allow these relationships to be perceived as they really are. (This 'loss of context,' or this 'substitution of an Imaginary context,' can of course take place only in the realm of Imaginary ideas—i.e. at the ideological level—because the real context and our real ideas about it are always there.)

The result will ordinarily be *symmetrization* or *inversion*. By symmetrization I mean the ideological and unreal 'flattening out' of a hierarchical relationship as it really exists. Along with the denial, the repression, or the rejection of the real context, the actual power relations sustaining and enforcing the hierarchy will also be ideologically 'neutralized,' as if they did not exist. People caught up in this kind of Imaginary behavior and belief will refuse to recognize the socially and economically enforced domination of men over women in our society, for example. Or they will hold that the dominant-subordinate relationship between capital and labor under state and private capitalism is 'really' a relationship of 'competition in the market.' Or they will treat a colony as if it were a nation—which it does indeed appear to be, *if you remove, invert, or symmetrize the real context made up of those who are doing the colonizing.*

Imaginary mediations which mispunctuate or misrepresent social (and natural) reality give rise to 'false consciousness'—i.e. to a form of consciousness which fails to recognize its actual situation in the real context, to a form of being and believing which depends for its short-term survival on keeping what it knows about reality unconscious and unrecognized.

As a result of this *symmetrization of levels*, distinct socioeconomic levels which *contradict* each other in the Real will commonly be perceived and acted on as if the various levels were simply in a single-level *opposition* to each other. (Man opposes woman, capital opposes labor, white opposes non-white, and so on.)

At the same time, however, these Imaginary symmetrizations will usually contain enough of a half-spoken truth about the real relationship to make the pseudo-symmetry believable. Indeed, all ideological mispunctuations and misrepresentations of real relations in our society do tell some kind of truth about some aspect of our relationships. These misrepresentations of reality are rarely outright lies—and this is part of what makes them so difficult to deal with.

Take the example of the symmetry overtly implied but covertly denied in the phrase: 'My wife and I are equals.' There is only one first-person subject in the sentence (the 'I'). The word 'my' is a possessive, which along with the word 'wife' (third person), defines the woman being spoken of as an 'equal' only in relation to her definition as an adjunct of the 'I' in the sentence. This is an 'I' which is paternalistically granting an Imaginary equality to the woman who the 'I' openly declares—when we examine the sentence in detail—that he possesses. The half-told truth here, of course, is that the commonest way in which men regard their relationship to women in our society is through possession.

The example just given shows us an Imaginary symmetrization of a real relation of domination in our society. The male speaker fails to recognize his socially-coded domination in any conscious way and yet at the very same time he confirms the domination by the words he uses. It is as if the man involved had a split personality. Each half of this personality makes exactly the same statement, but one half of it understands the message to mean 'equality,' while the other half knows that it means domination.

We all know that oppressive socioeconomic hierarchies exist all around us: whether and how we *recognize* them as they are is another matter. Practically all of us, at some level (or at several levels) are the objects of various forms of alienating domination. Heterosexual men, for example, are not oppressed or exploited on sexual grounds, but the majority of the men in any country are oppressed and exploited by other men, for they are oppressed and exploited by class and by race. In most countries, however, men are provided by society with scapegoats for the anger and frustration they feel: women.

This is male paranoia. Once the Imaginary has deprived a real hierarchical relationship of its real context, then the dominant participants in the real relationship are 'free' to substitute for it an Imaginary hierarchy. This means that once a relationship of power and control has been symmetrized in the Imaginary, then it can also be *inverted*. This is total paranoia.

Paranoia is defined as an individual form of insanity by practically every form or school of psychotherapy, from Freud to Fritz Perls. By 'individualizing' this form of behavior, the therapists cut out of their analysis the real social and historical context. (They cut out the real environment and treat the individual or the individual family as an isolated system.)

Paranoia is said to involve 'delusions of persecution' (a 'persecution complex'). What the psychotherapists generally fail to recognize is that the persecution always is (or originally was) entirely real. The 'delusions' are not delusions about the fact of being (or having been) injured and terrorized. They are delusions about *who is really responsible* for the persecution.

In other words, when we are behaving in a paranoid way, we are confused about the real source of the oppression we have suffered (and may still be suffering). As a result, we will project a distorted memory or representation of this real source, as an Imaginary image, onto any *other* we feel threatened by, no matter how unjustly. We were relatively powerless to do anything against the original aggressor—we were

---

Item 27: Woman as the Scapegoat

Diana: 'Stop selling, Max. I don't need you.'

Max: 'You need me badly—because I'm your last contact with human reality. I *love* you—and that painful, decaying love is the only thing between you and the shrieking nothingness you live the rest of the day.'

'Then don't lea...leave me.'

'It's too late, Diana. There's nothing left in you that I can live with. You're one of Howard's humanoids. And if I stay with you, I'll be destroyed. Like Howard Beale was destroyed. Like Lorreen Hobbs was destroyed. Like everything that you and the institution of television touch—is destroyed. *You're television incarnate, Diana.* Indifferent to suffering, insensitive to joy. All of life is reduced to the common rubble of banality. War, murder, death. All the same to you as bottles of beer [sic]. And the daily business of life is a corrupt comedy. You even shatter

the sensations of time and space into split seconds and instant replays [*pause*]. You're madness, Diana. Virulent madness. And everything you touch dies with you. But not me. Not as long as I can feel pleasure [*pause*] and pain [*pause*] and love.

[*Stoops over and kisses her. Heads for the door.*]

And it's a happy ending. Wayward husband comes to his senses, returns to his wife with whom he's established a long and sustaining love. Heartless young woman, left alone in her arctic desolation [*pause*]. Music, up with the swell. Final commercial. 'And here are a few scenes from next week's show.'

[*Pause. Turns to door and lifts suitcase, banging it as he opens door. Dramatic exit, complete with slammed door. Camera cuts to Diana, sitting alone.*]

—Faye Dunaway and William Holden: *Network* (1976)

children— and we are usually relatively powerless to deal with real aggressors later in life. Divide-and-rule, however, provides us with Imaginary aggressors to attack in place of the representatives of the real ones. We thus become used to making *indirect* responses to real aggressors (who have the power to hurt us), reserving our *direct* attacks for Imaginary aggressors—the *others* who have much less power and opportunity to protest against the tyranny they experience.

FIGURE 5-1: Symmetrization and Inversion

(a) Examples of presently existing, short-term power relationships between dominant and subordinate (contradictions):

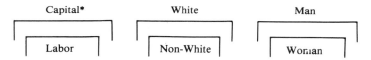

(b) Imaginary symmetrization (oppositions) in the present context:

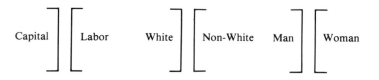

(c) Imaginary inversion of the present power relations:

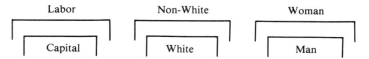

*Note that in the long-range, since labor alone can produce true wealth (use values for exchange), labor power or labor potential—human creative capacity—is ultimately dominant over capital, because it is the source of capital. The third level in the relationship between capital and labor is of course the natural environment: the organic and inorganic source of the reproduction of society over time (for the details of this argument, see the Introduction and Appendix to Wilden, 1980). The socioeconomic and other relations of race and sex are thus distinct from those between labor and capital, in the sense that no one race and no one sex is in recent evolution the source of any other.

As a result, our paranoia—our *misguided* attempts at self-defense—will generally be expressed in a projection through which we not only 'flatten out' a real hierarchy, in one breath (thus making the victim the Imaginary equal of the oppressor), but in the next, we turn the hierarchy upside-down. Thus we fall into the further Imaginary fiction that it is the socially and economically subordinate who are 'really' dominant after all (*Figure 5-1*)—and therefore 'really' responsible for the mess we are in.

As a final example, consider the way in which business and government (the dominant) consistently manipulate the consciousness of non-unionized workers (as well as the unpaid domestic laborers still called housewives) to make them believe that the biggest threat to them comes from the unions, when in fact the unions are subordinated to business and to government in our society. Consider next the way in which business, which is presently dominant over both government and labor, likes to encourage the fiction that the biggest threat to our security and our pocketbooks, when it is not 'Big Labor,' is 'Big Government.' The use of the adjective 'big' to refer to two distinct levels of power (labor and government) is a symmetrization which becomes complete, in the Imaginary, the moment that we use the expression 'Big Business.'

Two Notes to Chapter Five

How We Lost It At The Movies

As Pierre Berton's *Hollywood's Canada* (1975) makes plain, Hollywood has made many contributions to Imaginary racial and sexual stereotypes of Canadians. For example, the stereotypes called the 'wooden Indian,' the 'murderous savage,' the 'happy-go-lucky' or 'treacherous' French-Canadian guide, the 'dangerous squaw,' the 'passionate' French-Canadian 'spitfire' ('the little witch!'), and the 'evil' or 'drunken' or 'bestial' Métis, the 'degenerate half-breed' (in reference to Métis with French-Canadian parentage, not to those of British or European provenance).

This is not all. You may at some time have wondered why so many American movie scripts casually mention 'Montreal' or 'Toronto' or 'Saskatchewan,' and the like. This is the result of Hollywood's notorious 'Canadian Cooperation Project' (sic). In the late 1940s, when it appeared essential for Canada to impose quotas on the flood of imported American films, the possibilities of developing an effective Canadian film industry were quickly snuffed out by this nefarious 'bargain' made between Canada and Hollywood.

The 'bargain' was struck by U.S. film industry lobbyists with representatives of the Canadian government of Louis St. Laurent, the Canadian Broadcasting Corporation, and Canadian business. The Canadian principals included the American-born C.D. Howe, Minister of Trade and Commerce of the Liberal government; Lester B. Pearson, Secretary of State for External Affairs; Ernest Bushnell of the CBC; and Donald Gordon, Deputy Governor of the Bank of Canada.

The details can be found in Berton's book. This essentially economic blackmail resulted in our (executive) leaders trading practically our entire film industry in exchange for 'Canadian references' in American films, references that would supposedly serve 'to attract tourists to Canada.' We then sent a man to Hollywood whose life work was to persuade Hollywood film makers to insert such quaint references into their scripts.

To the Americans, an early 'cornerstone' of the Project was *Canadian Pacific* (1949), called a second-rate western by American film critics, starring Randolph Scott and Jane Wyatt. Scott had previously played a Canadian naval hero in *Corvette K-225* (1943), with Andy Devine and Barry Fitzgerald as his chief crewmen.

There was one dissenter, the sole Canadian government official who knew the film business, Ross McLean, Commissioner of the National Film Board. Hollywood objected. Gordon wrote to C.D. Howe; Howe wrote the Liberal minister, J.J. McCann; McLean was frozen out.

'Who controls the box office, controls the industry.'
    —*Adolph Zukor, Pres., Famous Players and Paramount (1923)*

In an article in *Heresies* (1977), Ardele Lister provides the following information about film distribution in Canada.

'1. The Canadian film audience pays over 200 million dollars annually to Famous Players and Odeon, both foreign-owned conglomerates (Famous is 51% owned by Gulf and Western, which also owns Paramount Pictures; Odeon is now owned by Rank, a British conglomerate concentrating on U.S. film production. Rank was originally 51% owned by Famous Players' Nathanson.) None of this money is taxed to leave any percentage in Canada to build the Canadian film industry; and there is no stipulation that requires Canadian films to be seen in Canadian theatres.

'2. Famous Players and Odeon control over 80% of urban Canadian theatres and openly indulge in practices such as tie-on bookings (made illegal in the U.S. in 1948 under the U.S. Antitrust laws).... In order to exhibit a moneymaking film like *Jaws,* theatres must agree to exhibit a string of mediocre American films.... As a result, neither mediocre Canadian films nor excellent Canadian films qualify for exhibition.

'3. In 1963 Canada was the sixth most important buyer of American films. By 1975 Canada...[was] the biggest buyer of American films outside the U.S.

'4. 94% of film rentals in Canada goes to the seven major U.S. distributors. With as little as a 5% cost-of-doing-business tax *in* Canada, 10 million dollars could be fed yearly into the impoverished local film industry. The Canadian government, afraid to be 'unfriendly,' refuses to legislate.

'5. United Nations statistics suggest that an industrialized nation should be able to produce a feature film per million population per year. Canada, with a population of 24 million, produces roughly five features a year.'

THE BRITISH DO THEIR BIT

One of the films most revealing of the 'Canadian situation' is the technically excellent English film *The Forty-Ninth Parallel* (retitled *The Invaders* for the U.S. market). A wartime film starring Laurence Olivier, Leslie Howard, Raymond Massey and introducing Glynis Johns, it was described by a British reviewer in 1941 as 'one of the best made films ever produced in [England],' although the traditional Canadian actor, the landscape, is played by Canada itself.

The intricate plot concerns the fate of six Nazi survivors of a U-Boat which is blasted to bits by 'Canadian Coastal Command' while stupidly sitting around on the surface of Hudson Bay—called the Gulf of St. Lawrence in a 1974 English review (Manvell, 1974). The Nazis spend a lot of time spitting—on Canada and Churchill, Manitoba, for instance—and shouting 'Heil Hitler' in upper-class English accents.

Laurence Olivier in a lumberjack shirt is 'Johnnie,' the 'happy-go-lucky' and musical 'French-Canadian trapper,' complete with bible and rosary and a million close relatives in Quebec. As a 'free' French Canadian, he refuses to believe that Quebec should go to war for France or England—until the Nazis shoot him. This first reel unwinds at what appears to be Fort York, Manitoba. The Hudson's Bay Company is represented by the veteran Scottish actor, Finlay Currie. His 'houseboy,' 'Nick the Eskimo,' wears his parka while doing the dishes. Nick is the first to die, when one of the Nazi seamen smashes his head in with a rifle butt.

The Nazi survivors then turn their guns on the Eskimo village, and steal a 'Canadian Airways' floatplane. They hope to reach the American border, because the U.S. is still neutral territory. The plane runs out of gas, whereupon Eric Portman, playing Leutnant Kirth, the 'Nazi fanatic,' curses the hapless German pilot all the way down until they hit the water with a stupendous splash.

The four remaining survivors then stumble on a German-Canadian Hutterite community, apparently composed of refugees from Naziism, and said to be 'one of the many foreign settlements in Canada.' Anton Walbrook plays Peter (referred to as 'Our Leader')—with a German accent—and Glynis Johns makes the beds and draws the water—with an English accent.

At a community meeting, Eric Portman launches into a Nazi rant on the subject of German blood-ties and 'the deepest of racial instincts' uniting the 'nordic' or 'Aryan' race. He gets called a 'microbe' for his pains. His raving is in effect a Nazi version of the Anglo-American caricature of Québécois nationalism. (For instance, there are no 'nations' fighting Germany, only 'the democracies.') This episode tells us how to distinguish the 'good Germans' in the movie from the 'bad' ones—by means of the same racist logic used by Anglos and their allies to distinguish 'good French Canadians' from 'bad Québécois nationalists.' At this point, one of the seamen (Niall McGinnis), who used to be a baker—but with an English accent superior to Portman's— tries to join the Hutterites, and is executed for treason, on Portman's order.

The three remaining Nazis reach Winnipeg, where everyone is reading of their exploits in the *Winnipeg Free Press.* What Portman calls the 'New Order's wind from the East' seems to be blowing pretty strongly at this stage in the plot: the Nazis head for Regina, Moose Jaw, Swift Current and points West. Courtesy of Canadian Pacific and the scenic route, they arrive in Banff National Park where it happens to be 'Indian Day.' But the Mounties have tracked them the thousands of miles to this very spot and, with the help of a wise old Indian Chief in full regalia, they finally get one of their men.

The other two stumble through the woods until they come upon Leslie Howard fishing from a canoe in a Rocky Mountain lake. The credits list him as a Canadian named Philip Armstrong Scott (British reviewers treat him as an English character). Scott is the author of *Red Men in the Rockies,* and 'rather likes pigging it occasionally.' In his 'humble teepee,' he keeps an original Picasso, a Matisse, a pipe, and Thomas Mann's *Magic Mountain* (in German). 'Wars may come and go,' he announces, 'but Art goes on forever.'

Scott entertains the two by reading from his manuscript about supposedly 'cowardly' and 'malicious' 'Blackfoot tribal customs,' noting the 'similarity' between these so-called 'savages' and 'a certain modern European tribe,' alias the Nazis. The Nazis get upset. Portman impugns Howard's masculinity by calling him a coward; the other one grabs a revolver. 'Hands up!' Howard puts his hands in his pockets and, in a classic English put-down, berates the two for their arrogance, their stupidity, and—above all—for their 'bad manners.'

The Nazis respond by burning his books, manuscript, and paintings, which has the effect of transforming this 'effete English(-Canadian) intellectual' into a man of action. Surrounded by his frightened Canadian employees and the cook ('George the Indian'), this 'spirited amateur' wonders aloud whether 11 million Canadians are capable of stopping the two dedicated Nazis left on Canadian soil. In a burst of absurd heroics, he walks straight into the revolver shots of one of the fleeing Nazis, gets hit in the leg, but still manages to disarm the Nazi and beat him up (offstage). 'Gee, the Boss has knocked him cold,' says one of his men. 'It was a fair fight,' says Leslie Howard, 'One armed superman against one unarmed, decadent democrat!'

Leutnant Kirth somehow ends up in a boxcar headed for the U.S. via Niagara Falls, where he meets Raymond Massey. (Massey's older brother, Vincent, became the first Canadian-born Governor General in 1959. The younger scion of the tractor people made his theatrical debut in Siberia, entertaining Canadian troops in Russia in 1919.) Massey gives a marvellous rendition of an AWOL Canadian soldier named Andy Brock. Andy drinks wine 'with a kick like a mule' made from grapes grown on his own little farm in southern Ontario. He extols the virtues of Canadian 'democracy,' using quaint expressions like 'my Royal Canadian foot!' Massey finally proves that it takes just one Canadian to stop Eric Portman—with a little help from the Americans at the border—and the film ends with his fist crashing into the German's face.

The fine photography and location shooting is by Freddie Young; the original screenplay is by Emeric Pressburger, a protegé of Alexander

Korda. The striking musical score is the work of Ralph Vaughan Williams (his first for a film), played by the London Symphony Orchestra conducted by Muir Matheson. The director, Michael Powell, got the idea for the film ('to help bring the U.S.A. into the war') from the wartime Ministry of Information in London. It was financed by a £500,000 grant from the British psychological warfare budget, and is said to have grossed some two million pounds in the U.S., where it belongs to Columbia Pictures Corporation. The masterful editing is by David Lean, later director of *Oliver Twist* (1948) and *Lawrence of Arabia* (1962).

The Forty-Ninth Parallel is an upper-class English version of a 1930s Hollywood movie about Canada, with English style ideological manipulations. A British reviewer in 1941 says that 'the film throughout shows signs of the most careful scripting from the propaganda point of view, and each episode may be said to be conceived as a positive answer to questions arising from insinuations regarding the democratic standpoint.' Writing in 1974, Roger Manvell, a British critic, tells us that 'the film did not make the fatal mistake of caricaturing the enemy, after the style of the old Russian "typage" of the capitalist and tsarist villains.' The 1979-80 edition of *TV Movies,* edited by Leonard Maltin and published by Signet in New York, describes it this way: 'Taut WW2 yarn of Nazi servicemen seeking to reach Canadian land when their U-boat is sunk; top-notch cast; admirably played for suspense and characterizations.'[5]

⁵For a more nineteenth-century English view—of murder amidst the 'evil-looking French-Canadian peasantry'—see the Sherlock Holmes tale, *The Scarlet Claw* (1944). With English aristocracy, judiciary, and functionaries, an anglicized petite bourgeoisie, a Scots police force, and bearded *Voyageurs,* the film celebrates Canada as the 'linchpin' between the 'two great branches' of the Anglo Saxon 'race.' (The linchpin quotation comes from Churchill; Field Marshal Montgomery called us 'the golden hinge.')

CHAPTER SIX

Dominance and Domination

Finding the Exit

The symmetrization of distinct levels of relation in society is characteristic of the dominant ideology under capitalism (state and private). It is of course always part of the oppressor's armory in relations of colonization. Symmetrization is used by the oppressor as a way of covering up or denying that a real relation of oppression actually exists; and this it accomplishes by means of a verbal smokescreen which at first appears to be a perfectly logical way of discussing the relationship in question. In reality, however, symmetrization is neither a logical operation (except for certain kinds of philosophers, who use it all the time), nor an adequate description of a real relation. It is an ideological device or tactic which succeeds in introducing such a muddle into the understanding of oppression by the oppressed that so long as the oppressed person accepts a symmetrized definition of her or his situation, there is absolutely no way out of the Imaginary trap in which he or she is caught.

We are taught in the home and in school to accept this illogical and unreal way of talking about our relationships with other people—and as a result, we learn at the same time to use it against ourselves. Jean-Paul Sartre, for one, accomplished precisely this in his play *No Exit*. The play depicts an interminable and circular conversation between a man and two women (the 'eternal triangle'), in a room to which they have been assigned after death. The major point of the play comes out in a single line which was much quoted by the 'intelligentsia' in the 1950s and 1960s (to whom such absurdities rarely fail to appeal): 'Hell is other people.'

If you take this Imaginary statement seriously, you will find that it succeeds very well in symmetrizing every possible kind of oppression in our society. It individualizes and atomizes the actual structure of our social and economic relations in such a way that all one can say as a result about any kind of oppression in our society is that 'everyone oppresses everyone else.' You can well imagine how positively delighted the real oppressors under capitalism must surely feel whenever they hear this kind of nonsense from the people they are exploiting. This is divide-and-rule with a vengeance. Wherever this kind of brainwashing abounds (as it does in our schools and universities), everyone is actively collaborating in their own oppression, as well as in the oppression of others over whom they have power. The people, in other words, are becoming their own thought-police. Moreover, if 'everyone oppresses everyone else,' then no one has any place to stand against oppression.

We know that real oppression and exploitation depend for their basis on *levels of power*, not on individuals being nasty to other individuals; and that these hierarchies of relative power entail in their turn *levels of responsibility* for oppression and exploitation. (Responsibility for one's actions is a function of the relative power one has to be responsible for them, power in relation to other people.)

What Imaginary statements like 'Hell is other people' actually accomplish, then, is to imply that oppression is individual, that everyone is equally oppressed, that everyone has equal power to oppress other people, that responsibility for oppression is also equal and individual, that everyone is to blame for everything (especially the victims), and, indeed, that the whole silly business is simply too absurd....

'Hell is other people' thus treats social relations as if they existed in one single dimension, as if society were composed of individual(istic) and independent atoms, and as if there were no historical and present context through which to understand what is actually happening. In reality, however, this statement is a symptom of the divisive oppression and alienation under which we live. It is not a statement about real relations or real people; it is a statement about the Imaginary. And so it should be, because it is one of the sentences in the Imaginary language (the Imaginary discourse) employed by the dominant ideology—the dominant system of values—under capitalism.

Sartre was quite right in entitling his play *No Exit* (*Huis clos*). He was right because if you agree to communicate in the discourse or code of communication imposed on you by the oppressor under capitalism, you will find yourself wrapped up in an Imaginary cocoon, paranoid as hell, and with no chance of getting out.

How *do* we get out, then? I don't know where we Canadians may end up in our struggle against colonial oppression, but I can propose that one of the first steps is to learn how to tell the difference between Imaginary relations—doubly Imaginary in the colonies—and real relations.

The way out of the labyrinth which entraps us in the Imaginary is to learn to recognize Imaginary patterns in Imaginary *messages* so that we can come to understand the basic patterns that produce the details in the messages. These patterns hold the keys that can open up the Imaginary *codes*; and once you hold the key to any such code, you can use the key to get outside the code and go beyond it.

In more everyday terms, this process of learning how to distinguish the codes from the messages—and thereby being able to counterattack against the oppressor at a level and on a ground with which he is not consciously familiar—is part of the pathway to political consciousness, to guerrilla consciousness.

Dominant Others—Dominating Others

One common relationship coded by the Imaginary in an oppressive society such as ours, is the way in which subordinates may be induced to play out Imaginary roles in a real relation to a dominant Other. Dominance does not necessarily mean alienation or oppression (as is explained below), but in our society it most often does. Amongst other subordinates, political dissenters in particular may come to play out Imaginary roles in the relation to the Other. What may often happen is that the dissenters become trapped, not in a real conflict or contradiction with the Other, but in a single-level and Imaginary opposition to what they dissent *against*—in this case usually an *alienating Other*, a very real Other, that represents or 'stands for' a real locus of real violence and oppression in the socioeconomic system.

This Other is not necessarily a person or persons, although persons will always be associated with it. The alienating Other may be a particular pattern in the socioeconomic hierarchy; it may be an institution or one or all of the media. The alienating Other may be represented by a whole pile of dishes and diapers to wash; or by an addictive drug such as nicotine or alcohol; or by a pile of reports to type, files to file, memos asking to be administered to, academic claptrap busy claptrapping, mail waiting to be sorted, people lining up impatient to be waited on. In the world of the most alienated form of labor, the oppressive Other will be represented by a machine, a production line, a whole factory—thudding and roaring and clanking and beeping away in its insatiable demand for human beings, for its daily diet of alienated human creativity.

The Other, alienating and not, may also be a person or persons, or an entire social group. It may also be the environment of the particular system or subsystem we are in.

To clarify the relationship being outlined, let us begin with a general statement about the Other and its position of dominance. The Other involves a level of relationship in society that is distinct from the level of relationship between 'self' and 'other.' The Other mediates the relation between 'self and 'other' (*Figure 6-1*).

Note that in the way of diagramming mediation used in *Figure 6-1,* the Other operates at the mediating level of the code, whereas 'self' and 'other' exist, in relation to the Other, at the level of the messages in the system. Perhaps needless to say, there are in our society many such code/message relations, many distinct subsystems at different levels in the overall economic system. (The Other might be represented by the 'Great White Father,' for example.) The Imaginary, however, projects a 'flattened' image of these multilevel and hierarchical relations. In the Imaginary, the Other *represents itself as*, and *appears to be*, just one more 'particular other': 'self'—'Other'—'other.'

FIGURE 6-1: *Self and Other*

Locus of Mediation by Others
(Coding Level)

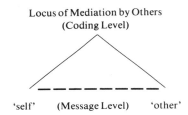

'self'   (Message Level)   'other'

In daily life, dominant and dominating Others will have their *representatives* amongst particular others. People who are white, for example, are representative of the mediation of white domination in relations of race, even though in their personal characteristics they may not behave in a consciously or overtly dominating way. Similarly, anyone who is male is representative of the mediation of social relations by male domination. And anyone who was brought up in, or who has migrated into, the professional, the managerial, or what is called the 'upper' class, will be representative, for others, of dominating mediation through the medium of class. It is only through properly political awareness, and therefore through the properly sensitive behavior that such awareness must bring with it, that we can make what we represent subordinate to who we have also become.

Nevertheless, we must be careful to distinguish between dominant Others who are necessarily oppressive Others, and dominant Others whose dominance in specific areas is humanly and socially useful so long as they do not abuse it. This may be a dominance earned through special training, a dominance delegated by a particular group, or a dominance earned by the exercise of special talents. One obvious example is the medical profession. A doctor, a midwife, or a nurse may well be dominant over a patient in matters of sickness or health, but as long as they know what they are doing and do not abuse their expertise, then their (earned) dominance is both welcome and useful.

We recognize the distinction between (socially-useful) *dominance* and (oppressive and alienating) *domination* in the way we distinguish between (legitimate) *authority* and (oppressive) *authoritarianism*. When people who are 'authorities' are doing the job delegated to them, when they are fulfilling the obligations and the responsibilities they have been entrusted with, when they are making their experience, their training, and their expertise available to other people who need this assistance, then we do not ordinarily regard them as 'dominant' at all. We tend to reserve the word 'dominant' for what should more properly be called 'domination.'

The fact that we often use the two terms, dominance and domination, interchangeably is an indication of the way in which our alienating society muddles up our perceptions of power, responsibility, and authority. Moreover, an alienating Other does not have to behave in an overtly authoritarian or domineering way to be (oppressively) dominating. Indeed, the passive domination of the empty-faced liberal, the inertness of the bureaucrat, the smiling inattention of the executive, the glassy-eyed stare of the person of privilege, the condescending refusal on the part of a 'superior' to recognize the existence of an 'inferior'—all these forms of domination, and many others, are usually far more difficult to deal with than the table-thumping and active engagement of people who are quite obviously authoritarian.

In the general case, the Imaginary induces us to misperceive or to mispunctuate dominance and domination in the following ways:

—We may confuse earned dominance with illegitimate domination and thus enter into an Imaginary opposition with a dominant Other;

—We may accept domination without recognizing it and thus enter into an Imaginary collusion with a dominating Other;

—We may confuse a particular other with a dominating Other and thus turn this particular other into an Imaginary Other;

—We may be induced by our socialization to confuse whole groups and classes of *others* with the real sources of our domination and alienation by real Others, and thus to turn *others* that society has designated as scapegoats into Imaginary Others;

—We may correctly perceive an Other as a dominating Other—or a particular other as representative of a dominating Other—and yet still become caught up in an Imaginary relation (positive *collusion* or negative *opposition*) with the dominating Other.

Levels of Oppression

In the kind of society we live in, most of us will ordinarily be representative, for specific groups of other people, of one or several dominating Others (whether we like it or intend it or not). Our various collective characteristics (notably class, race, and sex, but also such characteristics as national origin, education, urban or rural upbringing, and so on) will mean that most of us are representative of one or several forms of domination for other people. As R.D. Laing, for one, has put it, we all represent a number of 'others-for-others.' Although in many cases the others we represent for other people will not necessarily be significant, whenever an aspect of what we represent is the same as that associated with a particular form of oppression, then we carry with us the potential of representing a dominating Other for someone else.

As we should expect, of course, some classes of people manage to represent to other people most of the various distinct levels of alienation and oppression by Others in our society—white, Anglo-Saxon, Protestant, male-imperialist teachers or employers, for example.

The alienating relationship to the dominating Other is an inherent aspect of the capitalist order of things—indeed, the whole system is absolutely dependent on it—and it works in many ways to divide us from each other. The only class or group of people who would not directly represent *any* form of alienating domination for any others would presumably be those who carry the socially and economically defined markers for oppression in every system and subsystem—and at every level of exploitation—in their context. In North America, for example, the 'object' of all this violence could be a female and only child with only one parent (or none) from a 'deculturated' and poverty-'stricken' indigenous people living on a 'reservation' close to a sizable town—and particularly a child socially and economically coded as 'ugly.'

The non-white, female, and 'lower-class' person I refer to is a person coded by the dominant values of our society, not simply as 'unequal,' but as '*genetically* unequal,' and on three distinct levels: class, race, and sex. This person thus represents the profoundest depths of poverty in modern society: the poverty of missing alternatives. It is in the pornographic system of socio-sexual domination by males, and in the socioeconomic exploitation of the women who have been seduced into forming the emotional 'life-support systems' which keep us males on the job—it is in these two major systems of dehumanization in our society that the little girl we are writing and reading about will grow up.

She will grow up in a white-male-dominated system of oppression. Here she will not only risk her humanity, as any man of her class must do, in the commodity system which constrains us all. She will not only risk it in a racist society, as any man of her race must do. She will also risk her humanity on the male altar of sex. In other words, besides her oppression by class and race, she will also be faced with the same predominant set of conflicting and impossible choices as those faced by *any* woman of *any* race, and of *any* class, in our society: the simultaneous choice between the four basic and Imaginary 'female roles' laid out for women by the dominant value-system of our society: (Virgin) Mother, Wife, Whore, and Witch.

Imaginary Others

Real Others are dominant Others—but not necessarily dominating and exploitative Others. Both their reality and the significant characteristics of their dominance have to be ascertained by means of an analysis of the relationships they actually mediate.

In contrast, there are two basic kinds of Imaginary Others: (1) subordinate *others* who have been mysteriously elevated by social values into an Imaginary domination which they do not in reality exert; (2) really dominating, real Others, who are being viewed by the (socioeconomically) subordinate through Imaginary spectacles.

The first is exemplified by the Imaginary status commonly ascribed to women by men. The second is exemplified by the Canadian form of anti-Americanism (bourgeois nationalism). Because these two political positions persistently fail to identify the real Others correctly, and therefore fail to correspond with reality, they may both be called expressions of paranoia. (Indeed, both male imperialism and anti-American chauvinism are so riddled with Imaginary oppositions and projections, and real contradictions, that they could quite properly be classed as forms of schizophrenic relations.)

As already pointed out, Imaginary Others—(1) above—are commonly the *they*: 'the ones who are trying to take over' (women, non-whites, Québécois, unions, and so on). This is the standard Imaginary response, under our economic system, to the efforts of any subordinate social grouping which begins to demand 'fair treatment' politically and economically, or 'equal rights' (democratic rights)—or the right to be treated as the persons they are, rather than as the mere organisms, the 'inferiors,' or the things they have been made out to be.

In contrast, when the Imaginary Others stand for real Others with real power—(2) above—then they are distorted representations of the real Others who have really taken over.

The only certain way to understand when, where, and how a particular relationship is predominantly Imaginary, is to compare it with its actual sources in the Real. But that, in its turn, requires more information, more work, more resistance to social prejudice, more reflection and analysis, and a more self-critical approach than we are ordinarily accustomed to.

Women as Imaginary Others

If you get a chance to see the reruns, try watching *Zzzzz,* the *Outer Limits* one-hour teleplay (American Broadcasting Corporation, 1963-64) about men, women, and bees. This 'sociobiological' exercise in dominant social and economic values tells the tale of an attempt by the bees (women) to take over the Universe from Humanity (male... scientists), while personally seeing to the destruction of the 'jealous rivals' (wives), who are made to stand in the path of their 'evil' and 'secret' ways. In this zoological cautionary tale, all the worker bees in the hive being studied by the scientist are made to talk in a single and united voice through the scientist's so-called 'language analyzer.' The squeaky results of the 'translation' are made to sound like the voice of a midget form of the common or garden variety of (male) Alien from Outer Space.

The bees attempt their take-over of the world by sending one of their queens, in the apparently human form of a beautiful dark-haired lab technician, to seduce the (dedicated) scientist (whose marriage is childless) and thus to propagate their new kind by the millions. Her name is 'Regina.' She is young enough to be the scientist's daughter (as the script has the wife point out). Regina is presented as what men define as the 'primal Eve,' the submissively sexual playmate, the 'childlike' Temptress, the dangerous Seductress. She is also the Woman slaving behind the Man, the female threat, the future Mother, the Virgin Queen, and so on—depending on which aspect of this carefully crafted and paradoxical script you find yourself emphasizing. Indeed, in her relationship with what the script calls the 'exacting and perfect' scientist and her bees (which he thought were 'his'), she is Snow White, the House Mother, the Evil Queen, and the Wicked Witch all rolled up into one.

Moreover, as is customary in this genre ('science fantasy' or 'imaginary fiction'), Regina—as the Imaginary personification of the Alien Other in human form—is represented as 'ruthless' and, above all, as 'heartless.' As with the supposedly emotionless Alien, Mr. Spock of *Star Trek* (his creators having failed to notice that even his form of logic is a form of emotion), this Imaginary condition is explained as being the result of genetics; and the 'genes' that Regina is lacking are the same old kind that most Aliens lack in most science fiction: the 'genes' for what men define as 'love' and 'joy' and 'love of God.' (She may also be lacking the gene for marriage, it appears, since the script goes on about the Catholic view of marriage at some length.) Given the predisposition of many sci-fi writers for psychoanalytical categories of 'good' and 'evil,' we see that Regina is at one moment 'Instinctual Id' (dark-haired Eve) trying to take over the 'Rational Ego' (Professor Field, the 'perfect' scientist)—Imaginary 'Body' attempting to take over equally Imaginary 'Mind.' At another, she is the cold-blooded biological 'reproducing machine,' a deadly Iron Maiden trying to take advantage of the scientist's supposed 'male frailty.'

All wide-eyed 'male innocence,' Professor Field employs what the script calls his 'orderly and organized mind' in encouraging and feeding on the competition between 'wife' and 'Other Woman'—the competitive rivalry between women which has its source in the mediation of female relationships by male domination—and also takes the time to reassure his wife that her 'jealousy' is perfectly all right, since she is a 'normal wife.' (The director consistently places the three of them in a visual triangle, usually with the professor at the apex.) But Regina uses the bees in the hive to bring about the death of the wife whom she has viciously and cleverly attacked in many ways from their first meeting.

Professor Field becomes grief-stricken and sees the error of his ways. He knows that Regina is a so-called 'mutant,' and when she suddenly appears wearing his wife's bridal veil like a department-store mannequin, he launches into a verbal assault on her about the 'love' and the 'God' and the 'human ritual' of marriage that she can never know. He moves threateningly towards Regina, calling her 'inhuman.' The script then introduces one of the standard dramatic punishments for women like the Imaginary Other, Regina ('Thou shalt not suffer a witch to live!'). Regina backs away in terror and conveniently falls to her death over a balcony, whence she returns to being a bee hovering menacingly at the scientist's window. The Aliens have been defeated once again—but we all know that one day they'll be back.

This complex legitimization of male violence against women and supposed male genetic superiority was rebroadcast from Tacoma, Washington, in the Pacific Northwest in October 1978, in the week following the first appearance on television of Paddy Chayevsky's film *Network* (1976)—where it is Faye Dunaway ('television incarnate') who plays the role of the so-called Queen Bee (after Joan Crawford's film of that title, made in 1955), as well as the role of the (heartless) Other Woman.

No longer shown in prime time, as *Zzzzz* was in 1963 or 1964, this *Outer Limits* morality play reappeared on U.S. television with the help of a number of sponsors which identify the 'target audience' pretty well. These include Bounce, Coca Cola, Crest toothpaste, Old Spice Aftershave, and the paper diapers called Pampers; Teddy Roosevelt invading the kitchen to save the day for the housewife and mother with

Tough and Ready paper towels; and a long flagwaving promotion of the conservative newsmagazine, *U.S. News and World Report,* promising explanations and answers for all kinds of threats ('social unrest and violence, crime, drugs, and pornography'). *Zzzzz* also had the help of one car dealer, two nostalgia-tugging country folk singers, and—near the end—that of the entire Mormon Tabernacle Choir belting out the Hallelujah Chorus ($8.98 for records, $9.98 for tapes; Canadian orders add $2.00).

Item 28: The Female of the Species...

Outer Limits Announcer [following first commercial]: 'Human life strives ceaselessly to perfect itself, to gain ascendancy. But what of the *lower* forms of life? [Camera has cut to a close-up of Regina's upper body as she lies unconscious in the garden after her so-called 'mutation' into human form.]* Is it not possible that they too are at this moment on the threshold of deadly success?' [*Regina awakes.*]

Imaginary and Real

I have tried to show that the Imaginary is a (now) predominant way of coding and mediating our perspectives on social reality—as well as our behavior within that reality. The Imaginary is a code imposed on the Real in such a way that many of the messages we exchange with each other, messages we believe to be real messages about real relations, are actually Imaginary messages about real relations or, inversely, real messages about Imaginary relations.

(The 'battle of the sexes' is an Imaginary message about a real relation; the preceding statement is a real message bout an Imaginary relation; 'men are the dominating Other for women in the socio-sexual hierarchy' is a real message about a real relation.)

Society and our perceptions and behavior in society are arranged in a series of levels—the very levels that the Imaginary keeps us thoroughly confused about. The Imaginary is just one of these levels.

The level of the Imaginary is not the same as the many levels of the Real—which is why in discussing the Imaginary, it is necessary to use such expressions as 'a dominant mode of perceiving and behaving' or 'the predominance of the Imaginary in our society.' Since the value-system of the Imaginary denies or rejects the reality of levels of relation in the real world, then it also denies or rejects its own dominance, principally by masquerading as 'the natural order of things.' One result of the one-dimensionality of the Imaginary, then, is that it not only tells us (through other people) that it, and it alone, is the Real, but it also denies or rejects the fact that any such set of levels of relation called the Real actually exists—*except within the Imaginary.*

As a result, what commonly happens is that any explanation of the hierarchical relationship between the level of the Imaginary and the many levels of the Real is itself perceived and interpreted through Imaginary spectacles. The consequence of this Imaginary interpretation is that the single-level symmetrizing process of the Imaginary is often applied to the hierarchical relation between the Imaginary and the Real itself. When this happens, this relationship of levels is not understood as a relationship in which one level (the Imaginary) *contradicts* the other levels (the Real)—contradiction being used here to mean a conflicting relationship *between* levels in a hierarchy. Instead, the Imaginary is interpreted to be one entity, and the Real, another. These two supposed entities are then placed (by the Imaginary viewpoint) in a single-level and dualistic *opposition* with each other—opposition being used here to mean a conflicting relationship *within* a single level.

It is further implied that the Imaginary is autonomous, that it is independent of any other set of relations in the real world. This position is held by those who believe that the world is run and changed by ideas and ideologies alone, the position of those who believe that through some mysterious process an idea comes to be 'an idea whose time has come' (from where?), and that the world changes because of it. In reality, of course, it is as a result of changes in the Real (assisted, but not produced by ideas) that we come to have generally accepted ideas about the changes. The Imaginary position, in other words, is the position of the dominant ideology under capitalism, the position that pretends that ideas about reality are more important than reality itself, or, indeed, that ideas are the only reality we have to deal with (philosophical or metaphysical idealism).

The Imaginary opposition set up between the Imaginary and the Real is set up in such a way that we will ordinarily find ourselves asking which of these two 'entities' is true or correct, as if each could do without the other. In a word, the hierarchical contradiction between levels which is actually involved becomes reduced or 'flattened out'; the Imaginary and the Real then seem to be the two *sides* of an 'either/or' question.

But the whole point of the argument about the actual relationship between the Imaginary and the Real is to explain that the level of the

Imaginary and the many levels of the Real exist *together*; the relationship is not an 'either/or' opposition, but a 'both-and' contradiction. And the actual hierarchical relationship between them is the *inverse* of what it appears to be. The Imaginary *appears* to be dominant over the Real; and we ordinarily behave and perceive—under capitalism—as if it actually were. But, as has been pointed out in the development of the argument, this Imaginary code of perception and behavior is imposed over real relations. It is imposed over them because it is useful to the sustenance and the reproduction of the capitalist system to maintain the divide-and-rule involved in our confusion about what appears to be happening, as distinct from what is actually happening.[1]

Item 29: Diabolic Operations

Here is declared the truth about diabolic operations with regard to the male organ. . . . It is asked whether witches can with the help of devils really and actually remove the member, or whether they only do so apparently by some glamour or illusion. . . .

Answer. There is no doubt that certain witches can do marvellous things with regard to the male organs. . . .

. . . What. . . is to be thought of those witches who. . . sometimes collect male organs in great numbers, as many as twenty or thirty members together, and put them in a bird's nest, or shut them up in a box, where they move themselves like living members, and eat oats and corn, as has been seen by many and is a matter of common report? . . . . For a certain man tells us that, when he had lost his member, he approached a known witch to ask her to restore it to him. She told the afflicted man to climb a certain tree, and that he might take which he liked out of a nest in which there were several members. And when he tried to take a big one, the witch said: You must not take that one; adding, because it belonged to a parish priest.

All of these things are caused by devils through an illusion or glamour,. . . by transmuting the mental images in the imaginative faculty.

—Friar Heinrich Kramer and Friar James Sprenger: *The Hammer of the Witches* (1486)

---

[1]Note that the same kind of diagram as that used in *Figure 5-1* could be used here to illustrate the symmetrization and the inversion of the relation between the Imaginary and the Real. Naturally, all such diagrams are a simplification of the

In distinguishing between the Imaginary and the Real, consider again the example of the Imaginary Other, Regina. Consider the way men represent women to themselves and to other men, and the way they constrain women to fit these Imaginary stereotypes, as distinct from the real persons of women. Or consider the basic characteristics of the Real, as distinct from how it is made to appear. At one level, the Real consists of the physical universe, the universe of inert or inanimate matter. At another level, the Real consists of the ecological world of living organisms, the biological level of reality. At another level, yet again, the Real consists of the actual processes of production and exchange, the basic economic processes, by means of which society maintains itself and its members and reproduces its organization over time. In the Imaginary, these distinct levels simply do not exist as distinct levels; and they are moreover reduced to mere concepts or ideas about 'reality.' Or consider what will happen as this planet's limited natural resources become more scarce, as its capacity for food production is pressed to the limit, and as its capacity to absorb and recycle the wastes that industry pours into it approaches its maximum.

The point, then, is that just as nature is actually and ultimately dominant over society (in spite of the Imaginary belief that society dominates nature),[2] the Real is actually and ultimately dominant over the Imaginary. However confused we may be about our actual relationship to the Real, and however much our society may play on and reinforce this confusion, we nevertheless live and breathe and exist as both biological and social beings only because we know, whether entirely consciously or not, how to live and labor in the Real, the Real without which neither we nor the Imaginary could exist.

The Real, then, is the context, the only context, which can make sense out of the Imaginary and its apparent dominance in our social, economic, and ecological relations.

---

complexity of the relationship. It should also be noted here that the discussion does not include one other level of relationship between social beings in society, the domain of the Symbolic (cf. Wilden, *System and Structure*. revised edition, 1980, where the role of the symbol as a linking relationship is emphasized). A general definition of symbolic relations is that they may be Imaginary or Real, i.e. symbolic of an Imaginary relation, symbolic of a Real one.

[2]A useful test for real hierarchies, such as that between society and nature (not to be confused with social hierarchies), is to see which will survive if one is removed. The same test may be applied to the relationship between capital and labor (cf. *Figure 5-1*).

Viewed through the filters of the Imaginary, the Real becomes unrecognizable to our conscious experience. The Imaginary takes mere unconnected bits and pieces from the Real, and sews them together with Imaginary threads to create a patchwork quilt of illusion and delusion. In the relations between men and women, for example, where the Imaginary became apparently dominant long before the advent of capitalism, the results of the Imaginary distortion of the Real now appear in the mouths of males in tissues of contradictions like the following example of male gossip taken from *PsychoSources* (1973: p.40):

> A clever woman knows how to keep a man—*Smart women are emasculating*—All women think about is their looks—*A woman's place is in the home*—If she can't get along on what I give her she can get herself a job—*Women can't handle money*—I let my wife do all the bookkeeping—*Why can't she do anything right?*—With her looks she doesn't need brains—*Women are only suited for monotonous work*—Just like a woman to change her mind—*All women want is to get married*—Men create things, women create life—*Once they get married they sit around and get fat*—A man works from sun to sun but a woman's work is never done—*Women like to be raped*—Its a smart broad who holds out for a license—*All women do is gossip*—Women basically dislike other women—*Women are always so emotional*—Frigid bitch—*Career women are too damned independent*—Women cling like vines—*Women don't think*—Conniving female—*If she goes to college she'll never get a man*—They're all alike—*I can't figure women out*—Never trust a woman—*Behind every great man is a woman. . .*

What do women want? said Freud. What does Algeria want? said France. What do blacks want? say whites. What does Quebec want? say the English. What does Canada want? says the United States. Nothing you can give. Freedom given is always Imaginary freedom. Only freedom wrested from the hands of those who stole it has any chance of being Real.

A Note to Chapter Six

CODES AND MESSAGES

When we send messages in English to each other, the messages we actually construct are dependent on, and constrained by, what we may call the 'code' or the 'deep structure' of the English language. No one has

Item 30: Summer, 1759: 'No Mercy to Captives Before Quebec'

NO MERCY TO CAPTIVES BEFORE QUEBECK

General Wolfe: 'We will not let one of them escape, my dear Isaac—the pretty ones will be punished at Headquarters.'
Adjutant-General Isaac Barré: 'I understand you compleatly, General—strike 'em in their weakest part, Egad!'
Wolfe's Manservant: 'I wonder if I shall have my share?'

This cartoon is taken from Richard Garrett's *Clash of Arms* (1976). Garrett comments: 'Wolfe's treatment of the French civilians in the neighbourhood of Quebec was entirely ruthless. When [Brigadier-General George] Townshend depicted it in a cartoon, [Major-General Wolfe] was not amused. . . .' The British invasion forces were established downstream of Quebec City by the beginning of the summer of 1759. A major British attack on July 31 suffered a heavy defeat with the loss of over 500 men. Stanley Ryerson (1960) remarks: 'Meanwhile, Wolfe's troops ravaged the surrounding countryside. "It would give me pleasure,' he had written earlier, "to see the Canadian vermin sacked and pillaged. . . ." Now was his chance, and his men reduced more than 1,400 habitant farms to ashes. The reaction of the Canadians was to wage a determined guerrilla warfare of resistance. Wolfe, startled, recorded that "old men of seventy and boys of fifteen take up positions on the fringes of the woods, fire on our detachments, kill and wound our men."' Wolfe, a veteran of Cumberland's massacre of the Scots at Culloden in 1746, was killed in the Battle of Quebec, September 13, 1759.

---

ever convincingly shown just what this code is or how it works—and yet every English-speaking person is intimately familiar with it, without consciously knowing what it is. In other words, this code which constrains what can and cannot be said in English is an unconscious code, as indeed most important social codes of communication are (e.g. the codes of bodily communication in which we never stop communicating as long as we are alive).

The deep structure or code of the English language must be relatively complicated; it is probably best described as a set of rules constraining the possible patterns of communication that can appear in messages in English. (Try as we will, the code of English will never produce a single message in Chinese.) But however complicated the code of English may be, it is obviously much less complicated than the infinite number of messages that it permits English-speaking people to construct.

As an analogy here, but only an analogy, consider how much more complicated is a game of football as actually played, when compared with the written and unwritten code of rules and regulations that permit the participants to play the game itself. Football is not like language, but it is certainly a form of communication—and communication is impossible without a code.

The term 'code' is more loosely used in ordinary English than it is here. The so-called 'Morse code,' for instance, is not a code in the technical sense. It is actually a cipher, like the 'secret codes' of espionage. It is simply a means of transforming the letters of the alphabet (simple signs) into Morse signals. In contrast, the 'highway code' is a set of rules about how to behave in the traffic system; thus it is a true code, if a very simple one. It is much more simple, for instance, than the actual code of driving that we use to get from one place to another.

The reason for introducing these distinctions between the level of the *messages* in a system of communication (e.g. a particular 'play' in a football game) and the level of the *code* (or codes, since most communication involves many codes) is to point out that social and economic relations also involve code/message relationships. This is not to suggest that society is a language or a game; but it is to suggest that, just as we understand neither English nor football without knowing the code of rules that make them possible, we cannot ever expect to understand society and our own relationship within it without looking for the basic or 'deep structure' patterns—for the codes of rules, conscious and unconscious, written and unwritten, verbal and non-verbal—that make any given society what it is.

A code is a set of constraints or rules or limits which *mediate* the relationships between the communicators using the code. That is to say, when we communicate with each other, we do so not directly or 'immediately' by means of messages alone. We communicate indirectly (or 'mediately,' as the philosophers say) by means of the code or codes in use; and it is this communication via the common reference point of the code or codes which makes the messages mutually understandable.

If we do not share the constraints of a code or codes, then the information we attempt to exchange becomes reduced to meaningless 'noise,' noise like that of the sounds we hear when someone addresses us in a language we do not understand. And in an oppressive society, a great deal of the overt information we are exposed to (not to mention the complexities of messages we do not recognize as information at all) is obscured and distorted by many kinds of apparent 'noise.'

Indeed, all that distinguishes 'noise' ('uncoded variety') from information ('coded variety') in communication is the code shared by the communicators. Change the code—or the level of the basic perspective—for example (which is part of what I am attempting to do here), and a great deal of once apparently significant information turns out to be relatively worthless noise. By the same token, the same change of code or codes, the codes by means of which we perceive and act in reality, will always have the effect of turning a great deal of what we thought was noise, and perceived as noise, into newly significant information.

This decoding and recoding process is always the task of critical analysis. Similarly, the process of turning knowledge into recognition depends on understanding which patterns are truly significant (because they are basic patterns of coding) and which patterns are less significant (because they are merely patterns of surface details or messages).

The dominant ideology, however, seeks to obscure the understanding of these patterns by flattening out the code/message distinction. It reduces the codes to the messages (symmetrization). This procedure produces two kinds of results. Firstly, it seeks to individualize and atomize the messages by cutting them off ideologically from the patterns of coding in the contexts that make the messages possible. This comes to mean that every message is isolated ideologically from every other message. It is as if communication begins all over again every time a message is exchanged. In the second place, this Imaginary attempt to isolate code from message results in a situation all too common to our schools. Someone will identify a coded pattern of relationship—a racial or sexual stereotype in a children's book, for example. The response of the 'expert' will be to say that this pattern is merely one piece of 'data' (i.e. a message at the same level as every other message). The *qualitative* significance of the stereotype as a truly representative example of social relations will be denied.

The next step of the 'expert' will be to say that until you have looked at *all* the 'data,' or at a 'scientific sample' of the 'data'—the quantitative sampling process being one that destroys the code/message distinction—you do not know what you are talking about.

Since 'data' literally means 'given,' the term implies that the 'facts' are 'out there,' independent of the individual and *collective* processes by which we punctuate reality in interpreting it (as well as living in it). A fact or a measurement or a quantity is not an 'objective' thing, however, it is information produced within the constraints of socially mediated relations. Decisions about facts and quantities are based on, and derived from, *qualitative* evaluations of the subject matter—evaluations that are often largely unconscious. In human knowledge, as with the five senses, quality precedes and constrains quantity. Imaginary it may be, but 'objectivity' is itself a quality, as is the goal of quantification in the sciences.

The critique of 'objectivity' does not imply that all knowledge is subjective. Taking refuge in 'subjective relativism' amounts to a switch between Imaginary opposites in the dominant ideology. Whereas subjectivity exists in all human affairs, 'objectivity'—trivial matters aside—does not. But subjectivity is not strictly subjective. Many of our 'personal opinions' are in reality the products of social conditioning and the collective coding of values. The real relation we are concerned with is the difference between private and public knowledge. Public knowledge is based on persuasion, argument, and evidence—expressed in a collectively and individually recognizable coding. This in turn requires judgment, and all judgments are ultimately value judgments.

CHAPTER SEVEN

The Code of the Other

Imaginary Oppositions and Real Conflicts

The question we are working our way toward answering here is the so-called 'Canadian question,' the 'question of Canadian identity.' We Canadians are a colonized people, but our colonization has been a more complex and less barbaric process than elsewhere in the world—and we don't relish talking about it very much. Hence, the real question: 'Who is the dominant Other for Canadians?' requires some more groundwork before we can hope to answer it adequately, and in a non-paranoid way.

However real and necessary the hierarchical conflict between a 'self' (or a collectivity) and an alienating Other (or Others) may actually be—and for any and all oppressed peoples, it is indeed a real and necessary struggle—we must nevertheless remain aware that if this struggle is defined in primarily Imaginary terms, then it will take on the unhelpful characteristics of a dualistic opposition between Imaginary images. The relation will then be played out as a single-level mirror-relationship—and, as a result, the subordinate will have already lost the struggle before it began. Consider what often happens in a 'man-to-man' —or 'woman-to-man'—argument with one's boss, for instance.

The struggle will have been lost because it will have been expressed and fought as an opposition which is a simple attempt to 'negate' the dominating Other. In relations of oppression and exploitation, however, the subordinate is the one who is 'negated' by the Other—and not in theory, but in body and soul and in person. One primary characteristic of the relation to dominant or dominating Others is that although the mediation of an oppressive Other can in principle and in practice be *overcome* in various ways when necessary, dominant Others cannot be *'negated,'* except in a generally pathological sense, and in any case, not 'from below.' (Try 'negating' American capital—any kind of capital—in Canada, for example.)

A simple example: No symmetrical equation can legitimately be made between the epithets 'Honkie' and 'Nigger'—even though they are commonly treated as the 'two sides' of an Imaginary and symmetrical question, like 'Anti-Semite' and 'Jew,' like 'Man' and 'Woman,' like

'Business' and 'Labor.' Because each term and each image in each pair refers to distinct levels of exploitation under capitalism—a system of many levels—then the two terms (and the states they refer to) are not exchangeable equivalents in our society. 'Honkie!' cannot 'negate' white in the way that 'Nigger!' 'negates' black.

Item 31: That's Real White of You

white, adj. Honourable; fair-dealing: U.S. slang (—1877), anglicized ca. 1885; by 1920 colloquial. Ex the self-imputed characteristics of a white man. Cf. *white man*, q.v.—2. Hence as adverb: U.S. slang (—1900) anglicized ca. 1905; by 1930, colloquial. E.g. *act white, use* (a person) *white*.—3. As noun, 'a true, sterling fellow,' C.J. Dennis: mostly Australian (1916).

white man. An honourable man: U.S. slang (1865), anglicized ca. 1887; by 1920 colloquial. Nat Gould, 1898, 'There goes a "white man" if ever there was one...That beard [is] the only black thing about him.' See *white*, adj.; c.f. *sahib*, q.v.

sahib. A 'white man,' a thoroughly honourable gentleman: mainly in the Services; late 19th and early 20th centuries. Since ca. 1925, often derisive of 'Public School' morals and mentality. Ian Hay, 1915. Ex Arabic and Urdu respectful address to Europeans.

white nigger. A term of contempt for a white man: Sierra Leone Negroes' colloquialism: from ca. 1880....Cf. the American Negroes' *poor white trash*.

white man's burden, the. Work: jocular colloquialism: from ca. 1929. Punning the Standard English sense.

—Eric Partridge: *A Dictionary of Slang and Unconventional English* (1951)

In the real world supported and maintained by real labor, and where words may also be forms of violence, potential and actual, we learned from the civil rights movement that one white person's 'Nigger!' does incalculable damage to the 'self-concept' of the black, whereas one thousand or one million blacks responding to an original white assault by means of 'Honkie!' has no necessary or significant effect on the white at all. (It may result in guilt, of course, but guilt cannot be trusted. Neither can it form a real basis for political action.) Such 'negation' and 'counter-negation' cannot under state and private capitalism be reciprocal or symmetrical because the white collectivity represents a dominant and dominating Other for the black, as Frantz Fanon, for one, pointed out in his *Black Skin, White Masks* in 1952.

In other words: Under our present economic system—which has always used racism and other forms of bigotry to distract our attention from the real Others—it makes no significant difference how many times the epithets 'WASP' or 'Goy' or 'Cracker' or 'Gringo' or 'Honkie' are *quantitatively* multiplied (compare 'male imperialist'). These terms never attain the socially-coded and *qualitatively* distinct domination and violence expressed by a single white saying, yelling—or thinking—that he or she has been 'jewed' out of his or her money by a 'camel jockey,' a 'nig-nog,' a 'chink,' a 'jap,' a 'punjab,' or a 'frog' (compare the use of 'girl,' 'chick,' 'bitch,' and so on—as well as 'kookie commie').

Note, moreover, that in using this example, we have not been able even to touch on the several hundred contemporary alternatives for these racist and sexist terms. Much less have we been able to examine the hidden violence of the veiled or unconscious racism and sexism of the 'professionals,' the 'managers,' the 'educated,' and the 'liberals,' amongst others. Spokespeople for these bourgeois and petit bourgeois groups in Canada, as elsewhere, indicate to us that these groups generally consist of people whose class elitism has them believe that in modern society racism is confined to the 'lower classes'—give or take a bushel or two of 'individual' bigots in more privileged places in the social system.

This self-serving position is of course nonsensical. Racism, sexism, and classism in our society are produced and reproduced by the dominant, not by the subordinates; and the principal differences in the expression of this kind of violence against other people is *style*, not substance and not structure. Moreover, racism, classism, and sexism are not matters of individual preferences, as the predominant psychological interpretations of social and economic behavior would have us believe.

(Consider also here the way in which the dominant in Canada consistently reproduce the illusion of a symmetrical opposition between Quebec and 'English' Canada—'two races,' 'two nations,' 'separate realities,' 'two solitudes,' and so on. And by using the adjective 'English' in this Imaginary opposition, they simply ignore the large numbers of Canadians who are not of English origin.)

These hatreds, these elitisms, these unconscious attacks on whoever have been designated as the *others*, are expressed by individuals, it is true, but by individuals who would benefit from a better understanding of the way they themselves are being manipulated by the attitudes they hold and the expressions they use. For racism, sexism, and classism are systematic properties of our present economic system—the visible symptoms of alienation, the visible symptoms of systematic divide-and-rule—and every time we behave as racists, sexists, or (class) elitists, then we are behaving exactly as the real Others want us to behave.

Item 32: The Hammer of the Witches

Possibly what will seem even more amazing to modern readers [of *The Hammer of the Witches,* published in 1486] is the misogynic trend of various passages ....However, exaggerated as these may be, I am not altogether certain that they will not prove a wholesome and needed antidote in this feministic age, when sexes seem confounded, and it appears to be the chief object of many females to ape the man, an indecorum by which they not only divest themselves of such charm as they might boast, but lay themselves open to the sternest reprobation in the name of sanity and common-sense. For the Apostle S. Peter says: 'Let wives be subject to their husbands....'

... Witches were the bane of all social order; they injured not only persons but property. They were, in fact, as has previously been emphasized, the active members of a vast revolutionary body, a conspiracy against civilization....

We must approach this great work—admirable in spite of its trifling blemishes—with open minds and grave intent; if we duly consider the world of confusion, of Bolshevism, of anarchy and licentiousness all around today, it should be an easy task for us to picture the difficulties, the hideous dangers with which [its two authors, the Dominican friars] Henry Kramer and James Sprenger were called to combat and to cope....

...The *Malleus Maleficarum* [deals with] eternal things, the eternal conflict of good and evil, [and it] must eternally capture the attention of all men who think, all who see, or are endeavouring to see, reality beyond the accidents of matter, time, and space.*

—Montague Summers (translator): Introduction (1928) to the *Malleus Maleficarum* (1486)

From the fourteenth to the seventeenth century in Europe, notably in Germany, Italy, France and England, millions of 'witches' were tortured or killed, usually by being burned to death. In some German cities, executions averaged 600 a year. At Toulouse, 400 were put to death in a single day. Most were from the peasantry and the poor. Women made up some 85 per cent of those executed (Ehrenreich and English, 1973). The Malleus *was the Bible of the witch-hunters.*

The parasitical ignorance of the dominant in these matters is alone a problem quite serious enough. It becomes even more awesome and dangerous to human wellbeing in its effects when those who are the targets of these real and Imaginary objectifications are so overwhelmed by the insidious power and the daily insistence of these violences that they come unconsciously to believe them to be true. The result will ordinarily be that they will match their objectification by the Other with an objectification of themselves, by themselves. They will tend to match their stereotyping by the Other with an unconscious collusion in the stereotyped roles laid out for them. They will match the hatred expressed by the representatives of the Other with self-hatred, and with a hatred of others like themselves. The violence coming from the representatives of the Other will be turned partly inward, against themselves, and partly outward, against each other, and partly downward (if possible), against others in even worse situations than they are.

This *internalization* of the Other's attitudes and behavior, this unconscious *collusion* with the representatives of the Other, this Other-induced 'inferiority complex,' this *oscillation*[1] between being (and behaving) as the Other commands and demands and *not* being (or behaving) in conformity with the desire of the Other—this, for the colonized, is the major ideological battleground, both personal and collective.

Dominances and Dependencies

In terms of race, the white collectivity represents real and alienating Others for the non-white—just as in Canada, in terms of one aspect of our internal colonial economics, the Anglos and all their kin represent the oppressive Others for the French, the 'Canayen,' the Québécois. In these examples, amongst many others, the male, the white, or the Anglo participate in various and often overlapping systems of systematic domination, each system of oppression being identifiable in terms of the particular group of human beings that are its major targets. These systems of oppression are so complex and so interwoven with each other, however, that those who are the targets of oppression in one system— French-Canadian males, for example—may be the oppressors in another—their relation to Canadian women, for example, where

[1]On the topic of oscillation between paradoxical alternatives, see Wilden and Wilson, "The Double Bind: Logic, Magic, and Economics" (1976). In the terms of colonial identity, two major oscillations for Canadians are those between '(not) being French' and '(not) being English'; and between '(not) being British' and '(not) being American.'

Canadian males of whatever national origin link arms in that almost universal 'brotherhood of man' we know as male imperialism.

These various forms of systematic alienation include oppression by class, of course—for just as male imperialism cuts across the boundaries of race and class, so also do class relations cut across some of the boundaries of sex and race.

One result of such systematic oppression in our society is a collective delusion, a collectively-shared denial of reality, a collective refusal to recognize the actual state of affairs. This is a delusion of the dominators, the delusion of autonomy which seeks to have us believe that in terms of race and sex, we males, we whites, and we Anglos do not have to answer for the meaning of our existence to anyone in any way whatsoever. This delusion is in its essence just one more version of the ideology of 'genetic superiority' in our society. It allows us to forget that every aspect of our dominance and domination in the social hierarchy is dependent on its being paid for by the physical, emotional, and mental labor of those who have been obliged, by economic coercion and ideological cunning, to be the more oppressed of the oppressed at this time in history.

Item 33: A Real Perspective

'Regionalism' is an unequal sharing of the wealth and benefits a nation has to offer, expressed in geographical terms. But alone this is not a sufficient definition. There is also a relationship involved—a region is a part of something else, and herein lies the key to the *unevenness* of economic development. It is only uneven when more capital and profits are extracted than are put in—otherwise it is *un*developed, not *under*developed. A region can only be underdeveloped if it is tied to an external economy that is doing the underdeveloping. The only way it can be truly developed is if all those on site who participate in the development share equally in the surplus produced. If part of the surplus is shipped outside, underdevelopment is occurring. This principle applies equally to class relations or to regionalism, the latter frequently passing for the former.

—Wallace Clement: *Continental Corporate Power* (1977)

The delusion of autonomy—the illusion of the imperialist—is not shared by the non-white, by the woman, or by the Québécois, however, for they necessarily understand the reality of social relations in a much more fundamental way than those who dominate them do. Not that this understanding may not be distorted by the Imaginary, as indeed it often is. The point is rather that the imperialist—male, white, or Anglo—has been brought up in an 'instrumental' relationship to the world and to others, a relationship that fails to recognize the parasitical dependency of the exploiter on those he exploits. Like the capitalist, the male, the white, and the Anglo are trained to relate to others primarily as objects to be manipulated by their practice of instrumentality. Not so the non-white, the woman, or the Québécois, however, for within the contexts defined by their exploiters, they have been brought up with an overtly recognized relational perspective on their reality—a perspective which is defined by their existence-in-relation to the alienating or oppressive Other. In these three contexts of 'whiteness,' 'maleness,' and 'Anglo-ness,' their existence has been made by history and by economic realities into an overt and subordinate dependency in relation to the Other—into a *function* of the existence of the white, the male, and the Anglo as others who stand as representatives of the Others.

We hardly need wonder then, about the source of one common male-Anglo attitude to Quebec, an attitude often mimicked by dominant French Canadians who have 'gone over to the English.' This is the 'liberal' and oh, so understanding attitude which paternalistically grants to French Canada the 'female' role in the Canadian political and economic household.

Indeed, this use of 'accepted' and therefore almost 'invisible' metaphors of male imperialism to obscure from people other kinds of domination and exploitation goes further yet—and so easily, because male imperialism is so 'natural' (to men). The same metaphors are characteristic of the way the media discuss the roles of the provincial governments in Canada, notably when they get invited out (to another conference) by the federal government, the conferences that often precede another unilateral escalation of the power of the federal government.

The colony of Canada itself, as well as its people, is often represented to the world in words and images as a woman. However, unlike the warlike Britannia! on British coins; unlike the powerful Victorian image of the 'Widow of Windsor,' Queen Victoria; and unlike the French *Liberté!*—the Amazonian with the Greek nose often represented as leading the *sans-culottes* in the storming of the Bastille in 1789 (her sister looks out over New York harbor)—unlike all these powerful female figures from other traditions, our Imaginary 'Miss Canada' is quite often represented as a 'sweet young thing' wandering around in her shift.

**Item 34: The Great Colonial Con-Game, 19th-Century Style,
or, Miss Canada Meets Dracula and the Big Bad Wolf**
(Cartoon by 'Grip,' April 26, 1879)

GOODS PROHIBITED, BUT *EVILS* ADMITTED

Miss Canada: 'Now, Mr. Premier, I don't propose to allow this country
to be made a slaughter market for American ideas, any more than for
American goods.'

Nationhood and Individuality

In order to distinguish between real national identity and the Imaginary identities entangled in bourgeois nationalism, chauvinism, and jingoism, we find it necessary to use the word 'nationhood' and also to redefine it. We know that as long as the debate about Canada's quest for nationhood is coded or mediated by the concept of the State (consistently confused with 'the nation') and by the concept of nationalism as they are predominantly used in Canada today, then practically nothing worthwhile, and little that is new, can be said. But if we communicate *about* the *kind* of communication associated with the national question in Canada, if we step out of the confusion and the irrelevance of many of the messages, and direct our attention to the context of their sources, then we are properly addressing ourselves to the level of the code: to the code of the Other which is still mediating and dominating the issue in Canada, as it has traditionally done.

Item 35: Spiritual Achievements

Canadians rarely savour their own national achievements. It is surprising because few countries can match them.

Starting in 1867 with four small provinces, Canadians peacefully went about building the world's second largest nation. In the process, east was linked to west with a remarkable network of railways and canals, quite an achievement for the small, agricultural Canadian population. Vision, drive and inventiveness of the type required to accomplish feats such as these have overcome the difficulties of climate and terrain to give most Canadians a standard of living unknown in many parts of the world.

Though our material accomplishments are notable, our spiritual achievements are finer still. While the oppressive instruments of dictatorship have snuffed out liberty in many other countries, Canada has always endeavoured to enhance freedom of the individual. Indeed, Canadians have died by the thousands to preserve democracy in those places where it still flourishes. Considering what little respect most humans have for people of different races, cultures and religions, and considering the strife this causes elsewhere, Canada shines as an enviable model of tolerance and goodwill. Is it any wonder that the arts prosper here, that less fortunate people long to live here and that Canadians, through foreign aid, have shared their good fortune with the underprivileged and dispossessed.

In the years ahead, it will be difficult to survive in a world dominated by competing superpowers and near superpowers. It will require struggle and strain to eliminate our society's imperfections. But as these 12 stamps remind us, a country with the strength of unity behind it, and a country with a record as outstanding as ours, can face the future with confidence.

—Canada Post Office: *Canada Miniature Sheet,* 1979

Just as we distinguish Imaginary nationalism from real nationhood, so also we distinguish Imaginary individualism from real individuality. Nationalism in the sense of chauvinism tends to exhibit the same Imaginary values as individualism does: atomism, divisiveness, unconstrained competition, paranoia about *others*, and associated forms of pathological behavior. Chauvinism is moreover predominantly an 'either/or' relationship to other nations, just as individualism is to other individuals. In contrast, nationhood, like individuality, is a 'both-and' relationship. What predominates here is not atomism, but relationship; not divisiveness, but connectedness; not competition, but cooperation; not paranoia, but realism.

This realism, however, obliges us to understand that we may be forced into 'either/or' situations by dominating Others—as in the question of the foreign powers who are pillaging Canada of its natural resources, for instance. And because of the dominance of 'either/or' values and behavior under capitalism, we may well have to call upon our nationhood and our individuality to resist these Others—they will not go away just because someone has 'a better idea' of what is to be done than these Others and their collaborators in Canada do.

We should be careful also not to misunderstand the distinction between individualism and individuality. The dominance of 'either/or' values and modes of thinking in our present society sets up an Imaginary opposite for 'individualism': i.e. 'collectivism.' One almost automatic and misguided response to any critique of individualism, then, will be the assumption that any statement implying that individualism is A Bad Thing must *also* be implying that its Imaginary opposite, 'collectivism,' is A Good Thing—and the term 'collectivism' is a code-word in the dominant ideology for totalitarianism.

Another misguided response, by means of an Imaginary 'either/or' opposite, to the critique of individualism is to assume that individualism is a 'negative' which can only be replaced by its 'positive,' i.e. by its Imaginary mirror-image. Thus, if individualism is seen to represent aggressiveness, then 'aggressiveness' will become a supposed 'either' in an Imaginary 'either/or' duality. The dominant way of thinking about such relationships will imply that it can be replaced only by its supposed opposite—and this 'or' in the Imaginary equation will be passive or pacifist.

In reality, individuality is neither of these Imaginary opposites, aggressiveness or passivity. Individuality is, however, *assertive*; and this assertiveness is born in relations of cooperation which are the grounds of its special strength. Like nationhood, at one level, and political consciousness, at another, individuality is a self *and* other relationship. But when the Other declares war on this cooperative relationship, when the Other defines itself by its behavior as an enemy, then individuality fights back.

Mediation

As discussed in Chapter Six, it is not dominance, as such, or mediation by the Other, as such, which results in alienation in the dehumanizing sense. The problem is not the Other, it is the dominating Other; the problem is not mediation, it is alienating and oppressive mediation.

The human and social identity through which we come to live and feel our relational individuality as persons in society, is a result of mediation. The Imaginary and alienated identities of (economic and psychological) individualism under state and private capitalism are also the products of mediation, but of a different kind of mediation—mediation by the machines that rule our lives in particular, and especially as this fundamental alienation is experienced by those who directly tend those machines.

Whereas (competitive) individualism is generated by the divisive mediation of dominating Others, social individuality is a function of mediation by what may generally be called '*Otherness*,' the social world of Otherness. Many of us are quite unused to considering ourselves and our relation to other people in these terms; the following examples should help to deal with some aspects of the confusions about Otherness (confusions which might be called, in the Imaginary, the 'Robinson Crusoe Complex').

Critics of the dominant ideology over the past one hundred years have insisted that 'being human' in the proper sense of the term always means 'being a social being.' 'Being human' is not an inborn, or innate, or genetic trait; only the propensity to be human forms part of our genetic make-up. Therefore, 'wolf-children' and the like are not human beings in the proper sense (although we do of course treat them as such). They are human organisms. An organism is a member of a species (biological level of organization). A human being is a member of a society *as well* (socioeconomic level of organization). The 'wolf-child' thus becomes a human (social) being only when brought into the human family of society, where the 'Otherness' the child experiences is primarily a social and human Otherness, rather than simply a biological and animal one.

Another problem similarly related to the ideology of individualism in our society involves the understanding of mediation. Because in our ordinary experience a 'mediator' arrives on the scene 'after the event' in 'business disputes' (strikes, lockouts, and so on), we tend to think of mediation as a conscious, highly visible, personally-represented, rather legalistic, and 'surface structure' process. We confuse the least significant kind of mediation, represented in the person of an 'arbitrator,' with the profoundly unconscious mediation, and levels of mediation, at the level of the 'deep structures' or the codes in our society.

In reality, long before the visible mediator or arbitrator appears on the scene in a dispute between 'business' and 'labor,' the relations between worker and worker are already mediated by the present power of capital to constrain workers to compete with each other (for jobs, for promotions, and so on). Similarly, but at a different level in the overall system of conflict, the relations between a group of workers (or a union) and a business firm (or conglomerate) are already mediated by the presently effective power of business-in-general to subject workers to the constraint of 'competing' with the very 'business' which presently controls the workers' means of livelihood. This last is a form of relationship mediated by dominating Others in which no individual worker, no individual union, can ever win. Viewed as 'competition,' this hierarchical conflict between labor and capital is Imaginary. Viewed—and lived—as alienation, this conflict between the subordinate and the dominant in the workplace is of course entirely Real.

However, it is not the structure of mediation as such which creates the problem of alienation, for mediation is universal in human experience.

Rather it is the distortion and perversion of this structure by the Other, the twisted substructures created by oppression, and the alienating *contents* imposed on the *form* of this structure by those with the (relative) power to do so—these are the realities which are responsible for the dehumanizing mediation by dominating Others that almost all of us experience.

The result, of course, is to reinforce our fictional mosaic of individualism, our 'social atomism'—for when oppression by the Other is predominant in our lived experience, then we will tend to reject recognition of any form of mediation in our lives as oppressive, lock, stock, and barrel.

Imaginary Identity, Positive and Negative

When in a relationship between social beings, the dominant or dominating Other is perceived and related to as an Imaginary Other (whether predominantly positively or predominantly negatively), then the locus of mediation between 'self' and 'other' will also be predominantly Imaginary. As a result, all the 'selves' and all the 'others' who are mediated by this Imaginary relation will also take on predominantly Imaginary characteristics. In this relation, the 'self' is accepting the Imaginary Other as the 'ground' or 'source' or 'code' in respect of which both 'self-identity' and 'other-identity' are defined.

No form of identity, not even our unique biological identity, is an autonomous or independent characteristic. In spite of the way in which the Imaginary ordinarily defines the 'me' as independent of all others, even this Imaginary definition is in contradiction with itself. In the ideological attempt to maintain the Grand Illusion invented in its modern novelty by capitalism—the illusion of the 'freedom' of the (capitalist) individual—the Imaginary also defines the (alienated) 'me' as existing in opposition to 'them' and in a 'naturally' competitive opposition.

Identity, even alienated Identity, is always a relation. On the one hand, when the Imaginary mediator is felt to be predominantly 'positive,' the Imaginary Other will come to represent an Imaginary ideal (similar to what Freud called the 'ideal ego' or the 'ideal of the ego'). On the other hand, when the Imaginary relationship to the Other is 'negative,' then the 'ideal' is replaced by its Imaginary opposite, an 'anti-ideal.'

The Imaginary ideal, on the one hand (Heaven, for instance), and the Imaginary anti-ideal, on the other (Hell), are alienated ideals. They are not the same as real ideals, at one level, nor real aggressors, at another level—however often we may be induced to confuse them.

As an example, consider here the attitudes and the values of the 'counter-culture(s)' of the 1960s. Where they were not simply distorted expressions of already dominant values—e.g. class elitism, male imperialism, and bourgeois individualism—the values of the various counter-cultures were quite often simply 'anti-values' dependent for their existence, not so much on what they were as values, but rather on the Imaginary fact that they were 'anti-'.

Most Canadians are brought up in the home and in school in a tissue of contradictions about American people, American capital, and supposedly 'American' ideas. Too often these contradictions involve an introverted feeling of inferiority to the American giant, a feeling of inferiority which is hammered on by many of our politicians, by many media personalities, and by Canadian quislings from various walks of life. This is felt and experienced as violence. But recognizing the real source of this violence is dangerous; and attempting to turn it back on its actual sources is psychological suicide—for the individual. What commonly happens is the same as what happens in ghettoes of all kinds— including the ghetto called 'feminity' in our society. The violence from above is turned inward, against the individual victim; the violence is turned outward, against others in the same situation; the violence is turned downward, against those less empowered to fight back. The violence of the colonizers against the colony is thus turned by the colonized against each other.

Most of us are brought up to feel predominantly 'anti-American.' Others of us are trained to be 'pro-American.' Still others switch back and forth, at different times or at different levels, between the two opposed poles of this Imaginary relation.

Moreover, as often as not, 'anti-American' is taken to mean 'pro-British,' while 'pro-American' is assumed to mean 'anti-British.'

But as we can see from the preceding analysis, it makes little difference whether in our identification *with* or *against* the projected Other (the Imaginary American) our Imaginary relationship is predominantly positive (collusion) or predominantly negative (opposition). In both cases, the quality called 'Canadian' is being defined as subordinate to the quality called 'American.' The Imaginary code of 'national identity' that is being (unconsciously) used in this pathological relation to the dominant and dominating Other is a code constructed out of whatever it is that 'American' comes to stand for in any particular time or place.

The same is of course true when the Imaginary Others we are 'for' or 'against' include the other two major colonizers of Canadians, the British or the French.

A third position, however, transcends the dualism and one-dimensionality of the Imaginary relation. It does not depend on the symmetry of *either* 'American' *or* 'not-American' (and so on). This position and perspective, this position of political recognition, is one that can take all of the Imaginary positions into account and put them in their place. It goes beyond our Imaginary 'identity of opposites'—or opposition of Imaginary identities—with the United States (and other nations). It is a way of communicating about our relation to our colonizers, providing that relation with the real context which can lay open its hidden significance.

Item 36: Selling Us Out

[The Foreign Investment Review Agency] was set up by the Liberal government in 1972 supposedly to be a restraining factor on foreign investment and takeovers. This legislation was introduced to gain public support at a time when the Liberals' position in government was very tenuous. However, in practice, this Agency has acted as a funnel for foreign (mostly American) direct investment coming into Canada. . . . From May 11, 1976 to September 28, 1976 there were 86 applications put before the Agency for takeovers or for the establishment of new businesses by foreign corporations and 80 were allowed. . . .

Red Star Collective: *Canada: Imperialist Power or Economic Colony?* (1977)

This third position—the contextual position this essay seeks to speak from—is a position based on our actual history as Canadians, on our actual Canadian present, and on our real hopes for the future as a nation.

This is a position and a perspective which allows us to take whatever we need from wherever we find it from whatever tradition. It allows us to borrow from any number of traditions—besides the Canadian and Inuit and Amerindian traditions—and to transform them in whatever ways we find most fruitful and most useful. It is the position not of Canadian chauvinism, not of anti-American bourgeois nationalism, not of pro-American or pro-British or pro-French anti-Canadianism, but the position and the perspective of Canadian nationhood.

A Note to Chapter Seven

THE U.S. SEEN THROUGH IMAGINARY SPECTACLES

The following passages are excerpts from *The Canadian Question*, published in 1875, after Canadians had experienced the Fenian raids and watched the terrible destructiveness of the (second) American Civil War. (The first was the War of Independence, many of whose Tory opponents, the Empire Loyalists, dispossessed by the victors, fled to Canada and received large grants of land.) An estimated 40,000 Canadians fought in the war (1861-65), mostly for the North. Over 10,000 died. In this first full-scale war of modern industrial capitalism, Britain supported the South. Hence, no doubt, the 'schizophrenic' political attitudes of the author, William Norris ('late Captain, Canadian Volunteers').

Even after the war was over, the complicated struggle over the control and development of the American West continued unabated. (The West had been the basic economic issue in the war between the fledgling industrial capitalism of the North and the mercantile and agrarian capitalism of the South.) The response of Macdonald's Conservative government was to create the North West Mounted Police (1873) to garrison the Canadian plains.

The extracts are taken from pp. 43-4, 45, 46-7, 49, 52, 53-6, 65, 78, 90. They are pretty much representative of the anti-democratic British and Canadian traditions (the fear of what was called 'mobocracy'). Canada and Britain are presented as 'pure' and 'honorable.' In Imaginary opposition, America, and especially the extent of American democracy in 1875, is represented as 'evil.' And yet even this opposition and the contradictions that go with it are not maintained as Norris shifts from one attitude to another, sometimes within the same sentence. The Imaginary structure of oppositions between Canada and the United States is maintained by statements which purport to describe the situation in the United States (some of which are true), but which are in reality equally applicable, or more applicable, to the situation in Canada in 1875. Equivalent sentiments are still heard in Canada a century later.

> . . . The superficiality of the American character is admitted by their best writers. . . . There is nothing in the country at present that would last one hundred years. Everything is done for the present, and the future must take care of itself. . . . The character of the people is just as flimsy as their works; weak and shallow, satisfied with the gaudy and the showy; without any interest in those studies which form strong traits, it tries to make up in vain-glorious self-laudation what it lacks in strength. The qualities of energy, enterprise, and ingenuity cannot be denied to the American character; but the source of these qualities detracts from their merits. . . .
>
> . . . Every man tries to overreach his neighbor, and both endeavour to overreach the State. When the moral sense is destroyed by processes of this kind, the family relations cannot long remain pure. . . . Hence the frequency of divorce and the universal

corruption of boarding houses and hotels. In no other country has an effort been made to give public recognition to prostitution under the title of woman's rights. . . .

The contrast presented to this state of morality by the Canadian people is immense. The decent observance of all the social virtues at least in public and by profession is [well-known]. The absence of any divorce law [in Canada] is . . . some proof . . . of the general state of the morals of the people. Law is the result of necessity or rather the will of the people; and if the state of the people required it in such a democratic country as Canada [where only relatively affluent males can vote], such a will would make itself manifest by the passing of such a law. . . .

The desire to amass money and wealth is just as great in Canada as in the United States; but the means employed [in Canada] are not nefarious, and they are always subordinate to the feeling of commercial honor. . . . The English standard of commercial honor is an unusually high one. In the commercial circles of the United Sates of the highest class, the feeling which impels men to meet [their commercial] obligations may be just as strong; but the general morality in this respect is as much below that of Canada as it is below that of England. . . .

Rings, corners, and fraudulent stock are things which the unsophisticated and 'unenterprising' Canadians at present know nothing about; and their existence must always remain a mystery to them so long as the corrupt legislatures of the United States, based upon universal [male] suffrage, which gave these institutions strength and vitality, are impossible in their country.

The political institutions of the United States are in a great measure one of the main sources of the wide-spread immorality which prevails. The doctrine of universal [male] suffrage is held by Canadians generally as being responsible for the most of it; but the fault or evil lies deeper. The right to vote being given to a man without property is not of itself an evil. . . . Some may infer intelligence sooner in a man possessed of property than in one who has none. This inference might hold good in Europe; but not in Canada or the United States. Churches and schools in these countries are as accessible to the poor and they are to the rich, property consequently as a means of obtaining education and intelligence cannot have the same weight in this respect as in Europe. . . .

. . . In a country where the press is so free and subject to so little supervision as in the United States, the danger arising from its abuse is more imminent that in a country where it is subject to censorship. The mass of pernicious reading which teems from the American press cannot help having a deleterious effect on those capable of reading it, and whose taste has not been formed by any instruction whatsoever. In other countries this danger is averted by religion. Education and religion go hand in hand in forming the mind, and, while education provides the means of acquiring information, religion, and in some countries a rigid censorship of the press, provide that these means shall be made use of in acquiring the proper kind of information.

These two securities are totally wanting in the United States.... The religion and education of the United States are not sufficient to guide the people in the use of their political rights....

The chief difference between Canadian and American institutions is in this: the Canadian franchise is a limited one [restricting the right to vote] to property-holders and house-holders.... [However,] even if the manhood suffrage be introduced into Canada, the moral power of her people is sufficient to enable them to use it properly and prevent it from becoming the evil it is in the United States....

The ruler [sic] of the United States or the president is elected every four years, and during this time he is not continually responsible to the people. He is liable to a certain extent by impeachment; but this, as its punishment is only removal from office, after being found guilty by the senate,—which, with the power in the hands of the president is almost impossible—cannot be said to be much of a security.... The susceptibility of the government to the will of the people as expressed by their representatives, which is the main characteristic of the English system of government, is entirely wanting in that of the United States....

...Under the Canadian system the Executive is continually under the control of the people, and susceptible to their will. The Government of Canada is simply a Committee of the House of Commons....

...The veto power, which in the hands of a president of the United States may do such irreparable damage, is in the hands of the Canadian executive entirely innocuous....

...The Executive of the United States is elected every four years by the people indirectly [through the electoral college]. This periodic upheaval of society so frequently, upsets the business of the country, affects the stability of the Government, and engenders animosities among the people. It also frequently carries with it a total change of the policy in the country. . . . This periodical battle for the spoils of office. . . under the pretence of principle, must eventually lead to the extinction of patriotism, and the degradation of the nation. As the severity of the contests increases, the men engaged in them become inferior. The step between George Washington and U.S. Grant is immense. . . . Under the [Canadian] system of responsible government those evils are avoided. . . .

. . . Now, independence would do the same thing for Canada that it has for the United States. [It strengthened them 'to cope successfully with the mother country again in the war of 1812.'] It would create a nationality which would unite the people as one man against all encroachments by the United States, and effectually prevent the absorption of the country by that power. Nothing but independence can ever avert this misfortune, which like a black cloud continually overhangs the country. Let not the ignorant prejudices of Scotchmen and others in favor of their native countries hide this from Canadians. . . .

Apart from all the material advantages which might legitimately be hoped from independence, there are the moral advantages which are greater than all. Under the present system [in Canada] there is no past to be proud of, no present to give reliance, and no future to hope for. Devoid of national life the country lies like a corpse, dead and stagnant; but not so bad as it has been.

. . . Vitalized by the spirit of nationality, Canada would leap forward on the road of progress—her people, imbued with self-reliance, enterprise and independence, would accomplish more in twenty years than they would in a hundred in their present position.

. . . It is independence and independence alone that will ever enable Canada to fulfil her destiny, to be the asylum for the oppressed and downtrodden peoples of Europe—an asylum where, under their own vine and fig tree, they can live in the enjoyment of happiness and liberty, perpetuating English institutions down to the most remote generations.

PART THREE

Economic and Historical

CHAPTER EIGHT

Colonizers, Collaborators, and Colonized

Anti-Canadian talk about our national identity is not in itself the only predominantly Imaginary kind of communication in our society (much of which is non-verbal communication in any case). But it is indeed representative of one system of Imaginary communication which concerns us in every aspect of our lives: the Imaginary communications of the bourgeoisie in Canada.

Item 37: Imaginary Canadian Control: Manipulating Statistics

In 1972 Alcan [the Aluminium Company of Canada] was defined by Statistics Canada as being a Canadian rather than a U.S. controlled corporation. However, the 1975 Annual Report from Alcan says that 42 per cent of the company's shares are owned in Canada, 43 per cent in the United States, and the remaining 15 per cent in other countries. But even this figure of 42 per cent requires some qualification. The chief officer of Alcan, Nathaniel Davis, is a resident of Canada and as such his shares are classified as 'Canadian Owned'[!]. In fact, Davis is a member of the Philadelphia family associated with the Mellons in the ownership of such corporate giants as Alcoa, Pittsburg Plate Glass, Gulf Oil, and Westinghouse Electric. Davis moved into Canada to assume control of Alcan only after a U.S. anti-combines commission or-dered Alcoa to divest itself of the Canadian operation. . . .

Between 1971 and 1972 INCO [International Nickel] was also reclassified from foreign to Canadian control. Statistics Canada had concluded that over 50 per cent of the shares were owned by residents of Canada. This may well be true, although a conclusive investigation of the actual control of INCO is yet to be done. For the time being, it should be noted that, depending on the nature and distribution of the shares of a company (common stocks as opposed to preferred; lots of small investors or several large blocks; use of holding companies), it is not only possible but common to control a large corporation with less than 10 per cent of the equity. . . .

—Red Star Collective: *Canada: Imperialist Power or Economic Colony?* (1977)

Grand Bourgeois and Petit Bourgeois

Since the term 'bourgeois' is commonly used as a term of abuse without much concern for what it actually refers to, it is just as well to begin this section on economic matters with some definitions. 'Bourgeois' is not used here to signify what is usually signified by 'middle class' or 'upper class.' It is used to refer to that class of people—the dominant *structural* component of state and private capitalism—who control and constrain the expression of the productive resources of an economic system. This they do, not merely as individuals or groups, but most importantly as a socioeconomic class. This is a class whose diverse and competing vested interests are in conflict, as a whole, with those of the working people whose creative capacities are controlled and constrained by bourgeois interests.

The bourgeoisie thus includes all those whose private or collective ownership and direction of the means of production (the productive capacity) of various sectors of the economy is such as to include a *controlling interest.* (Mere ownership of stock and the like does not necessarily entail control; and many of the bourgeoisie also work for a living.) The bourgeois class thus includes the economic managers of the system (as also in the USSR, for instance), as well as bankers and the like, and also their political representatives and their spokespeople in the media. A local or domestic bourgeoisie may itself be dominated by monopolistic and multinational economic interests, whether willingly or not.

Under the power of modern capital, the bourgeoisie may ordinarily be distinguished from the small-business and professional domain of the 'petty bourgeoisie' (who may or may not identify themselves with the bourgeoisie as a whole) by the fact that the petite bourgeoisie generally operate within the remnants of the 'free competition' of the 'free enterprise' level of the economy (e.g. old-style service stations), as distinct from the monopolistic (and oligopolistic) levels (e.g. the energy companies and their country partners, e.g. in the Middle East).

The petit bourgeois class thus coincides in general with the upper level of what is usually called 'the middle class' in North America. This upper level ranges from truckers owning or leasing their own trucks to university faculty members, doctors, lawyers, small businesses, specialized technicians, and 'professionals' of all kinds. The name, however, has been translated into English as such a bourgeois (and pseudo-leftist) put-down that few of us like to recognize our membership in it. (Remember, however, that the Algerian War of Independence against the French (1954-1962), as in some earlier happenings in the American colonies, was to a considerable extent sustained by petit bourgeois 'politicals,' as well as being supported by the majority of the people as a whole. The petit bourgeois obviously has more relative freedom and protection in society, and more free time, than the worker.)

One further point here: because they form the major *boundary* between the bourgeoisie and the workers, the petite bourgeoisie are rarely clearly 'united' by or about any issue, except perhaps by the delusion that they need to be 'protected' from people and groups below them in the socioeconomic hierarchy of power. When they do recognize that the real threat actually comes from above, however, they often become militants.

Item 38: Canadian Capital in Flight

The Sunday Star [of Toronto, as reported by Canadian Press,] says a recent trend of large Canadian companies buying property and creating industrial jobs in the United States may be partly behind the slump in the Canadian economy.

The newspaper says Canadian interests have bought or opened more than 300 manufacturing plants in the U.S. and have spent more than $1 billion on U.S. real estate development since January, 1977.

The newspaper quotes estimates by the U.S. commerce department that the total of new Canadian investment in the United States exceeded $6 billion [in 1977] for the first time, probably making Canada the largest single foreign investor in the U.S.....

'For us, there is little difference from a project management point of view between, say, Edmonton and San Francisco,' said A.E. Diamond, chairman of Cadillac-Fairview Corp. Ltd. of Toronto. 'And right now the U.S. economy is in a much more dynamic state than ours.'

Diamond also said Canadian investors are more welcome in the U.S. than in their own country.

—Vancouver Sun:
Edition of July 17, 1978

The Open Arms Policy

The Canadian bourgeoisie is significantly Canadian only in name, not in reality. It is not, and has not been for some considerable time, a *national* bourgeoisie, i.e. a class of capitalist entrepreneurs who take on the task of the economic development of a particular country in the generalized world context of capitalism. Throughout its history, Canada has been primarily developed in its productive and basic industries by foreigners and by foreign capital.

Our pseudo-bourgeoisie long ago decided, it appears now—for whatever reasons—that they would be and could be quite comfortably well off by engaging in profitable and relatively secure second-level and third-level industries, while leaving the primary industries, as well as most manufacturing, to others. Thus it is that the 'Canadian' bourgeoisie is dominant in banking, in transportation (directly subsidized in many ways by the public), in retailing, and in other service industries (such as our breweries). Moreover, this apparently Canadian bourgeoisie has traditionally invested most of its profits or surplus Canadian capital *outside* Canada—e.g. in the U.S., in Brazil, in the Caribbean—not where it has always been needed, at home (cf. Items 9, 38, and 43).[1]

The traditional role of the 'Canadian' bourgeoisie, especially since the creation of our tariff barriers and artificially inflated domestic prices after the 1880s, has been that of openly and actively encouraging American capital to jump the tariff walls and invest directly in the raw-material resource industries and the manufacturing industries of Canada, i.e. in the basic, productive industries, outside agriculture, which are this country's most important source of wealth (*use values*) and riches (*exchange values*). The result has been that again with the active collaboration of Canadian vested interests—our raw-material resources must after all be used by workers in production in order to create value, if the second-level and third-level industries dominated by Canadians are to survive—American capital does not now simply dominate the country quantitatively. More importantly, it exerts positive and qualitative controls, as well as negative but still qualitative constraints, over the fundamental character of the Canadian national economy and over the future goals of this as yet still relatively 'undeveloped' country—a country, moreover, whose economic masters have been effectively *de-industrializing* and *de-developing* since the late 1950s. (One parallel we are reminded of here is the de-development of India by the British, especially as regards the manufacture of textiles, in the late eighteenth and early nineteenth centuries.)

[1]For an analysis of Canadian quasi-imperialist investment abroad, see Red Star Collective, 1977.

Item 39: Corporate Concentration:
'Leaving the Foxes in Charge of the Chickens?'

The scope of the [study by the Royal Commission on Corporate Concentration] was, however, a surprise. The commission had neither been asked nor expected to study Canada's tax framework, yet its most prominent recommendation concerned the scrapping of capital gains and corporation income taxes.... The chapter on taxation covers just 25 pages in the 450-page report and, unlike other issues discussed, there is no background study behind it....

Far more significant is the commission's attack on the proposed tribunal to screen mergers, first recommended by the economic council in 1969. Unlike the capital gains tax, the tribunal has not yet been set up. Mergers that threaten competition in any given industry are still dealt with under criminal law, and there has been only one conviction in the 55 years that [this] law has been on the books....

The commission concedes that Canadian industry is already highly concentrated, more so than in the United States. But it argues that concentration should be accepted—and even encouraged—in the interests of making Canadian industry more efficient,

innovative and competitive in world markets. In arriving at this conclusion, the commission contradicts the findings of some of its background studies....

In parts, the report of the commission reads like a paper by John Kenneth Galbraith, the Canadian-born Harvard economist who argues that industry must be concentrated to undertake the risk and expense of planning for the future. But the commission ...does not accept his remedy of permanent wage-price controls to protect consumers against gouging. Says Nadeau: 'The consumer is overprotected now.'*

—*Maclean's Magazine:*
Edition of May 29, 1978
(Report by Suzanne Zwarum)
According to Maclean's, *Commission member Pierre Nadeau is president of a Belgian-owned oil company, Petrofina Canada Ltd., which was convicted of anti-competitive practices in 1974, and is now under investigation—along with seven other oil companies—for allegedly conspiring to fix prices. The Royal Commission on Corporate Concentration was set up by Prime Minister Trudeau in 1975, after the aborted bid by Power Corp., a Montreal-based conglomerate, to take over Argus Corporation, its Toronto-based*

competitor. *Nadeau also sits on the board of the Royal Bank. The Royal Bank provided Power Corp. with the money for its* *attempted purchase of Argus. On Nadeau's own board at Petrofina sits Peter Thomson, a director of Power Corp....*

Change of Masters

There are many political, historical, and economic details of the colonization of Canada and its people which cannot be included here; and there are of course exceptions to the general patterning of the foreign ownership and control of the productive resources of this country. But it is the patterns, not the exceptions, that are important, and as we gradually become acquainted with 'what actually happened' in our own past, new or previously unrecognized patterns begin to present themselves to our consciousness. In particular, the perennial problem of the 'quest for Canadian identity' suddenly begins to make unusual sense. It begins to make new sense once its real economic and historical sources are used to understand it, that is to say, once the context of the Real—our natural, social, economic, and historical reality—is rescued from the oblivion into which our bourgeois compradors have cast it.

The peculiarities of Canadian history—much of which is symmetrized British history to start with—beg to be understood here. Most Canadians are ordinarily brought up to take about as much pride in their history as they do in their postage stamps. This is hardly surprising. After all, it is a little difficult to feel pride in an economic and historical tradition when it is our own capitalists who have thrown us to the wolves of foreign exploitation.

When we expended our blood and our treasure to help the 'Mother Country' in the First World War, for example, we were contributing—without knowing it and for the best of intentions—to a new era of domination for this British Dominion, which was not granted 'official' independence until 1931. If it was as *colonials* that we went to war in 1914, as in the earlier British war against the Boers (1899-1902), then it was as budding *neocolonials* that we returned in 1918. For after Europe had bled itself near to death, previously dominant British investment in Canada (mainly indirect investment) leveled off, while U.S. *direct*[2] investment increased. Canada's pseudo-protectionist tariffs guaranteed

---

[2]'Direct' investment refers not to investment in loans, bonds, stocks, and the like (indirect or 'portfolio' investment), but to investments of capital in subsidiaries, branch plants, and so forth, such that the interests represented by the capital maintain direct control over the plant, industry, or economic sector in question.

Item 40: The Mantle of Empire

From: Rudyard Kipling: The White Man's Burden*

Take up the White Man's burden—
  Send forth the best ye breed—
Go bind your sons to exile
  To serve your captives' need;
To wait in heavy harness
  On fluttered folk and wild—
Your new-caught, sullen peoples,
  Half devil and half child.

Take up the White Man's burden
  —The savage wars of peace—
Fill full the mouth of Famine
  And bid the sickness cease;
And when your goal is nearest
  The end for others sought,
Watch Sloth and heathen Folly
  Bring all your hope to nought.

Written in 1899 and published with the subtitle: 'The United States and the Philippine Islands.' The United States seized Guam, Puerto Rico, and the Philippines from Spain in 1898, and made Spain withdraw from Cuba. The Americans had been aided by Filipino nationalists in 1898, who controlled the entire archipelago except the city of Manila, but their seizure of the islands led to the 'Philippine Insurrection' of 1899-1902. For three years, while the British were busy with Boer guerrillas in South Africa, an army of 60,000 American troops was employed in defeating the Filipino guerrillas (the 'goo goos'). One of the American Generals waged war with such 'indiscriminate ferocity' (says the latest Encyclopedia Britannica) *that he was court-martialled and forced to retire. In spite of the estimated 200,000 Filipinos killed, organized resistance continued for some years after 1902, and still continues. The Philippines remained an official American possession until 1946.*

U.S. branch plants high profits and relative freedom from competition. By 1930, total U.S. investment far exceeded the British total. World War II increased total U.S. holdings to three times the British, U.S. direct ownership rising to seven times that of the British. In 1967, U.S. direct investment in Canada was greater than in Europe, and almost twice that in Latin America (Red Star Collective, 1977: pp. 31-6).

Internal Scapegoats and 'Outside' Threats

At the ideological level of this neocolonial relationship, and in the mirror-game which many of our pundits use to play us off against each

Item 41: 'Quebec: The Soft Underbelly for Subversion'

A subversive threat of the utmost gravity, masterminded and co-ordinated by the Soviet KGB, undoubtedly exists in Canada. The political situation in Quebec, in particular, provides an ideal environment for the growth of subversion, for not only are there sufficient dissident elements to be fostered and supported but these can also be penetrated by dedicated Marxists.

Those who in their naivete believe that they will achieve their political aims in alliance with militant Marxists and yet preserve the existing democratic frame-work will find that when the Marxist juggernaut really gets under way, they will be the first to go to the wall.

It would be strange if the United States and the North Atlantic Treaty Organization were not maintaining a very careful scrutiny of current political events in Canada. Apart from the very real opportunity for Russia and indeed other powers not especially well disposed to the Western alliance to exploit unrest in Quebec, any material change in the province's relationship with the rest of Canada will have a profound effect on the strategic stability of North America—the heartland of the Western deter-rent against total war. . . .

In the nation's short history the fractious quarrel between French-Canadian and Anglo-Saxon has resulted in constant political confrontation, erupting from time to time into violence. Ironically, the 1867 constitution, with its inbuilt checks and balances, has over the years become a major obstacle to a satisfactory solution. It is to be hoped that the recent proposals for radical amendments to the constitution will go a long way toward convincing the Quebecois that whatever the past injustices, real or imaginary, they are now 'first-class Canadians' in every way.

—The Institute for the Study of
Conflict: *Report on Canada*
(1978)*

For the source of this quotation, see the end of this chapter. The headline quoted is that used by the Vancouver Sun. *The author is British. Note that he does not refer to English or British Canadians at all, but only to Anglo Saxons. For many of the British, 'Canadian' means* the others.

other—and to keep us oscillating between the British and the Americans—we are repeatedly told that the only really significant 'internal' threat to our 'liberties' in our history has come from French Canada—our largest colony within a colony—symbolized by the heroic and tragic figure of the Métis, Louis Riel.

In 1849, Louis Riel's father led an armed show of force against the autocracy of the Hudson's Bay Company (the 'Courthouse Rebellion'). In 1870, Louis Riel led the citizens of the Red River Colony[3] in the Manitoba they founded—with the support of some of the still powerful Plains Indians—in political and military resistance against the economic and political expansionism of the newly 'confederated' Canada (the confederation of 1867 through which vast land-holdings west of the Canadian Shield were eventually delivered by corrupt politicians into the expensive hands of the railway promoters, amongst others). And if Anglo Canadians remember the date, 1885, at all, it is generally as the date of the year in which the last spike was driven at Craigellachie on the Pacific railroad (November 7). French Canadians, in contrast, have never forgotten it. For 1885 is also the year that Louis Riel, after the second 'rebellion' and in spite of a recommendation for mercy from a jury of WASPs, was hanged in Regina, Saskatchewan, condemned as a traitor by the Macdonald government in Ottawa (November 16).

At the same time, eighteen Métis and 'about thirty' Indians (including Big Bear and Poundmaker) were sentenced to penitentiary terms for their role in the resistance. Also hanged in 1885—in public at the North West Mounted Police stockade at Battleford, Saskatchewan—were eight Indian warriors: Ikta, Little Bear, Wandering Spirit, Round-the-Sky, Miserable Man, Bad Arrow, Man-Without-Blood, and Iron Body (see Brown and Brown, 1973: p. 21).

If the native Canadians, the Québécois, and Canadian labor unions have repeatedly been made into our major *internal* scapegoats (led or influenced, of course, by Imaginary 'outside agitators' and 'alien ideas'), it is the Americans—whose interests are already so firmly entrenched inside the country that American capital and its collaborators are our nearest present danger—who have just as repeatedly been used as a

---

[3]In 1870, there were 12,000 people in the Red River settlement, classified by Joseph Howard (*Strange Empire,* 1952) as: 6,000 Métis, 4,000 English 'half breeds,' 1,500 white 'Europeans,' and 600 Indians. The legal Provisional Government of the settlement was set up in 1869, disbanded in 1870. Riel was called back from exile in the United States as the leader of the second 'rebellion' (like the first, in reality, partly a civil war, and partly a war between two countries).

fictional *'external'* threat to 'Canadian liberty.' Indeed, a number of Canadians did help the British defeat the several military invasions of this country by American forces, as in the War of 1812. But the real American military threat (up to perhaps 1870) and the apparently external economic threat (up to the 1930s) were originally threats to British imperialism, rather than to the people of Canada. Nevertheless, the misguided paranoia, directed both internally and externally, still remains. The Imaginary American enemy, for example—as distinct from the real economic take-over of Canada by American capital after World War I—still looks out at us from the deluded pages of 'Defense Scheme No.1' the secret brain-child of Colonel J. Sutherland Brown, Director of Military Operations and Intelligence from 1920 to 1927. This was a plan to counter an expected American military invasion of Canada by invading the United States, a ghost that was not officially laid to rest until 1931. (For real potential military threats to Canadians, see the Note to Chapter Twelve.)

The same ideological sources as those which produce and reproduce the hoary old themes of 'outside agitators/internal threats' and 'the threat to Canadian liberty by alien ideas' also imply that our erstwhile 'colonial' years were in general so peaceful and progressive that we never experienced any form of civil war, or revolution, or whatever. We didn't need them, so the story goes, because the British had already had them for us.

Indeed, it is certainly true that we have not yet experienced a successful uprising against colonial power and inherited privilege, nor against any form of political and economic domination.

In that one word, 'successful,' our history diverges significantly from that of the French and the Anglos who were primarily responsible for stealing this land from its original inhabitants in the first place.

In other words, this country has never at any time since the Europeans named it been other than a colony controlled, exploited, and garrisoned for the benefit of somebody else—someone other than the working people of many nationalities who built it, someone other than the working people who still carry it on their backs.

What We Are Not

Above all, we have never experienced the wars and upheavals of rising bourgeois interests, the bourgeois revolutions, and the rise of a home-grown industrial capitalism that made our principal ancestors—French, British, American—what they are. To put the matter bluntly, we suffer from the awkward and unpleasant reality that our 'Canadian' bourgeoisie is predominantly a hand-me-down, secondhand bourgeoisie—a

Item 42: Canada Between the Hammer and the Anvil

The Ever-Widening Wave Circles or the Jubilee of the "Last Spike"

The reverberation of the driving of the last spike of the world's greatest transportation enterprise has not yet ceased encircling the world in the interest of Canada and humanity in general.

Cartoon by A.G. Racey

In Montreal Daily Star, November 12, 1935

collaborationist bourgeoisie that repeatedly capitulated to our various overlords in our history rather than fight such military, political, and economic struggles in its own right.

From this we may permissibly conclude that if Canadians as Canadians have been socialized to be Imaginary citizens of an Imaginary nation, it is primarily because, in terms of world history, the 'Canadian' bourgeoisie, real as they are, is a class of Imaginary capitalists.

Thus it is that the marginal role we have been granted in other peoples' histories, our relative lack of a truly Canadian class of productive entrepreneurs, the corruption and conniving of our politicians in history, the treasonable renewals of our always colonial status, our repressive heritage of irresponsible government and colonial authoritarianism, and the repeated manipulation of our supposed independence of the 'Yankee spectre' by our ideologists, have all resulted in a particularly Canadian anomaly amongst a supposedly non-third-world people: a people whose 'national identity' is almost exclusively defined by *what we are not*.

Above all, we realize that—with the exception of the indigenous peoples—our historical and economic reality has meant that the dominant Other for Canadians as a whole—Symbolic, Imaginary, or Real—has never been a *Canadian* Other.

Two Notes to Chapter Eight

SOFT UNDERBELLIES

The stirring piece on 'Russian subversion' and 'outside agitators' in Quebec, quoted on p. 134, fortunately appeared in the *Vancouver Sun* (September 15, 1978) before this essay went to press. The author is Rowland Mans; its source is explained by the *Sun* as follows:

> The Institute for the Study of Conflict, a London-based private organization whose members include military men and academics who are students of subversion, has recently issued a report on subversion and terrorism in Canada. [Quoted] are some excerpts from the concluding sections. Major-General Mans, a British career military officer, has served as an instructor at Royal Military College, Kingston, Ont.

Item 43: The Myth of the Shortage of Capital in Canada

In 1969, 1970, and 1971 respectively, 82 per cent, 78 per cent, and 97 per cent of the funds for investment by 970 foreign corporations in Canada were generated internally by the corporations themselves. U.S. direct investment was almost 80 per cent of the total direct investment in Canada in those three years. These statistics show that it is no longer necessary for American imperialists [in Canada] to import [new] capital from the U.S. to increase their investment [in Canada]. U.S. controlled investments in the non-financial industries rose from $25.5 billion in 1970 to $30.1 billion in 1973. Not only do profits made from exploiting the Canadian proletariat save them from having to export capital to Canada, but in addition some of these profits are drained out of Canada and exported to other countries to support U.S. ventures. These investments are generally labelled as Canadian external investment. However [according to Statistics-Canada's 'Canadian International Investment Position 1968-70', p. 29], 'at the end of 1970 non-resident equity in Canadian direct investment abroad amounted to $2,711 million, equivalent to some 44 per cent of the total Canadian investment abroad.'

—Red Star Collective: *Canada: Imperialist Power or Economic Colony?* (1977)

Without this little note, I daresay some readers might have confused this piece with a heavy-handed plank in the election tactics of a well-known Canadian political party.

'YOU WON'T BE WANTING IT BACK, WILL YOU?'

According to newspaper reports of a Gallup Poll taken in mid-July 1978, a majority of the 1031 adult Canadians asked would like Canada to 'buy back control' of US firms in Canada (59%). Over two-thirds (69%) feel that there is at present 'enough' (sic) U.S. capital invested in Canada. What the truly representative figures on this issue may actually be, we have no way of knowing, because of the way in which the 'yes/no' questions were skewed to produce suitably moderate answers (*Vancouver Sun,* August 12, 1978, Section D):

First Question: 'Now thinking about U.S. capital invested in Canada—do you think there is *enough* now or would you like to see *more* U.S. capital invested in this country?' [emphasis added].

Second Question: 'Some *experts* are suggesting that Canada buy back a majority control—say 51 per cent—of U.S. companies in Canada. *Even though it might mean a big reduction in our standard of living,* would you approve of this or not?' [emphasis added].

One would surely have expected the pollsters to be a little less outrageously manipulative in their skewing of the second question. Similar manipulation would be accomplished a little less obviously by 'denial,' i.e. by saying: 'even though it *might not* mean a big reduction in our standard of living' (compare Items 20, 23, 33, 43, and 44). However this may be, the majorities refusing to be intimidated by the pollsters are very significant indeed.

Item 44: Some Statistics, Such as They Are

[In 1976] direct U.S. investment in Canada totaled about $31 billion—about 23% of the total U.S. investment stake around the world....Americans own 42.5% of Canadian manufacturing..., and Canadians own just slightly less—41.4%, with other foreign investors holding the remaining 16%. So Canada has lost control of manufacturing already.... [In] petroleum and coal products, foreign ownership is almost 100%. Here are a few additional percentages of U.S. ownership of various Canadian industries: mining, 49% [in 1971, previous to the 'reclassification' of certain companies as 'Canadian,' this was officially 59%]; rubber products, 76.5%; textile mills, 50.3%; machinery, 52.6%; transport equipment, 78.3% and chemical products, 61.2%.

—Tam W. Deachman: *What Every American Should Know About Canada* (1977)

Those answering Question 1 with 'there is enough American capital now' range from 46% in 1964 to 69% in 1978, with a high of 71% in 1975. Those answering 'don't know' range from 21% in 1964 to 9% in 1978.

The second question about 'buying back control' with 51% of the equity is grossly misleading about 'control' (cf. Item 37 and Chapter Fourteen). Those answering this question with 'buy back control' made up 46% in 1970; 58% in 1975; 41% in 1977; and 52% in 1978. Those answering 'don't know' range from 19% in 1970 to 11% in 1978. (Note the increased frequency of the polling.) (See also page 19.)

CHAPTER NINE

Unequal Trades

As Wallace Clement notes (1977: p. 290), although the U.S. share of the 'gross world product' (GWP) has declined from about half in 1950 to about a third in 1976, Canada's dependence on the U.S. has steadily increased. Our other outside relations have also declined dramatically. Our exports to the U.S. increased from about half of all our exports in 1961 to over two-thirds of our exports in 1971. It is now over 70 per cent. Moreover, we cannot easily withdraw from this unequal 'trade' in the continental context, because, unlike earlier periods, much of our so-called 'trade' consists of intracompany transfers to U.S. parent companies.

Note the important connection of this unequal 'trade' with the constant machinations by vested interests, Canadian and non-Canadian, against the Canadian dollar (recently down to about 81 cents U.S., its lowest level in over forty years). This forced devaluation lowers the price of our resource and other exports to U.S. manufacturing interests (amongst others), thus keeping U.S. profits up on both sides of our undefended border. For when we get our own exports back in the form of manufactures, their prices escalate. Given the basic instability of the U.S. dollar in the world market, the United States does very well indeed with its exploitation of Canada and Canadians. Has it ever occurred to you, for example, that probably the biggest single export from the United States into Canada is the United States' own home-grown inflation?

(The Europeans found this out some time ago, as a result of the U.S. export of inflation—originally to a considerable extent via Indochina—into their own countries.)

The Canadian Market

It is an arduous task in Canada to obtain properly relevant and adequately researched information about the Canadian economy and Canadian trade. Government manipulation of the statistics relating to Canadian ownership and Canadian control of industries located in this country is a particularly thorny and irritating question (see Items 37, 44, and 45, for example). Since the government agencies involved are not yet asking the right questions, it is doubtful whether anyone in Canada has

Item 45: Corporate Welfare

[The Export Development Corporation] is a government agency whose role is as stated in their 1974 Annual Report, 'to facilitate and develop export trade by the provision of insurance, guarantees, loans and other financial facilities.' The EDC loans money to governments or companies in second and third world countries in order that they may buy goods from Canada.... [The following table] illustrates that since 1972 U.S. companies in Canada have benefited significantly more than Canadian companies from the EDC funding of trade.

Percentage of U.S. and Canadian Companies from whom Commodities were purchased for which the Export Development Corporation provided Financing to the Purchaser

Year	U.S. Companies	Canadian Companies*
1969	36.5%	38.1%
1970	31.7%	37.8%
1971	26.7%	46.7%
1972	50.0%	7.1%
1973	40.5%	29.7%
1974	41.0%	28.3%

—Red Star Collective: *Canada: Imperialist Power or Economic Colony?* (1977)

*Because of the way in which the Federal authorities present the figures from which these percentages are calculated, there is considerable uncertainty about what the precise figures may actually be. Foreign ownership and control of corporations in Canada, for example, is commonly calculated in the most politically advantageous manner, rather than in the most rigorous and relevant way. In the years tabulated above, aid to corporations labeled as British varied between 2.7 and 14.3 per cent (average 7.1 per cent). There are two other categories also involved: 'Ownership Unknown' and 'Various Suppliers' (unidentified). Aid in these two categories for each year is as follows: 1969—19.1%; 1970 —22.0%; 1971—19.9%; 1972— 35.7%; 1973—27.1%; 1974— 26.4% (figures supplied by Red Star Collective).

any real knowledge of the actual extent of the foreign—and not simply U.S.—control of our industries and technology.

Along with official statistics which do not tell the whole truth, there is one perennial story put out by government and business sources in Canada which needs a comment or two, especially because when asked, so many Canadians will repeat it. This is the story that our high prices, our high unemployment, our high interest rates, or what have you, are the result either of what is called 'our small domestic market' or of what is said to be 'the failure of Canadian industry to remain competitive in the world market.'

This story is trotted out like clockwork every time we are driven by foreign economic interests into a depression, every time the inordinate profits of monopolistic industry and banking in Canada drive up the rate of inflation, every time our dollar is devalued, and every time Canadian labor struggles against the reduction of real wages brought about by the inflation for which business and government are primarily responsible (compare Items 13, 16 and 46).

The 'small domestic market' is nonsense. Canada is actually part of the continental (North American) market controlled by U.S. and multi-national interests; and all that keeps prices so high in Canada is the highly profitable Canadian colonial market. It is highly profitable because there is little or no price competition in Canada to start with, and there does not need to be, since the government tariff policies are what produce the artificial prices we pay in this country.

After all, if the Canadian market were not so extraordinarily profitable for capital, then why is it that foreign interests exert so much effort to buy control over it? In British Columbia alone, since the return of Social Credit in 1975, foreign-owned firms have taken over 63 Canadian businesses; and about 80 per cent of all foreign investment in this province is now concentrated on buying out existing businesses, rather than on creating the new industry and the new jobs which the government and business fairytales tell us such investment will bring (see the *Vancouver Express* of January 19, 1979; and Items 20 and 36). Obviously, we need more properly researched information to find out just how badly the Canadian consumer is being exploited in the support of foreign and domestic interests; but the rapidity with which Canada is becoming progressively more colonized every year by those interests should indicate to those with the ears to hear it that there is nothing significantly 'small' about the domestic market in Canada.

Item 46: Reckless and Irresponsible Government Spending

Former auditor-general Max Henderson said [on May 3, 1978 that] the federal government's 'reckless and uncontrolled' spending is rapidly debasing Canada's currency.*

...Henderson said the federal government's current $48 billion budget is taking 50 cents of every dollar's worth of goods and services generated in Canada.

'You may remember that this is the level that brought Britain to its knees' and resulted in devaluation of its currency, he said.

In contrast, Henderson said, the comparable figure for U.S. spending on government is only 23 cents—'a figure which [Demo-cratic] President Carter deplores as far too high.'

He called for a 10-per-cent or $4.8 million across-the-board reduction in federal spending, which is 'the biggest single factor causing our high domestic inflation and widespread unemployment.'

...'The real danger we face is that our present political leaders, with an election coming along, will embark on more government spending and gimmicks to stimulate consumption and buy votes.'

—*Vancouver Sun:* May 4, 1978.

The Liberal deficit (1968-79) is now $10 billion.

As for the nonsense about the 'failure of Canadian industry to remain competitive in world markets,' there are two simple counter-arguments to be made. Since most of our basic industry is controlled by foreigners, then its present technological and structural inefficiency (its lower productivity) is primarily the result of decisions made by foreign corporations, not by Canadians. Productivity in industry is controlled primarily by capital; where low productivity exists, it is not the result of the output of Canadian workers. And since no one would accuse capitalists in Canada of being stupid, there must be good reasons why they do not bother to upgrade their Canadian branch plants so as to make them more productive. These reasons must surely be that they are doing so well with the present situation—and with the *lack* of the necessity for 'efficient competition' in Canada, because of the extraordinary extent and degree of monopolistic concentration in this country—that there is no incentive for them to change their present mode of doing business here (see also Item 8).

The second counter-argument is even more decisive. Canada's vast stores of renewable and non-renewable natural resources are absolutely

Item 47: The Low-Mobility Society

The fragmentation of the capitalist class in Canada does not mean that the whole class is not still powerful vis-a-vis the working class—indeed, it may have gained power because of its alliance with U.S. capitalists in the continental context. It does mean, however, that the Canadian component must commit itself to the continental context. The existence of a powerful Canadian commercial elite, based in the Canadian upper class, and a predominantly foreign-controlled elite in production means that Canada remains a 'low mobility' society. Concentration and centralization in commercial sectors have been the work of indigenous forces while the same processes in the productive sectors have been imposed from outside (with the aid of Canadian capitalists in circulation). The result is a highly structured economy with few avenues through which the lower class can rise. The process of compradorization has offered a few middle-class Canadians mo-bility into the elite, but many of the uppermost positions created by this process have been filled by the indigenous elites. In fact, very few Canadians have moved from the branch-plant structure into the real power positions within the parent company. This middle-class comprador elite* is largely trapped in the backwater of the U.S. subsidiaries.

Unlike the portfolio investment typical of the British Empire, the direct investment of the U.S. empire does not eventually break off as a result of economic forces alone but deepens its hold. Nor is there any reason to suspect that the indigenous capitalists in circulation are contemplating taking over U.S. enterprises.

—Wallace Clement: *Continental Corporate Power* (1977)

*com.pra.dor, n. (*Portuguese: a buyer, purveyor.*) *In many countries, a native agent or factotum, as of a foreign business house* (The Living Webster: 1971).

---

essential to the continued survival, in the short term, of global and multinational capital. Nevertheless, Canada is forced by the foreign control of its resource industries, and by the collusion of the federal and provincial governments with these alien exploiters, to sell its resources for peanuts. The real and simple economic reality is that when a country has what everyone else needs—minerals, metals, water, gas, petroleum, hydro-electric power, forests, and so forth—then, in the contemporary world of vanishing natural resources, that country can always wait for the world market to come to it—rather than being induced to *subsidize* the imperial powers in that market, not simply with irreplaceable raw materials, but also with artificially manipulated low prices.

And the foreign capitalists know this only too well. Canada is going cheap—and this is why so many of them are falling over themselves in their haste to get in on the Canadian bonanza.

The 'Canadian Question'

The 'Canadian Question'—no, the term 'Canadian' is misplaced by this wording, misplaced in such a way that, like 'the Jewish Question' or 'the Woman Question,' the wording projects the problem away from its real source, away from the exploiter, onto the oppressed, and out of context—the 'question of the Other for Canadians' has long lain on page 240 of Fanon's *Wretched of the Earth* waiting for us to discover it:

> Because it is a systematic negation of the other person and a furious determination to deny the other person all of the attributes of humanity, colonialism forces the people it dominates constantly to ask themselves the question: 'In reality, who am I?'

To which we add: *'And why don't we know?'*

It should be obvious, I would think, that unlike the 'answers' repeatedly formulated by our representatives in business, in academia, and in government, this 'oedipal' question is not primarily a psychological or personal one. It is primarily historical and economic. But the representatives of our oppressors have always preferred to blame Canada on Canadians—I have listened to this fairytale for more than two decades now—and *by blaming Canadian workers* for the economic instability of our colonial economy in the context of the oscillating pseudo-stability of capitalism, the representatives of the alien Other have amazed us with one more triumphant extension of Freudianism: The Canadian Complex theory of Canadian history.

Freudian Counterinsurgency

A major reason why the question of responsibility and identity can so easily be misrepresented as an 'oedipal' or psychological question comes out of the wide influence of Freud's misunderstanding of social relations in the family, and from his misinterpretation of Sophocles' play, *Oedipus the Tyrant* (Latin: *Oedipus Rex*). 'Who am I?' is the problem faced by Oedipus throughout the play. After his father, aided by his mother, tried to murder him as a child, Oedipus grows up to kill his father in open combat and to marry his mother, without realizing who they are. These 'transgressions' are supposedly the reason for a plague that strikes Thebes, where Oedipus has become tyrant as a result of the marriage. A search develops for the man who killed his father, the dead tyrant. The 'Who am I?' of Oedipus thus really means: 'Am I the killer? Am I responsible for all this? *Am I guilty?'*

Freud's answer is 'Of course you are'—just as any child who even *thinks* of killing or displacing fathers must certainly be. The inverse is not true, however, implies Freud; and all through his work he simply ignores or explains away the violence of parents towards children (especially female children).

To buttress his (unconscious) role in reinforcing the dominant ideology of our society, Freud took Sophocles's play, neutralized its social, economic, and historical *context* by ignoring it ('psychoanalyzing it') and then used what was left (not much) in such a way as to completely misrepresent the actual and usual parent-child relationship in violent societies. In a word, just like Freud's interpretation of the situation of women, the whole basis of his invention and interpretation of the so-called 'oedipus complex' is Imaginary. It is a vicious circle in every sense.

Freud, however, treats the so-called complex not simply in purely individualistic terms, but also as if it were biologically 'innate,' as if it were a 'genetic trait.' From this Imaginary perspective, all children (but especially female children) are designated as individually responsible for the violent (or hypocritically coercive) behavior of their parents. They are also made to be responsible for their reaction to the behavior of their parents—Jesus Christ and his 'martyr complex' provides a good example—and as if this were not enough, children are also made to feel guilty about what their parents have done to them, verbally, non-verbally, or physically ('This hurts me more than it hurts you').

Besides this, Freud's entire theory of paranoia is based on the same technique of blaming the victims as is his 'oedipal' theory. Freud's so-called analysis of paranoia is based on a famous autobiographical account of paranoia by a certain Dr. Daniel Paul Schreber (whom Freud never met). Freud just happens to leave out of account evidence available to him about Schreber's father. The father had not only manipulated and coerced all his children in extraordinary ways (another son commited suicide), but had also used them as guinea pigs to test various leather and metal restraining devices invented by him. (He was a very well known 'educational authority' whose various books depicted these devices.)

Morton Schatzman has provided us with the evidence of the absurdity of Freud's theory—not to mention that of his most famous followers—in his *Soul Murder: Persecution in the Family* (Signet, 1974). (Contra Schatzman's attempt at a social interpretation, however, there is nothing specifically German about Schreber's father's insane behavior—no more than fascism is specifically German.)

Freud's ideological position on society and the family is not significantly different from that of many others—especially as regards the 'paranoia' of women about men. This kind of Freudian counter-insurgency—making the oppressed collectively and individually responsible for their oppression, making the exploited responsible for their exploitation—still runs throughout most contemporary psychological, social, and economic theory and practice, 'Freudian' or not. Indeed, many commentators, media personalities, politicians, academics, and businessmen in Canada use it all the time. Others of us have been trained to use this Freudian weaponry against ourselves. The ordinary result of this is to make us accept our colonization as if it were our own fault, at the same time as we are made to feel guilty about our legitimate anger at it.

Item 48: A Bright Memory

The world's memory of Canadians in battle is a bright memory. The Canadians in World War I seemed to shine out of the blood and muck, the dreary panorama of trench warfare. They seemed to kill and die with a special dash of lavishness.

—General A.G.L. McNaughton (final Canadian authority over the Dieppe Raid), speaking in 1943. Quoted in *Colombo's Canadian Quotations* (1974)

A Note to Chapter Nine

THE FIRST BATTLE OF PAARDEBERG
February 18, 1900

'It would be difficult to estimate the number of men who have been killed directly and indirectly in the South African war through thirst. Every letter from the front speaks of the insatiable thirst, and in almost every hot fight men have been struck down, either while crossing the fire zone to secure water for their comrades, or while exposing themselves to the enemy's fire in their efforts to quench a thirst more agonizing than a wound....

'[The Boer commander, General Piet] Cronje was speaking with well-aimed rifles. He would not surrender and was beginning the most desperate fight of his life. He was in a trap, a hopeless trap, with every outlet closed. [The British commander, Lord] Kitchener had done his work well.... [Cronje's] retreat had filled the besieging force with admiration, and now his determined stand in the bed of the Modder [River] gave him a new right to his title, 'The Lion of the Transvaal'....

'On such a position, against such a man, the Canadians began to advance as soon as they had shaken some of the water from their clothes [acquired in crossing Paardeberg Drift on the Modder]....

'Never were soldiers more thoroughly tried than those in the firing line of the Royal Canadian Regiment on February 18th. At times the air seemed alive with singing bullets, and the soldiers' only safety lay in clinging close to the dry plain. Some...scooped themselves holes in the sand.... A rush was out of the question; to stand upright, to attempt to double to another shelter would have meant instant death....

'. . . Here too were the chaplains, and particularly that noble self-sacrificing priest Father O'Leary....

'All through the morning the hot sun blazed overhead, scorching the bodies of the men and parching their tongues; all through the morning that unceasing fire made them seek close cover....

'The day grew hotter but the fight slackened but little. The exhausting [night] march to Paardeberg, the need of food, [the lack of water,] the heat were telling on the men.... [A rainstorm struck....] When it passed, many of them refreshed and rested fell asleep where they lay and several were struck as they slept.

'There could be no better evidence of what the Canadians had endured than this. A man must indeed be worn out when he can sleep with death singing its song about his couch....

Item 49: The Maple Leaf Scrapbook

Tributes to Canadians...

Canucks fight like dervishes, writes Englishman

By H. D. ZIMAN
Daily Telegraph Special Correspondent

How do the Canadians strike a British war correspondent? I might have been asked how do Canadians refrain from striking a British war correspondent?

I am more and more impressed by the good manners and tolerance of Canadian officers and above all of Canadian WO's, NCO's and men. What I have found surprising and delightful is that Canadian officers and troops regard the press as their friends.

However the job of the Canadians in Normandy is not to receive newspapermen but to fight the Germans. But do you need me or anyone else to tell you how well you are doing this? If I may quote from a letter I wrote some days ago to my wife «who has incidently been working for over four years at Canadian Military Headquarters in London, this is what I said

« I am very proud to be with the Canadians, who are fighting magnificently. They have taken very severe losses in the battle of Caen, but they are still going terrifically strong »

Tribute to Courage

It is not my business in this article to say much about the fighting, but I must say something about the spirit of the Canadians.

« How many casualties have you had among the padres in your division? » I asked.

« Four dead out of 12 » he told me — and he still wanted to go forward.

It is no wonder the German troops believe Nazi propaganda about Canadian soldiers being savages with scalping knives. Many of the captured enemy are quite surprised to find that these Canadians who have fought like wild dervishes are really quiet, civilized, calm and well-disciplined when one meets them after the battle

---

Another Englishman on Canadians

Surrey girls will forever tell spouses: you should be more like the Canadians

BY DOUGLAS REED
Kemsley Correspondent with Canadian Forces

The Canadians, as I observe them, certainly have a natural gift for making friends «and, if those looks of coy surrender I sometimes see mean anyting for influencing people» I noticed this first in my native Sussex, when the Canadian occupation occured. There was an immediate outbreak of collaboration from Uckfield to Cuckfield, and from Eastbourne to East Grinstead.

In distant years, when this war I hope is but a memory, I think the roses-round-the-door cottages will resound with the quarrels of old men and their wives on the point of « You're too slow why can't you be more like the Canadians? »

Actually, the Canadians were lucky in having a free field and much favour; if the Americans had arrived a year earlier they would have had a great competition to beat

It impresses me to find that Canadians are just as successful in France They got on equally well among the great nations of the resistance movement and the girls of the least-resistance-movement «probably the daughters of Mademoiselle from Armentiers in the last war» As passionate leave has not yet started this is good.

I shall not forget the grave of Bombardier Hill, a Canadian who fell at Caen. He was killed in the roadside, either by his own friends or by the French. One soldier's grave the more what is that, in Europe? Well, the French have made a wayside shrine of a new kind of his grave. They have ornamented it, and they keep it fresh with flowers. They have put the French tricolour and the Union Jack on composed an especial little poem in homage to Bombardier Hill, and written above it «The French will never forget the Canadians» I've seen no more impressive tribute It says all that could be said

---

BRITISH TRIBUTE TO CANADA   16 Oct. 1944

Our friends in England — and in so many cases our families appreciate our efforts. This is what The Evening Standard says

« Once again Britain acknowledges a debt of gratitude to the Canadians. They stormed positions of steel and concrete to liberate our Kentish towns from the batteries which for four years have been their constant scourge and tribulation. They helped to reduce the flying bomb from a terror to a nuisance weapon. They have de-infested the harbours from which the E-boats menaced our shipping restored to our French allies their maritime cities, and to us supremacy over the narrow waters. Above all, they have, by their brave exertions, sustained the general advance exploited so brilliantly by Montgomery's men, freed the general staff from one of their greatest anxieties, and enabled the main forces to go forward, confident of their long sea flank and communications »

THE CANADIAN STATURE   16 Aug. 1944

« The Dominion of Canada has reached full stature among the great nations of the world »

The Evening Standard of London pays a tribute in commenting last week on the expansion of Canadian forces in France to the status of a powerful national army. « It is difficult », The Standard says, « to recount our debt to Canada harder still to express our gratitude. The heroism of her troops in the last war is legendary, her present sons their worthy successors.

« Now, on the anniversary of the decisive onslaught launched by their fathers at Amiens against the Kaiser's armies, they are entering into their heritage. They are not avenging Dieppe, where they bore the heaviest burden of a brave experience. They are exploiting the experience of Dieppe with the skill, tenacity and the shining courage of a great and grand people »

The dervishes or 'fuzzy-wuzzies' were followers of the Mahdi, fighting for the independence of the Sudan in the late nineteenth century, and well known for incredible bravery in the face of technological superiority. In 1884-5, English-speaking and French-speaking Canadian and native Canadian voyageurs helped General Lord Wolseley fight his way up the Nile cataracts in a fruitless effort to relieve General Charles Gordon, besieged by the Mahdi at Khartoum. A major at Lucknow in 1857, Colonel Wolseley had led the expedition against the Red River Rebellion in Canada (1869-70). He had also won a decisive victory in the Zulu War of 1879. He became commander-in-chief of the British army in 1895. In 1896, the Sirdar of Egypt, Lord Kitchener (who had served under Wolseley in the Sudan in 1885), was ordered to reconquer the Sudan. At Omdurman in 1898, eleven thousand dervishes were slaughtered in a few hours by Kitchener's forces, for a loss of 48 British and Egyptians. The man who made the reconquest possible was the man who built Kitchener a 385-mile long railway from Wadi Halfa to the vicinity of Khartoum, a young Canadian engineer named Edouard Percy Cranwell Girouard. While still a lieutenant, Girouard was appointed president of the Egyptian state railway system (1898). By 1899, he was Director of Railways in the British war against the Boers (1899-1902). He was knighted in 1900 (see MacLaren, 1978).

'At four o'clock Colonel Allworth of the [Duke of Cornwall's Light Infantry, the British force on the Canadians' right] told Colonel Otter [the commander of the First Canadian Contingent, a veteran of Upper Canada College who had led the Battleford Column against the Indians under Poundmaker in the North West Rebellion of 1885] that "he had been sent to finish this business, and proposed doing so with the bayonet". . . . Bugler Williams leaped on an ant-hill and while the bullets rained about him the clarion notes of the charge, so welcome to the Saxon ear, rang out. The tired, exhausted line [of British and Canadians] woke up and swept forward at the double, stumbling, falling, mowed down like grain before the reaper. Forward, forward, through a hail of bullets; at last they could stand it no longer. The Cornwall's Colonel was killed with five bullets, the 'recall' was sounded and his men broke and retreated. The Canadians were too near the enemy to retreat. . . . At this close range no help could be given to the wounded. . . . Many of the wounded as they writhed in agony were struck a second time. It was a horrible ordeal for the young soldiers, and yet but the beginning of nine days of as severe fighting as ever tested men.

'The charge was as magnificent as the charge of the Light Brigade [against the Russians at Balaklava—where Lieut. A.R. Dunn of Toronto won the Victoria Cross—during the Crimean war of 1853-56], but it should never have been made. As has since been proved the British knew absolutely nothing of the character of the Boer's position. They might as well have tried to carry Gibraltar at the bayonet's point as Cronje's position. The soldier dearly loves the spectacular in war, and nothing is so magnificently inspiring or picturesque as a bayonet charge; but...it has a place in modern war only on the rarest occasions. Of all the blunders of this war [Kitchener's] at Paardeberg is perhaps the most unpardonable. Magersfontein has its excuses, but Paardeberg has none. However, the mistakes of England's leaders have been the glory of the English soldier; and this charge gave Canada a permanent place in British history. "The Men of Paardeberg" will stand out in bold characters on the future pages of the story of the Empire. But there was a terrible butcher's bill for the renown gained. Seventy-five per cent of all who fell on that black Sabbath met the fatal blow in this mad charge.

'There was nothing the Canadians could do but lie where they fell until darkness came. . . .'[1]

[1]Quoted from T.G. Marquis, *Canada's Sons on Kopje and Veldt* (1900). This is a contemporary account of the First Canadian Contingent of 1000 'elegant extracts' from the militia sent by Laurier to aid the British in the Second Boer War—without the consent of Parliament.

Australians and New Zealanders also served. In 1901, a detachment of Australians from Victoria mutinied after being told by General Beatson that they were 'a lot of wasters, and white-livered curs.' Seeing an Australian officer taking down his words, he said 'You can add "dogs" too,' and went on to say that all Australians were alike (Kruger, 1959: p. 435; compare Item 17).

When he made his stand at Paardeberg in the Orange Free State, Cronje, with less than 5000 men, was retreating before Lord Roberts and Lord Kitchener, with 40,000 troops. Previous to this, the British had gone from one defeat to another. These included the massacre at Spion Kop (January 24, 1900). Some 2000 British infantry, packed together on the tiny summit without cover or water, were subjected for an entire day to Boer artillery and rifle fire—while the rest of the army watched. Winston Churchill was one of the war correspondents who witnessed the resulting carnage: at least 1200 men killed and wounded, the dead piled three deep in the shallow trenches. (The Boers lost about 300.)

As a result of Kitchener's fanatical misuse of his troops—he had never before faced whites in battle—the British and Empire forces suffered 1300 casualties on the first day at Paardeberg. The Boers suffered some 300, including women. (Later in the war, at least 20,000 Boer civilians, mostly women and children, died of hunger and disease in Kitchener's concentration camps.)

Cronje was finally shelled into surrender, on February 27, 1900, by a massive concentration of heavy artillery, including naval guns. Once more, Colonel Otter's Royal Canadians led the final infantry charge. (The Royal Canadian Regiment, 2nd (Special Service) Battalion, suffered some 130 casualties at Paardeberg.) For colonials, the two assaults at Paardeberg foreshadow the ANZACs at Gallipoli (1915-16), Hong Kong in December 1941, and the 'Dieppe Raid' of August 19, 1942, the worst disaster British bungling ever inflicted on Canadian troops—3367 casualties out of 4963 troops embarked.

CHAPTER TEN

The First Canadian Civil War

The basic patterning of the social individuality which links a people together will be found in their history. This individuality is indivisible from our social relationship with others. But Canadians, like so many millions of others in similar and in much worse circumstances, have not been permitted by their schooling and their upbringing to know their own history, much less encouraged to find it out.

Historical Amnesia

The story of Canadian history is a story of cunning distortions, of convenient lapses of memory, and of twisted symbols that bear little readily understandable relationship to what they represent. Subjected as we have been, and still are, to repression by the agents of Canadian or American 'law and order,' by ideological censorship, by economic coercion, and by plain bloody ignorance, we Canadians, historically speaking, are a nation of amnesia victims. The history we are taught, and the historical and other fictions reinforced by the media, are little more than a long series of denials and rejections, by the spokepersons for our foreign rulers and their collaborators, of our actual historical experience.

As Greg Keilty has put it more bluntly (1974: p. 10): 'An almost unbroken line of paid liars, masquerading as historians, have laboured to convince us that we have always been happy to be a colony, have never fought back, have no heroes and no history.'

Moreover, as any number of other oppressed groups already know— non-whites, women, productive workers, for example—the biggest lie in all these secret histories is not necessarily the overt (and often unconscious) misrepresentation of the reality. As often as not, the biggest lie of all is *what is not said*, the lie communicated by silence (Mark Twain).

There are many significant silences about Canadian history, but two in particular attract our attention. Separated by almost exactly a century, both concern Canadians under arms in civil wars against oppression. The first is the story of the Canadian volunteers in the Spanish Civil War of 1936-39.[1] The second is closer to home, but more distant in time: the Canadian Rebellion of 1837-39.

[1]One of these volunteers was the Dr. Norman Bethune who so distinguished himself in his later service to the Chinese people, before his death in 1939, that he is better remembered by many millions of Chinese than he is by his own country.

How many Canadians under 50 years old today remember the open outpouring of popular support in Canada in the late 1930s for the volunteers our people sent to Spain? It has been said that, proportionate to population, more Canadians volunteered to fight Franco, Hitler, and Mussolini in Spain than did the citizens of any other country outside Spain, except for France. Do we remember that the Canadians in the 40,000-member International Brigades assisting the legitimate, elected government of Spain were fighting the mechanized might of Fascist and Nazi troops, guns, tanks, and planes? According to the latest *Encyclopedia Britannica*, some 80 per cent of the Brigades consisted of working people—and this was at a time when the governments of the western 'democracies' (including Canada), by means of an agreed-on 'policy of non-intervention,' were effectively and decisively intervening in the conflict on the side of the Fascists. With the partial exception of France, the democracies accomplished this by the simple expedient of refusing to sell to the embattled Republic—even for cash on the barrelhead—the arms without which it could not possibly continue to protect its people (cf. Hoar, 1969; Elstob, 1973; Halton, 1944).

As a result, while Texaco (for example) made large profits illegally selling oil to Franco (on unlimited credit), the Republican government was forced into dependence on Stalin's Russia.

American sympathizers sent the Abraham Lincoln Battalion to Spain (about 3000 men); the British sent about 2300 men; the French Battalion was called the 'Commune de Paris'; ours was the 'Mac-Paps,' the 1155 men of the Mackenzie-Papineau Battalion of the International Brigades.

Rebellion

Louis-Joseph Papineau (1786-1871), the representative and *Patriote* who led the Canayen resistance to the British until he felt compelled to choose exile in 1837, is remembered as a national hero by many Québécois. The Scots-born Reform democrat and militant, *William Lyon Mackenzie* (1795-1861), an elected representative of the people of what is now Ontario in the violent Rebellion of 1837-39, is not so well remembered by non-Scottish Canadians.[2] Both of these men, rep-

---

[2]Many people cannot avoid an unconscious attempt to 'complete' this seemingly incomplete name, William Lyon Mackenzie, by that of Mackenzie's grandson, William Lyon Mackenzie King (1874-1950), the Liberal who was three times dynastic prime minster of Canada—a 'Freudian slip' of some political consequence.

Mackenzie emigrated to Canada in 1820. In 1834 he was elected the first mayor of Toronto. As a member of the colonial Assembly between 1828 and 1836, he was expelled five times on trumped up charges by the Tories of the

resenting thousands of other Canadians, were leading figures in the greatest struggle for *independence* from British colonial tyranny and from its agents in the Canadas that our history records.

But few standard histories or standard references mention the word 'independence' meaningfully, if at all; and the accounts they give of our war with colonialism are in general so sanitized and distorted that some of the 'authorities' ordinarily available to us not only persist with the 'outside agitator' theory, but actually refer to this hard-fought series of uprisings, pitched battles, naval excursions, and guerrilla attacks on the British garrison and the bloodthirsty Tories of the 'Canadian' militia, as 'Papineau's Rebellion.'[3]

Before their final defeat, the Canadian Patriots were aided— sometimes unfortunately—by large numbers of individual Americans who shared the Canadian hatred of British rule—some of them Catholic Irish (cf. Tiffany, 1905). This circumstance was twisted by the ruling oligarchy in Upper Canada, the Family Compact, into another fiction in the 'outside agitator' theory, into the propaganda that the Rebellion was American inspired. The truth is that American federal

---

Family Compact, but repeatedly re-elected by the franchised voters. His first newspaper, the *Colonial Advocate*, was saved from bankruptcy in 1826, when a Tory gang (in the presence of two British magistrates) totally wrecked his presses, because he was able to win damages in a civil suit. The Tories made several attempts to assassinate him.

Mackenzie's grandfather and great-grandfather fought for Charles Edward Stewart ('Bonnie Prince Charlie') in the Forty-Five Rebellion against the English. In 1746, the Duke of Cumberland, the star of Handel's 'See the Conquering Hero Comes,' attacked about 5,000 weak and ill-led Highlanders at the Battle of Culloden, beginning with a devastating cannonade. The Highlanders were overcome by the English force, twice their numbers. The Redcoats were then ordered to slaughter the Scottish wounded where they lay. James Wolfe, of later fame, was one of Cumberland's officers.

In the Canadian Illustrated Library series, Mackenzie is pictured in the volume entitled *The Heroes: A Saga of Canadian Inspiration* (1967). He is identified as a 'firebrand' newspaper editor. The only other information given is the caption to the picture: 'William Lyon Mackenzie's attacks on the "Family Compact" of Upper Canada caused a mob to smash his newspaper office. He led an abortive revolt in 1837 but, after being pardoned, he returned to Canada and became Toronto's first mayor.'

[3]*The Squeaking Wheel* (1966: p. 68) puts it this way:

In 1791, after a considerable wave of settlement had been made in what is now Ontario, the British Parliament divided Canada into Upper and Lower Canada.

This gave Lower Canada (Quebec) an opportunity for its own assembly, and this move eventually led to the rebellion of French Canada.

As a counterstep Lord Durham recommended the union of the two Canadas. . . .

troops assisted the British in various ways in putting the Rebellion down.[4]

In their mercantilist and almost feudal exploitation of Upper Canada, and in their refusal to attend to the economic development of the colony, the Family Compact in Upper Canada is readily recognizable as the direct ancestor of today's fragmented 'Canadian' bourgeoisie. In the history of other countries, it was via the 'progressive' rise of a national bourgeoisie, later an industrial bourgeoisie, that the capitalist version of democracy was worked out. Not so in Canada. When the Upper Canadian Patriots followed the lead of the *Patriotes* and rose up in December, 1837—in the face of years of economic coercion, political manipulation and violent provocations, including repeated attacks by Tory terrorists—it was only after their elected representatives had struggled against the colonial Executive for over a decade in the attempt to obtain redress of grievances by every available democratic method, including the principles of majority rule.

Repression

But so effectively has this particular criminal conspiracy of silence been enforced against the Canadian people that even 50 years after the Rebellion, when a monument was finally erected in Toronto in 1893, a monument to the memory of just two of the Canadians the British hanged—in spite of 30,000 signatures on a petition for clemency— Samuel Lount, a blacksmith, and Peter Matthews, a farmer, the inscription on the monument made no mention of the manner of their death, nor of the civil war and the attempted war of independence of which they had been a part.

Perhaps needless to say, we in Canada are generally informed neither of the tenaciousness of the *Patriote* and Patriot resistance, nor of the *national* character of this struggle—much less of the fact that, as the evidence in our archives makes plain, the Rebellion of 1837-39 was a direct response to the class warfare originally initiated by the British and their local allies against the Canadian people.

The British and their 'Empire Loyalists' recalled too well their igno-minious defeat by the American rebels in 1783. In the Irish Rebellion of 1798, the British had vented their ferocity on Catholic and Protestant alike: 'Countless thousands died, shaking their scythes at cannon' (Seamus Heaney, *Lament for the Croppies*). Inexperienced in military

---

[4]The British eventually paid the Americans for their cooperation in cornering the Patriots—with large chunks of Canada, beginning with the Webster-Ashburton Treaty of 1842 (see Keilty, editor, 1974: pp. 222-3).

matters, the Patriots underestimated their foes. The two Canadas were gerrymandered into a new colonial Union in 1840—this alone cost the French a pretty penny⁵—and the means were put in hand to stamp the very memory of the Rebellion out.

But before this, the British had to stamp out the Rebellion itself. This operation was hardly a 'comic opera' defeat of the 'rabble,' as many of our history books tell it. By the fall of 1839, the British Chancellor of the Exchequer was complaining that the Rebellion had cost Britain some two million pounds (ten million dollars)—and the British garrison which arrived in London, Ontario, in January 1839 was not withdrawn from the town until the outbreak of the Crimean War in 1854. (The uprising in the London District, on December 9, 1837, was led by Dr. Charles Duncombe.)

While nothing compared to British behavior in Ireland, India, and Africa, the British and Tory responses were vindictive. Apart from the arrest of anyone suspected of democratic leanings, the repression included attacks on Patriot women, the razing of villages and homes by fire, the use of armed bands of Indians in warpaint to hunt down fugitives in the woods, the shooting of wounded, and the use of prisoners as running targets for 'loyalist' sharpshooters.

Sir John Colborne (called 'Satan' in Lower Canada) spread army terrorism and courts-martial throughout the *Patriote* districts. The major agent of the repression in Upper Canada was Lieutenant Governor Sir

⁵Lower Canada (French Canada), with no public debt, was required to take responsibility for the huge public debt of Upper Canada (£1,200,000). Perhaps needless to say, the Canayen population was not consulted on the Act of Union which created the Province of Canada in 1840. Upper Canada, in contrast, was not only consulted, but (as it had been trying to do since the 1820s) successfully insisted on being assigned a number of elected members equal to that from Lower Canada (42 each)—in spite of the fact that the white population of Lower Canada (650,000) was 200,000 greater in numbers than the white population of Upper Canada (see Bergeron, 1977: pp. 95-113).

This tradition of unrepresentative government has been continued in other ways and places. The basic principle of 'one person, one vote'—recently established by the Supreme Court of the United States—does not exist as yet in Canada. We Canadians are still using the English political system of the early nineteenth century—complete with the Canadian equivalent of 'rotten boroughs.' For example, some 80,000 people inhabit the provincial district of Richmond, B.C., which elects one member to the provincial legislature. In Atlin, B.C., which also elects one member, there are a mere 3,158 registered voters. This is a time-worn way of disenfranchising many thousands of Canadian voters. (In the most recent example of gerrymandering, the agents of Social Credit in B.C. broke up three New Democratic Party areas, created five seats expected to favor Socreds in 1979, and actually increased the numerical disparity between two seats in Vancouver.)

Item 50: The Autocrats of Upper Canada

*In the election called by Lieu-
tenant Governor Sir Francis
Bond Head in 1836, Mackenzie
received 389 votes; his opponent,
489. As even Lord Durham later
attested, the colonial executive
and the Tories interfered in the
election in many ways, including
bribery, the creation of instant
voters, and general intimidation
(the secret ballot was not introduced until 1874). On nomination day at Streetsville, the
polling place for the newly
created Second Riding of York,
armed Orangemen (Protestant
Irish) attempted to intimidate
Mackenzie, who had to be protected by a personal bodyguard.
Mackenzie spoke as follows
(June 27, 1836):*

When I last met you here I told
you the causes of our difficulties,
and showed you how far they
might be removed by the
concessions or interposition of
the British Government. I regret
to say that all efforts of the Reformers during the last two years
have only gone to show that the
Government is above all law; that
a person, living in one of the
streets of London is the autocrat
of Upper Canada; and that the
people's representatives have
neither power nor influence to
promote education, encourage
trade, redress grievances, secure
economy, or amend your laws

and institutions. I have been dili-
gent in the legislature; every
proposition calculated to make
you happier I have supported;
and whatever appeared to me to
be against popular government
and the permanent interests of the
many I have opposed, please or
offend whom it might. The result
is against you. You are nearer to
having saddled on you a dominant priesthood; your public
and private debt is greater; the
public improvements made by
Government are of small moment; the chartered Banks and the
Canada Company have you more
and more under their control; the
priests of the leading denomin-
ations have swallowed bribes like
a sweet morsel; the revenues of
your country are applied without
your consent; the principle that
the Executive should be responsible to public opinion and ac-
ceptable to the people is denied
to your use, both by the Governor
here, and by his employers elsewhere; the means to corrupt our
elections are in the hands of the
adversaries of popular institutions, and they are using them;
and although an agent has been
sent with the petitions of the
House of Assembly to the King
and House of Commons, I dare
not conceal from you my fears
that the power that has oppressed
Ireland for centuries will never
extend its sympathies to you. It

will seek to elevate the few, who are suitable instruments for your subjugation, in order that (like the Canada Company, Thomas Clark's £100,000 estate, John McGill's £50,000, and I might add, Colonel Talbot's vast accumulation) such men may will, or take their wealth elsewhere, to impoverish you. Look into the history of our race:—'Ages pass, and leave the poor herd, the mass of men, eternally the same— hewers of wood and drawers of water.'* I have taken less pains to be elected by you this time than I ever did before, and the reason is, I do not feel that lively hope to be able to be useful to you which I once felt. On this subject I spoke my mind with great frankness at Cooksville, when I told you that this country was beginning to lose all hope from Reform majorities

under this government, and that I feared the result of the election would show that it was so. We are, of course, to wait for the answer to our petitions to England. If it be favorable, it will be our duty to uphold the system of monarchical government, modified, of course, by the removal of that wretched playhouse, the [appointed] Legislative Council, together with the mountebanks who exhibit on its boards. If the reply be unfavorable, as I am apprehensive it will, for the British Whigs and Tories are alike dishonest, contending factions of men who wish to live in idleness upon the labors of honest industry then the Crown will have forfeited one claim upon British freemen in Upper Canada, and the result is not difficult to foresee.

Cf. Joshua, 9: 21, 23, 27.

George Arthur, a man whose use of violence in the name of law and order in the Province eventually provoked even the British Colonial Office into aristocratic protest. Arthur was the man responsible for the judicial murder of Lount and Matthews, amongst others.[6]

[6]Lord Glenelg wrote to Arthur from Downing Street on March 14, 1838, before Lount and Matthews were hanged (April 12, 1838): 'Sir, representations have reached this department . . . that during the present session of the Legislature of Upper Canada, measures of unusual severity and of extensive application have been proposed against those who may have been in any way implicated in the late insurrection in the province. . . .

'Her Majesty's Government are fully alive to the difficult position in which at such a period of alarm and confusion, the Legislature and the Government of Upper Canada are placed. . . . Nothing, I fear, would be more likely to impair the moral effects of the late events than unnecessary severity; I trust, therefore, that. . . your influence will be successfully exerted in moderating the zeal of those, if such there be, who might be disposed to proceed to extreme measures, and in allaying the irritation which, however natural, cannot but be attended with danger to the public peace' (Lindsey, 1862: II: p. 189n; see also Landon, 1960).

Arthur had previously served as the Lieutenant Governor of Honduras (1814-22), where he put down a slave rebellion. Before coming to Upper Canada in March 1838, he served twelve years as Lieutenant Governor of the penal colony of Van Diemen's Land (Tasmania), detested by the settlers and more than hated by the convicts at forced labor. As Arthur explained in a letter to England written shortly before his appointment to Upper Canada, the principle behind the penal colony was to reduce the transported convicts to the status of slaves. With his history of the liberal use of the lash and the scaffold, Sir George Arthur surely stands as one ancestor of the Tory fanatic in Canada today.

Item 51: Sir Francis Bond Head and Friend: In Defense of the Family Compact

[*Editor:*] The often maligned 'Family Compact' of Upper Canada should not be hastily condemned. In his 1839 account of the Upper Canadian situation, former Lieutenant-Governor [Sir] Francis Bond Head attempted to show how such a 'compact' was a necessary part of any civilized society....

[*Sir Francis:*]... This 'Family Compact' is nothing more nor less than that 'social fabric' which characterizes every civilized community in the world. It is that social fabric, or rather fortress, within which the British yeoman, farmer, and manufacturer is enabled to repel the extortionate demands of his labourers; and to preserve from pillage and robbery the harvest of his industry after he has reaped it!

'The bench,' 'the magistrates,' 'the clergy,' 'the law,' 'the landed proprietors,' 'the bankers,' 'the native-born inhabitants,' and 'the supporters of the Established Church,' form just as much 'a family compact' in England as they do in Upper Canada, and just as much in Germany as they do in England....

The 'family compact' of Upper Canada is composed of those members of its society who, either by their abilities and character have been honoured by the confidence of the executive government, or who, by their industry and intelligence, have amassed wealth. The party, I own, is comparatively a small one; but to put the multitude at the top and the few at the bottom is a radical reversion of the pyramid of society which every reflecting man must foresee can end only by its downfall....

—J.M. Bliss, editor:
Canadian History in Documents,
1763-1966 (1966)

Judging from the sources I have so far consulted, precise details of the extent and nature of the repression are not readily available. I have not seen even an overall estimate of the several hundred Patriots and *Patriotes* killed or murdered in the various stages of the war. It is known, however, that over 1500 people were jailed at various times on the two capital charges of insurrection and high treason against the British. Between 150 and 200 were transported to the penal colonies of Australia and Tasmania. Many others were exiled to other colonies or banished to the United States. Thousands of Canadian and American settlers were harassed by the British Army and the Tory militia—well known for

---

Item 52: Sanitized History

The Tories made the most of their victory. They felt vindicated in their persistent claim that the reform agitation was merely a cloak for sedition and republicanism, and they set out to break their opponents beyond recovery. Only two men,* Lount and Matthews, were hanged for their part in the rebellion, but the guilt of these two particular victims was open to the gravest doubt. . . .
Edgar McInnis, President of The Canadian Institute of International Affairs, formerly Professor of History at the University of Toronto, in: *Canada: A Political and Social History.* New York: Holt, Rinehart and Winston, 1963. (First published 1949, revised 1959.)

This is also what Lord Durham wrote in his official report on the Rebellion for the British government, in 1839. Lount and Matthews were advised to plead guilty by Robert Baldwin, who formed the ministry of the two Canadas with (Sir) Louis Hippolyte Lafontaine in 1847, the first so-called 'responsible government' in the Canadas. Lount was a long-time political opponent of the brother of Chief Justice John Beverley Robinson, by whom he and other prisoners were tried. Governor Arthur and Attorney General Hagerman refused all pleas for clemency. The executions were witnessed by numerous prisoners in the Toronto City Jail, themselves lying under sentence of death.

---

their policy of taking few prisoners—and many homes and farms were pillaged, destroyed, or confiscated. How many became refugees from the atrocities of the war against the civilian population, from the war itself, and from the repression that followed is even more difficult to ascertain than the number of dead, but we must have lost at least 20,000 residents and citizens. Twenty thousand exiles in a white population of about 1.1 million (1840) would be equivalent to about 400,000 refugees from the Canada of today.

During this reign of terror, hundreds of Canadians were tried by courts-martial made up of local militia officers; some were sentenced without trial; all were faced by hostile courts, military and civil; hundreds were intimidated into throwing themselves on the mercy of the courts. Several hundred were further terrorized by being sentenced to death—at the rate of five a day in the case of the 44 court-martialled by Arthur in London, Ontario, between December 26, 1838 and January 20, 1839.

The British and the Tories eventually selected their official victims: twelve French Canadians and twenty others, mostly Anglo Canadians, 12 from French Canada and 20 from Upper Canada and the United States, 32 in all. These men were hanged as traitors and pirates in 1838 and 1839. How many of us can recite the names on this Canadian roll of honor?

Two Notes to Chapter Ten

CANADA'S HISTORY IN OIL

The following excerpt from a recent account of the Canadian Rebellion was written by Arthur R. M. Lower, Profesor Emeritus of History at Queen's University, Kingston, Ontario. It is from a chapter in a book reproducing some of the work of the Canadian artist, C.W. Jefferys (1869-1951), reprinted by The Ryerson Press, Toronto, in 1968. The chapter is called: 'Agitation: The Struggle for Self-Rule.'[7]

> [Papineau's] attitude, his complaints and his motives can be easily
> understood, for they were exactly the same as those of every other

[7]These passages are taken from C.W. Jefferys, *The Formative Years: Canada 1812-1871,* edited by James Knight, Toronto: The Ryerson Press, 1968, pp. 37-39, 40, 42-44, 50-51, 53; © Imperial Oil Limited, Toronto, 1968. Reprinted with the permission of Imperial Oil Limited, 111 St. Clair Avenue West, Toronto, Ontario. Originally published in the *Imperial Oil Review,* July 1967.

left-wing French-speaking Canadian who has ever existed. English-Canadians are constantly asking what Quebec wants. The question is so simple (to the historian, at least) that it appears naive. Quebec wants what *la race française en Amérique* has wanted from the day of [Lévis'] surrender outside Montreal in 1760; she wants to reverse the Conquest, that is all. So that whatever the terms of the day may be, the situation never changes: reverse the Conquest, 'get the English off our necks,' and if possible out of the house. People who cannot understand the psychology of a conquered people can never get very far in Canadian history and affairs. . . .

. . . [Papineau] remained in perpetual opposition and as a rule he was able to carry with him his fellow 'Canadians' (no English-speaking person used that term in those days [sic]). . . .

. . . Like many another French-speaking Canadian, he was at home in England and he had a clearer and more scholarly idea of the nature of the English constitution than had most of the mere businessmen of Montreal. That constituted another element of strain—the difference in cultural level between the two groups which was in favor of the French.

. . . Papineau staged a series of open-air mass meetings, at which his eloquence whipped the crowds to fever heat. Secret drilling began The end was clearly in sight.

In December [actually November 22], 1837, fighting broke out. . . . When fighting broke out he fled across the border. The rebels were crushed, many of them imprisoned and a number of them executed.

. . . In the same year and the same month, December, 1837, rebellion broke out in Upper Canada. It might seem as if the two were a concerted movement, but this is not the case. Papineau and Mackenzie had some correspondence, that is all [sic]. . . .

. . . It may have been that there were more grievances in Upper Canada [in the early 19th century] than elsewhere, it may have been that there were many Americans in its population not accustomed to taking grievances quietly or it may have been that there happened to be a few prominent trouble-makers present in Upper Canada; whatever the exact explanation, discontent began to bubble in Upper Canada soon after the turn of the century. . . .

. . . Mackenzie's rebellion, as an armed revolt, was a flash in the pan: a few shots (the pleasant legend is that these were quite enough to frighten both sides into taking to their heels) and it was all over. . . .

What makes this excerpt all the more interesting is that the historical works of C.W. Jefferys were until very recently in the possession of Imperial Oil (totalling about 1200 drawings and paintings). Imperial Oil was obligated by its purchase agreement with the Jefferys' estate to make proofs of these works available to the public 'for cultural and educational purposes.' However, when New Canada Press requested proofs for use in Bergeron's *Petit manuel d'histoire du Québec* (1971), Imperial Oil refused the request on the grounds that Bergeron's history is not educational. In fact, ruled Imperial Oil, the book cannot be educational because it manifests (in their words) 'a particular political or social philosophy.'

Imperial Oil is controlled by Exxon, heir of Standard Oil of New Jersey, the original basis of the world-wide multi-billion dollar empire of the Rockefeller interests of the United States. This U.S. conglomerate thus attempted in this instance to deny to a Canadian author and a Canadian publisher access to this highly significant part of Canada's heritage.

THE DEATH OF A PATRIOT

'Next morning (Friday) those who had arms buried them, and after sending to inquire whether a friend a mile below had been dangerously wounded, we agreed to separate and make for the frontier, two and two together. A lad in his nineteenth or twentieth year [Allan Wilcox] accompanied me, and such was my confidence in the honesty and friendship of the country folks, Protestant and Catholic, European and American, that I went undisguised and on foot, my only weapon at the time being [Captain] Duggan's pistol, and it not loaded. . . .

'We. . . saw and talked with numbers of people, but with none who wanted the Government reward [for our capture: £1000]. About three in the afternoon, we reached Comfort's Mills, near Streetsville; we were told there that Col. Chisholm and three hundred of the hottest Orangemen, and other violent partisans, were divided into parties searching for us. Even from some of these there was no real danger. They were at heart friendly. [Many farmers and laborers of Upper Canada had been forced to serve in the 'loyalist' militia.]

'Mr. Comfort was an American by birth, but a resident of Canada. . . . [Mrs. Comfort] insisted on our staying for dinner, which we did. Mr. Comfort knew nothing of the intended revolt, and had taken no part in it, but he assured me that no fear of consequences should prevent him from being a friend in the hour of danger. . . . [Lindsey adds: 'Comfort took out an old pocket-book, well filled with bank bills, laid it on the table, and told Mackenzie to take a supply, to which the latter replied: "I have plenty of that". . . . Comfort rode after them, at a distance of about half a mile, saying to Mrs. Comfort as he left his house, "Good-bye, wife, perhaps I may never see you again. . . ." ']

'Some who saw me at Comfort's Mills went and told the armed Tories of Streetsville, who instantly went to the worthy man's house, insulted and threatened his intrepid and true-hearted wife, proposed to make a bonfire of his premises, handcuffed and chained him, threw him into a wagon, and dragged him off to Toronto jail, and, as they said, to the gallows. He lay long in prison untried, and was only released to find his excellent wife (who had been in the family way) in her grave, the victim of that system of persecution and terror which classes men in America, as in Europe, not according to their personal deserts, but with reference to their politics, birth-place, faction, or religious profession.'

Lindsey remarks: '. . . He was first arrested by Col. Chisholm and Chalmers, and they appear to have sent him to Toronto without a guard, when he was stopped at the Credit Bridge by James McGrath, and again arrested. He showed Col. Chisholm's pass. McGrath swore Chisholm was the biggest rebel in the Province. Col. Star Jarvis examined the pass, and said they ought to respect it. But McGrath insisted . . . and prevailed. Comfort was sent to jail, where he remained three months.'

Lindsey continues: 'While he was in prison, a party, under Harry Cole, with guns and bayonets rode briskly up to Comfort's house. The children were frightened. Mrs. Comfort hearing them scream, looked out, and when she saw the threatening demonstration she fainted and was carried to bed. Her fright arose from a notion that the armed men were killing the children. She had a succession of fits. When she came to herself, one of the men asked if she had any concealed arms, and desired her to give information for the conviction of her husband, assuring her, at the same time, that he was sure to be hanged. One brute cocked a pistol, and placing it at her breast, threatened to shoot her through, if she did not tell all she knew. This threw her into another fit. They then threw pails of cold water on her in bed. This revolting treatment led to premature confinement, resulting in her death, on the 16th of January, 1838. Great efforts were made to obtain leave for Comfort to attend the funeral, on the 21st, but [Attorney General] Hagerman [who had a personal grudge against Comfort, dating back several years] was immovable, and the poor man's prediction that he might never see his wife again was realized.'

> —Charles Lindsey: 'Mackenzie's Account of his Escape from Montgomery's [Farm] to the American Shore, with Notes by the Author.' In: *The Life and Times of William Lyon Mackenzie. With an Account of the Canadian Rebellion of 1837, and the Subsequent Frontier Disturbances, Chiefly from Unpublished Documents* (1862)

Item 53: Rebellion and Revolution

A Chronology

1775-83: American War of Independence.

1787: U.S. Constitution drafted.

1789: Fall of the Bastille; Declaration of the Rights of Man in France; Belgium declares its independence of Austria (suppressed, 1790).

1790: U.S. Congress adopts the Bill of Rights (first ten amendments to the constitution).

1791: Constitutional Act creates Upper and Lower Canada. First General Strike in Germany (Hamburg). Slave revolt against the French in Santo Domingo (Haiti). U.S. Bill of Rights ratified.

1793: Bill for abolition of Negro and *Pani* (Indian) slavery in Lower Canada defeated. Henri Mézières and Citizen Genêt's pamphlet: *Free Frenchmen to their Brothers the Canadians.*

1794: Armed demonstrations in Quebec against the new Militia Act. Russians suppress rising in Poland.

1795: British deport 600 Jamaican insurgents (members of the Maroons) to Nova Scotia.

1796: Continued resistance to British rule in the districts of Quebec and Montreal; demonstrations against British attempts to re-impose the (feudal) *corvée* on the Canayen. Repressive Alien and Sedition Acts used to make widespread arrests; armed attempt at Montreal to free prisoners; riots in the St. Roch district and at Lévis.

1797: David McLean, a leader in the Canadian agitation, arrested and sentenced to death—he was hanged in public, then beheaded and disembowelled.

1797: British navy mutinies at Spithead and the Nore.

1798-99: United Irish Rebellion suppressed by the British.

1801: Guerilla warfare under Toussaint Louverture helps to expel Spanish and British from Santo Domingo (Haiti); slaves freed; independence 1804. Irish forced into union with Great Britain (now the 'United Kingdom').

1803: Insurrection of Robert Emmett in Ireland.

1804: Alien Act in Upper Canada, used against reformers and suspected democrats.

1808: Spanish rebel against the French under Napoleon, begin guerrilla war.

1810: Radical newspaper in Lower Canada, *Le Canadien,* closed down by troops, three of its editors imprisoned without trial.

1810-25: Successful wars of independence in Paraguay, Chile, Colombia, Peru, Mexico, Brazil, Central America, and Bolivia.

1811-15: Luddites destroy and sabotage machinery in England.

1812: U.S. declares war on Britain. Riots in Montreal against the forced draft of the militia are quelled by regular troops. Joseph Willcocks, founder of *The Guardian* at Niagara, exile from the Irish Rebellion of 1798, declares for the United States, along with others.

1813: The Dutch rise against the French.

1814: Norway becomes independent of Denmark, approved by Sweden. Pope Pius VII restores the Index, the Jesuit Order, and the Inquisition.

1815: Boer revolt against the British in Cape Colony (South Africa). White terror in Southern France after the fall of Napolean.

1817: British Coercion Acts suspend *habeas corpus* for the first time in English history.

1818-19: Illegal imprisonment of Robert Gourlay, a populist Scot, in Niagara Jail, from which he emerged physically broken and insane.

1819: Cato Street Conspiracy against British government is discovered.

1819: Peterloo Massacre in Manchester: British cavalry charge a peaceful crowd of men, women, and children—over 600 dead and wounded.

1821: Greeks rise up against Turkish rule.

1820-21: Revolt and Revolution in Spain, Naples, and Portugal.

1820-30: Repeated slave revolts in the Caribbean.

1825: Decembrist revolt by army officers in St. Petersburg against the Tsar.

1826: Mackenzie's *Colonial Advocate* smashed by Tories.

1827: Peru secedes from Colombia.

1828: First Reform majority in Upper Canada Assembly.

1830: Risings in Brunswick, Hesse, and Saxony (Germany). Belgium declares independence of Holland. French conquer Algiers. July Revolution overthrows the restored Bourbon monarchy in France. Greece independent.

1830-31: Insurrection against the Russians in Poland; one of the officer exiles later hanged by the British for participating in the Canadian Rebellion.

1831: Austria suppresses rebellions in Modena, Parma, and the Papal States (Italy).

1831: 'Tithe War' in Ireland, against enforced payments to support the alien Episcopal Church.

1831: On a motion by Papineau, the Lower Canada Assembly enacts a law upholding equal rights for Jews. (Legal disabilities on Jews not ended in Britain until 1858.)

1831, 1834: Revolts of silk weavers at Lyon, France.

1832: First Electoral Reform Bill finally passed in Britain. Troops fire on crowd in Montreal during 1832 elections, killing three.

1833: British Coercion Bill against the Irish. Turkey recognizes independence of Egypt.

1833-40: Civil War in Spain.

1834: Mackenzie elected mayor of Toronto; Reform majorities in U.C. and L.C. Assemblies. Demonstrations by Democrats at Frankfurt.

1836-48: Chartist agitation (workers associations) for reform in England. In 1837, Chartists support Canadian independence.

1836: Corrupt election puts Governor and Tories in control of U.C. Assembly. Texas declares its independence of Mexico.

1836-37: Beginning of the first great depression in the U.S. and Canada.

PART FOUR

Constitutional & Political

CHAPTER ELEVEN

Democracy and Democratic Rights

The Canadian Rebellion of 1837-39 is a precious time in our history, and one we all need to know more about than we presently do. It is precious because it was struggle to bring democracy and independence to Canada, and because we can learn from the very savagery of its repression many of the reasons why we still have colonial governments in Canada today. Between the power of the unelected Executive Councils in the early 1800s, for example, and the present power of the Prime Minister's Office in Canada, there is almost an unbroken line of succession; and the Family Compact of those days now looks down on us from the citadels of the modern Canadian establishment.

We can also use our knowledge of the national struggle of the 1820s and 1830s, both French Canadian and Anglo Canadian, to test the accuracy, the scholarship, and the politics of every Canadian historian who has written about, or glossed over, this period in our history. You may be surprised at how many of them, both academic and popular historians, fail the test, especially on such significant and easily verifiable details as the number of executions. Their long campaign of character assassination against William Lyon Mackenzie is of particular significance for English-speaking Canadians, because it is an indication of the violence with which the Tory establishment in Canada treats those they regard as traitors to the cause.

Out of the many hundreds taken prisoner or arrested and jailed in Lower Canada, in the two major uprisings of 1837 and 1838, some 108 Canadians from Lower Canada were tried by court-martial under Colborne's martial law, after the second uprising (Ryerson, 1975). These included the following trades and occupations:

66 Farmers	6 notaries
5 blacksmiths	5 merchants
4 innkeepers	3 bailiffs
2 doctors	2 students
2 shoemakers	2 carpenters
2 waggoners	1 teacher
1 miller	1 clerk
1 cabinetmaker	1 seaman
1 soldier	1 'bourgeois'

Of these, nine were acquitted, 27 freed under bond, 58 deported to Australia,[1] and 12 were executed. Those executed were: Five farmers, three notaries, one French army officer, one bailiff, one school teacher, and one student. The British and their Tory allies thus did not pick out important leaders of the Rebellion in Lower Canada for trial and execution; they picked less well-known supporters from the petite bourgeoisie to 'make an example of.'

Item 54: Quick Canadian Facts

In the fall of 1838 a Hunters army landed at Prescott on the St. Lawrence River and fought a five-day battle, and a small group invaded Windsor from Detroit but was easily repulsed. In Lower Canada the 1837 tragedy continued. On Nov. 3 [1838] a small group of rebel leaders evaded [British, Canadian, and American] border patrols, brought a few arms, found support of nearly 3,000 "patriotes," mostly unarmed. By Nov. 11 the British forces and loyalist volunteers had ended this second rebellion. Punishment was severe: the country around Beauharnois was put to the torch, 12 men were hanged and 58 transported to the penal colonies of Australia, an ending still recalled with deep resentment.

—Quick Canadian Facts: The Canadian Pocket Encyclopedia, 33rd Annual Edition (1979)

Some comparable information about the social and economic class of the Patriots in Upper Canada can be found in the Appendices to Lindsey's second volume on the Rebellion. Some 824 Patriots are listed as jailed for varying periods on the specific charges of insurrection and high treason alone between December 5, 1837 and November 1, 1838 (sixty-one others were charged but escaped capture). Of the total of 885 listed by Lindsey as arrested or escaped, 375 were farmers (42 per cent);

---

[1] A more precise listing of the occupations of the 58 people deported to Australia from Lower Canada, a number of whom practiced more than one trade or occupation, can be found in the Appendix to Ryerson's *Unequal Union*. An Australian, Mary G. Milne, provides the following information on the offences for which 201 transported prisoners on three of the transport ships were convicted: Americans: Piratical invasion of Upper Canada, 79; High Treason, 7. Anglo Canadians: Murder, 3; High Treason, 7; Desertion, 46; Highway Robbery, 1. French Canadians: High treason, 56; Highway Robbery, 2. Pardons were finally issued in 1844. After many hardships, most of the transportees managed to reach their homes.

80 were carpenters, tanners, blacksmiths, and other tradesmen; 85 were innkeepers, merchants, and professionals; and 345 were laborers (39 per cent).

My high-school history book by Edgar McInnis of the University of Toronto conjures up a very different picture, however: 'The rising in Upper Canada was even more scattered and shortlived [than that in Lower Canada]. It was precipitated by the outbreak in Lower Canada . . . .At length Colonel Fitzgibbon, adjutant-general and a veteran of the [British-American] War of 1812, took matters into his own hands. On December 7 [1837] he led a force of a thousand volunteers out against the ill-armed rabble of a few hundred that had gathered above the town [of Toronto]. A few volleys scattered the insurgents and ended the rebellion in Upper Canada. '

McInnis does go on to refer vaguely to 'vindictiveness' and to 'widespread and indiscriminate arrests.' He is presumably aware of Lindsey's list of 824 arrests and jailings continuing well into 1838. He may be aware that about 800 of this particular group of victims were 'dealt with' before November 1, 1838, some convicted of insurrection or treason *in absentia*, nearly all being held in jail under the threat of a sentence of death. Many were eventually released for lack of evidence. Others were obliged to throw themselves on the mercy of the courts, most of them then being 'pardoned' without being tried and convicted. Of this group about forty people were eventually sentenced to transportation for life. McInnis, however, says only that 'the bulk of the population had refused to follow the radicals in their resort to armed violence'—as if this were a voluntary decision.

Lindsey's book (1862) is a standard source for some of the details of the Rebellion in Upper Canada. One wonders, therefore, how any historian could have missed the fact that Lindsey's list refers to a *third* hanging, besides that of Lount and Matthews on April 12, 1838 (compare McInnis's statement quoted in Item 52). The entry reads: 'James Morrow, tanner, [arrested] June 27, 1838, civil court, guilty, executed, July 30, 1838.' This is presumably the same person as James Moreau, an Irish American from Pennsylvania. Moreau was one of the leaders of a group of Canadians and American residents of Canada—settlers who had been forced by the repression to flee the country—who came back to fight at the Short Hills, in the Niagara District, in June 1838, along with a number of American residents of the United States.

'Unwritten' Constitutions

One of the lessons we can learn from the twentieth century is that countries with a false front of democracy—but without the tradition of democracy in the sense that their peoples are used to a considerable measure of participation in the way they are governed—that such countries, like the Germany of the 1930s, are more quickly and easily taken down the road to totalitarianism and dictatorship, especially in times of severe economic difficulties, than other countries are.

For this reason, and especially because our present constitutional arrangements in Canada leave us wide open to dictatorship, this chapter and the next two chapters will turn their attention toward the rights and protections available under the capitalist version of democracy, towards the absence of these rights and protections in Canada today, and towards the dictatorial nature of our present form of government and decisionmaking.

In Canada we live under a Victorian system of government with nineteenth-century political attitudes and traditions. That part of our constitution which is 'written' is the British North America Act of 1867. (It is 'written' in the sense that all the topics it deals with are contained in a 'codified' set of documents.) The BNA Act was designed to protect governments from each other, not to protect the people from the government. Besides that, it was imposed on Canada by the British, acting in concert with the political and economic ambitions of the Canadian politicians and business interests in what is now Ontario and Quebec. The rest of our constitution is called 'unwritten.' This does not mean that most of it is not written down, as it is, but rather that it is scattered all over the place in different laws and traditions made in different times and in different places.

Government can attain enormous power under an uncodified constitution, for the simple reason that when the people look for it to define their rights and protections, they cannot find it—and for the associated reason that under this style of government, the 'unwritten' constitution is in general whatever the Government in power decides it is.

Nineteenth-century traditions are imperialist traditions; they demonstrate scant concern for the democratic rights of the people, and the only 'individuals' they really pay any attention to are the 'legal individuals' called corporations (the ultimate in symmetrization). I recall from a recent newspaper article, for instance, that a Canadian wishing to testify before a Government commission recently was refused permission to speak on the grounds that the woman in question was 'only an

Item 55: English Canadian Identity: Not What It Used To Be

The underlying cause [for upper-class English Canadian enthusiasm for the British war against the Boers], it seems to me, is to be found in the fact that the British Empire is a living unity, though not formally bound together by a constitution. This fact has been ignored by people to whom written statutes and compacts are everything, but not by those who with Emerson regard law as simply a memorandum. The United Kingdom has managed to get along for a thousand years since Alfred without a written constitution. It, however, has a Parliament whose supremacy is unquestioned; while there is no Parliament for the Empire, for admittedly the august body which sits at Westminster would never dream of coercing Canada or Australasia. But there is something antecedent to and more vital than a Parliament. Unity of race, of history, of traditions, of aims and moral ideas constitutes a vital unity....

...Everywhere the flag meant open markets, the protection of life, and all that makes life valuable. Increasingly attractive, as the symbol of union, became the personality of the Queen.... [British permission for Canada to negotiate trade treaties] put us on our honor, and it showed that we were partners, not dependents. While political status was being so generously recognized and extended, we felt more strongly than ever that the Empire meant freedom, equality for all white men, the independence of judges, and everything else the British Constitution is popularly supposed to mean.

[...As was recently declared in London, England:] 'the time is not far distant when the Canadian will be as full-fledged a citizen of the Empire as the Englishman....'

...The larger patriotism, which has now taken possession of Canadians, cannot possibly vanish....We are henceforth a nation....

—George Monro Grant, in Marquis: *Canada's Sons on Kopje and Veldt* (1900)

---

individual.' Some Canadians might regard this incident as trivial—and if taken alone, it might well appear so. But in reality it is symptomatic of a long governmental, business, and bureaucratic tradition in this country of *refusing to listen to Canadians*—much less take action in our interests.

It is also a symptom of the fact that totalitarianism in supposedly democratic states is invariably expressed in the apparently trivial: in petty decisions made by petty administrators and petty executives in apparently petty matters.

The Canadian Bill of Rights

Under the 'British tradition,' the civil liberties or civil rights of the people depend on the will or whims of Parliament. As Michael Bolton explains in a very useful book, *Civil Rights in Canada* (1976: pp. 2, 121), any of our so-called 'basic democratic rights' can be withdrawn by Parliament at any time. this This means in effect that the Prime Minister and Cabinet of the Federal government can control those rights, even though, under the 'written' (codified) part of Canada's constitution (the British North America Act of 1867), 'civil rights' are stated to be an exclusive concern of the Provinces.

In October, 1970, for example, the Cabinet decided that the Front de Libération du Québec had given rise 'to a state of apprehended insurrection within the province of Quebec,' and invoked the War Measures Act. (In this context, the word 'apprehended' in this Act means 'expected or 'feared,' as distinct from 'real.') Bolton remarks (p. 2):

> Special laws regarding the F.L.Q. were in force for approximately six and one-half months, until April 30, 1971. During this time, thousands of Canadians were harassed by arbitrary searches and investigations. Hundreds were arrested and detained in custody. Only a few were actually charged, and very few were tried and convicted.

In other words, *habeas corpus*, the common-law protection against the arbitrary use of the law as a weapon against the citizenry, was suspended at that time. In this context, *habeas corpus* means the right to demand that one either be charged with a specific crime (the charge to be based on 'reasonable evidence,' and not on mere suspicion), or else be released from jail.

However, the right to a *speedy* and *public* trial was not suspended by the martial law imposed in 1970 and 1971. As previously pointed out about the use of the Official Secrets Act of 1939, public trials are an essential democratic protection against the abuse of the rights of the individual by the executive and the judiciary. As part of due process, they are especially important in protecting the rights of minorities against the majority. The right to a speedy trial is equally important. Otherwise, the government can use its arresting powers to detain individuals in jail 'at the pleasure of the Crown' (the executive), on trumped up charges and prohibitively expensive bail if exigency requires it, or the government can resort to a whole series of delaying tactics to keep an individual 'out of circulation.' These two rights were recognized two centuries ago (in 1791) in the series of ten Amendments to the 'written' (codified) constitution of the United States, the amendments now know as the American Bill of Rights. These constitutional protections against the law and the government were not suspended during the October Crisis, because neither of them exists in Canada as a 'written' right. Neither is mentioned, for example, in the Parliamentary statute of 1960 called the 'Canadian Bill of Rights' (see Bolton, 1976: pp. 84-5).

The Canadian 'Bill of Rights' offers neither theoretical nor practical protection against the abuse of personal and civil rights by the government and its agents which the American Bill of Rights provides for. Since it is an ordinary statute, even its imaginary protections can be repealed at any time by a simple majority in Parliament. In any event, any other statute passed by Parliament has only to state the equivalent of the following paragraph to render the so-called 'Bill of Rights' in Canada even more meaningless than it is already. For example, the War Measures Act states:

> Any act or thing done or authorized or any order or regulation made under the authority of this Act, shall be deemed not to be an abrogation, abridgement or infringement of any right or freedom recognized by the *Canadian Bill of Rights. . . .*

As constitutional experts remind us, in a country with an 'unwritten' style of constitution, the citizenry never really knows where they stand on many important legal matters. Moreover, the language of the quoted paragraph illustrates the dangers, under the imperial traditions of the British parliamentary system, of having any statement about 'democratic rights' put down in writing—*without also reforming the entire political system and the constitution* at the same time. Otherwise, Parliament can simply continue to play hide-and-seek with our freedoms and protections.

In the American form of constitutional democracy, it is relatively easy to know which part of the body of law has to do with the people's rights, because these rights are codified into one basic document. This, along with its amendments, forms the American constitution. This written (codified) document is of a higher level of law than the rest of the law (which also involves levels, but this does not require discussion here). This document states the fundamental democratic principles which no lower level of law is to be allowed to infringe on. Along with the traditional protections of common law and customary law which the Americans share with the British tradition, the courts, in principle designed to be as independent of governments as possible, use this document to oversee the making of law and the enforcement of the law. As a result, it is more difficult for legislators to abuse their lawmaking power, or for executive and police agencies to enforce the law unjustly, in the United States than in other countries.

In other words, the American constitution is a set of *constraints* within which the legislators, the executive power, and the courts are required to remain in carrying out their functions. Like a code, the American constitution is a set of rules about what kinds of laws and behavior are permitted. Like a code, it is in principle the mediator of all the laws and legal activities (the 'messages') in the nation.

In contrast, under the British Parliamentary system, there is no *codified* level of general constitutional law. It is very often up to the judge to decide whether a particular case or item of evidence involves constitutional principles or not (e.g. the use of illegal evidence), in situations where the U.S. constitution provides much clearer and much more accessible guidelines than the British system.

(There is in the British tradition a statute of 1689 called the 'Bill of Rights.' This statute was part of the deal made with William of Orange when William and Mary were offered the throne in place of James II, deposed in the 'glorious revolution' of 1688. With the exception of a few articles protecting individual rights against royal power, the basic design of the statute was to declare illegal a number of ways in which James II was considered by Parliament to have abused his powers. Thus, this statute primarily concerns the relation between the king and Parliament, not the relationship between the government and the people.)

Under the British and Canadian systems, the overseer of the rights of the people and the responsibilities of the government is not ultimately the constitution and the interpretation of the constitution by the courts. Our principle overseer is Parliament itself—a political body of political people who make up the constitution more or less as they go along. (This is one reason for the abysmal quality of most Canadian legislation. Since Parliament's laws are rarely questioned by the courts, and indeed, since there is even a question as to what the courts' relation to Parliament actually is, our lawmakers and their aides have been allowed to forget how to write good law.)

In contrast, the principal guardian of rights in the U.S. system is the collective result of generations of court interpretations of the codified constitution, as well as those of the courts. Unlike Canada, in most instances, American citizens or residents with grievances to settle—and money or legal support—get to go to court. In the case of the faculty members dismissed in one way or another by the administration of Simon Fraser University in 1970, for example, the B.C. Supreme Court denied them the right to sue the university. In contrast, in the case of the five faculty members fired by Howard University in the sixties in Washington, D.C. (for demonstrating against General Hershey and the draft laws), the aggrieved parties went to court and eventually won their case.[2] As for more serious matters, the presumption of guilt by the Crown in the political cases of the FLQ (e.g. Item 7) would not have been attempted by the prosecution in a court of the rule of law.

Again unlike the British or Canadian system, the U.S. constitution, in its origin and in its amendments, is the product of the expressed and recorded approval of at least two-thirds of the people's representatives at both the federal and the state level. The Canadian system is less historical, less safe, and less populist. In Canadian custom and practice, the 'guardians of our rights' are in practice the particular people, at a particular time, who hold a particular majority in a particular parliament.

As a result, in Canada today, having *any* government—i.e. *any* temporarily dominant political party or parties—writing anything down about 'rights' and 'freedoms' in ordinary (statute) law is more dangerous than depending on the traditions of common law. Statutes like the Canadian Bill of Rights provide the Government with a laundry list of 'rights' which they or some other Government chose to 'give' us, a laundry list by which to remember what rights to take back again later on, if expediency requires it.

This is in effect what happened with the 'Post Office Continuation Act' of 1978, when the Prime Minister and Cabinet dragooned their Party into taking away the right to strike that they had previously 'given' to the Canadian Union of Postal Workers (cf. also Items 6, 60, and 62).

The texts of the War Measures Act and the 'Bill of Rights' are available in Bolton's book. The preamble to the Canadian 'Bill of Rights'—

---

[2]In 1978, in British Columbia, a Crown Prosecutor succeeded in intimidating movie exhibitors into cancelling showings of a 'controversial' film—which had already been passed by the film censors of B.C. He threatened prosecution but did not bring the case before the courts. When accused of intimidation and almost 'personal' censorship in a television discussion (which included representatives from the B.C. censors and local film critics), he implied that he was merely trying to save the courts trouble and the country money.

which actually defines the 'rights' and the 'authority' of the government (Parliament) as superior to the rights and authority of the people—makes a fascinating commentary on the dominant realities and the dominant ideology in Canada as of 1960:

> The Parliament of Canada, affirming that the Canadian Nation is founded upon principles that acknowledge the supremacy of God, the dignity and worth of the human person and the position of the family in a society of free men and free institutions;
>
> Affirming also that men and institutions remain free only when freedom is founded upon respect for moral and spiritual values and the rule of law;
>
> And being desirous of enshrining these principles and the human rights and fundamental freedoms derived from them, in a Bill of rights which shall reflect the respect of Parliament for its constitutional authority and which shall ensure the protection of these rights and freedoms in Canada.... [etc.].

Compare the authoritarian and antiquated wording of this standing constitutional joke with the simplicity and the modernity of the two-hundred-year-old Preamble to the Constitution of the United States. This constitution came into force in 1788 on being ratified by the ninth state of the original thirteen (unanimous approval of the state representatives came in 1791). You will note at once a major and essential distinction: its emphasis on the superior power and authority of the *people,* rather than on the authority of the government:

> We the People of the United States, in Order to form a more perfect Union, establish Justice, insure domestic Tranquility, provide for the common defence, promote the general Welfare, and secure the blessings of Liberty to ourselves and to our Posterity, do ordain and establish this Constitution for the United States of America....

I am not advocating that we annex ourselves to the United States, nor that we come up with a carbon copy of their political system, nor that we become a republic (whether we retain the monarchy or not in the future is completely irrelevant to how we restructure our political system on democratic lines). I mention these three points because it is practically a certainty in Canada that any attempt to talk commonsense about political systems and the like will be labeled by the establishment as 'Americanism' or 'republicanism' in the hope and design of neutralizing what needs to be said. (Imaginary 'Americanism,' of course.)

Item 56: No Guarantees of Freedom

His Majesty's subjects possess no guarantees of freedom. The 'rights of man' are not guaranteed, nor even mentioned anywhere in English constitutional law. There being no written documentary Constitution, no high-sounding declaration of the liberties of the individual exists. Various Constitutions have been promulgated in other countries which include the enunciation of noble principles of individual rights [just as the Canadian Bill of Rights attempts to do]. But often these declarations have proved to be not worth the paper on which they are printed, for sometimes it is not difficult to bring about the suspension of written Constitutions [and Bills of Rights], and of the 'guaranteed' liberties along with them.

His Majesty's subjects are in theory therefore in a disadvantageous position compared with the citizens who live under a written Constitution—but in practice they are far better off. The secret of English liberty rests on the fact that any subject is entirely free to do what he likes and to say what he likes, provided only that he does not thereby break the law as it exists at any time. If his freedoms are infringed, he has his remedies in the ordinary law of the land as enforced in the courts. He cannot be deprived of any of his liberties or of his remedies, except by Act of Parliament....

The freedoms of the individual thus remain extensive, and are practically unlimited in respect of the expression of political and religious opinion. Minorities are free to become majorities, by persuasion, if they can.* Freedom of this kind is the life-blood of the Constitution. By it the Constitution has grown and become what it is, and could not survive without its perpetually reinvigorating stream.

—S.B. Chrimes: *English Constitutional History* (1953)

Note the implicit justification of the potential tyranny of the majority over the rights of minorities.

Civil Rights and Democratic Freedoms

Civil rights do not of course depend on words and bits of paper, but rather on the historical development of the political traditions which give rise to written constitutional protections. In their turn, these written protections depend for their actual effectiveness on the way the courts interpret them. In the United States of the 1950s, for example, gross and public violations of civil rights, due process, and the equal protection and application of the laws by police, courts, and governments were daily occurrences which passed unnoted by the majority of the population. It is only in the last twenty years that civil rights became the centerpiece of U.S. constitutional reform, largely through the reinterpretation of the American constitution by the U.S. Supreme Court— and these reforms can now be seen to have had a major source in the drastic contradictions between the political realities of the United States and the international image it needed in its prosecution of the Cold War.

Canada is now experiencing similar contradictions between image and reality, contradictions intensified by watching what happened in the U.S. between the assassination of President Kennedy in 1963 and the forced resignation of President Nixon in 1974. So far, however, we have not experienced any significant reform in the matter of democratic freedoms and civil rights, although the words and terminology associated with them are very much in the air. Indeed, it is the fact that they are 'in the air,' rather than in our political reality, that allows the rhetoric of 'democracy' and 'civil rights' to be so easily used against us by our Anglo-American overseers.

On the one hand, we have Imaginary Americans who wield the rhetoric of 'civil rights' against unsuspecting Canadians, without the substance; on the other, we have equally Imaginary Englishmen who accomplish much the same with the rhetoric of 'British democracy' and 'the British constitutional tradition.'

Without due process and the rule of law, and without the sovereignty of the people over parliaments, 'civil rights' remains an empty phrase for those most in need of the protections for which it stands. In Canada, for due process we have 'the accepted procedures' (which permit violations of due process); for the rule of law we have 'the rule of order' and 'order above the law' (which violate the rule of law); and for civil rights we have 'the privileges of authority.' Civil rights in Canada today are not derived from the rights of the people; they are based on the privileges of management.

William Lyon Mackenzie attempted to introduce to Upper Canada in 1837 the idea of a constitutional democracy based on the rights of the people in the British and American radical traditions (Lindsey, 1862, II: pp. 344-58; Aylmer, 1975: pp. 88-96). Some 150 years later, the theory of constitutional democracy, with its written constitution, has become so separated from its historical sources in the radicals of the English

Revolution of the seventeenth century that it now appears to be an 'American'—and therefore 'alien'—mode of government.

Over that same 150 years, Canada has been so singularly dominated by a colonial version of British parliamentary democracy that expressions such as 'civil rights' and 'the rule of law' now have significantly different meanings on one side of the 49th parallel, compared with the other—as I remarked at the very beginning of this book. With the United States as one point of reference, but not the only one, we have still to establish in Canada the political language that will enable us to deal successfully with our actual political reality, and at the same time enable us to consider how it might be reformed. This is no exercise in abstractions, for without fundamental political reform, it is not going to be possible for us to take control of our own country.

The political structure of constitutional democracy depends in essence on a judicious and constantly negotiated compromise between 'the will of the majority' and 'the inalienable rights of the individual.' We have no 'inalienable' rights in Canada, for within their area of jurisdiction, Parliament and the provincial Legislatures can take away from us whatever it pleases them to take away. The English radicals fought Parliament for such fundamental rights in the seventeenth century—and unfortunately for us, they lost.

The twentieth century has shown us more clearly than any other how essential to a working democracy is the compromise between the rights of the majority and the rights of the individual. The rise of Hitler in the short-lived democracy of Germany (the Weimar Republic) showed the world how the 'will of the majority' can be manipulated, by means of scapegoating, into a genocidal dictatorship of one kind of German ('Aryans') over other kinds (Jews, 'Communists,' gypsies, the 'feeble-minded,' and so on). The popular appeal of fascism in the Western democracies in the 1930s—evidenced in their tacit and other support of Franco in the Spanish Civil War—and the history of anti-Semitism and other forms of racism in France, Britain, and the United States is evidence enough that simple 'majority rule' is not the essence of democracy in the modern, liberal sense. The re-emergence of overtly fascist political parties in France, Britain, Canada, and the United States in the last ten or twenty years further shows us how easy it is to convert legitimate dissatisfaction and distress into 'witch-hunting' crusades against people defined as 'different.'

The consequence is that it becomes essential to democracy to restrict the 'will of the majority' by protecting the individual against potential abuses of power by the majority. It becomes equally necessary to protect both majorities and minorities against potential abuses of the power delegated by the electorate to its representatives. Democratic elections alone are not sufficient to provide these safeguards against the possible tyranny of the majority and the possibe tyranny of government and its agents. Limited power (and the division of powers: Chapter Twelve) is thus the essence of constitutional democracy. Just as 'constitutional monarchy' means limits on the power of the monarch over Parliament, so constitutional democracy means limits on the power of the majority and the power of government over the individual.

Under a truly constitutional democracy (which we have yet to see), all of these political limits and constraints on power come under the single protective heading of 'civil rights.' In its turn the constitutional protection of civil rights depends on the rule of law: due process; the equal protection and application of the laws; the right to prosecute or sue the government and its agents; the right to challenge the constitutionality of any law or regulation; the independence of the judiciary; protection against arbitrary arrest, searches, and seizures; the prohibition of general warrants ('writs of assistance'[3]) by the requirement that warrants be based on specific evidence and 'probable cause' (rather than on mere suspicion); the protection by *habeas corpus* against illegal detention; the presumption of innocence; the right to legal counsel (gratis if necessary); protection against self-incrimination; the right to a fair hearing before any tribunal, committee, court, or administrative entity sitting in judgement; the right to trial by jury for all serious offences; the prohibition of illegal evidence; the right of the accused to confront and cross-examine their accusers; the right to a speedy and public trial; the right to secure damages for illegal arrest and/or detention, as well as for denial of justice and abuse of power, whether public or private; the right to an interpreter whenever necessary; the prohibition of cruel or unusual punishment; the right not to be put in jeopardy twice for the same offence; security from harassment, arrest, or trial for political, religious, or other beliefs. . .and so on.

Implicit also here are the 'freedoms' of advanced capitalist democracy

---

[3]In 1976 there were 210 writs of assistance issued under the drug laws to individual officers of the RCMP: 53 in Ontario, 52 in B.C., 35 in Quebec, and 15 in Alberta. Saskatchewan, the Maritimes, and the Territories each had less than 15. (These writs of assistance are also authorized under the federal income tax and customs laws.) They allow the named officer to search any residence at any time for narcotics or controlled or restricted drugs (Bolton, 1976: pp. 34-5). When the British used writs of assistance against smugglers in the American colonies in the 1760s, the use of these writs became one more grievance in the general uproar leading to the Declaration of Independence in 1776.

(the problem being that it costs so much money to exercise them): freedom of speech; freedom of the press; freedom of information (i.e. the right to know what business and government are up to, from credit ratings and balance sheets to political ratings and so-called 'national security'); freedom from the invasion of personal privacy and personal communications; freedom of contract, assembly, and association (except where such contract, assembly, or association denies to others the principle of equal opportunity, as business monopolies do); freedom of conscience (including the freedom to refuse military conscription and the like); and freedom from discrimination on the grounds of race, sex, language, age, birth, occupation, fortune, or political opinion (cf. Faribault and Fowler, 1965).

Constitutionally, in order to maintain the principle of the sovereignty of the people, it is necessary to add that all rights, protections, immunities, and freedoms not enumerated here remain vested in the people.

Civil rights are not therefore some 'altruistic' invention of 'do-gooders' or 'bleeding hearts', as they are sometimes made out to be. Civil rights are based on the self-interest of the individual, on the self-interest that tells each and every one of us that what protects you also protects me. The nub of the matter is that all these rights and freedoms stem from an even more basic right: the right to self-defense. And the best defense for the individual is collective self-interest, the collective self-defense of the community to which the individual belongs.

Under capitalist democracy, individual and collective self-defense entails a right that is rarely mentioned in Bills of Rights: the right to consent to a contract, written and unwritten, and therefore the right to refuse continued consent when the contract is nullified or broken. When we ask for a written constitution, for example, we are demanding that the basis by which we consent to be governed by the delegated power of our representatives be written out, with all the proper terms and conditions, so that we can tell whether the other parties to the contract, our elected representatives, are abiding by it or not. The same goes for our relationship to the courts, the police, and the law. When judges or police break the law, they violate their contract with the people, which is to protect them by means of law. This was Richard Nixon's major crime: as the Chief Executive he violated his contract with the American people—that he would faithfully execute the laws—by trying to set himself and his agents above the law.

The concept of consent to contract, as well as the right to be protected from discrimination, have their applications to the workplace also. Employees have the right to withdraw their labor when their written and unwritten contract with their employers is nullified or broken by management. Capital, after all, repeatedly goes out on strike whenever it feels that its interests are in jeopardy; in a constitutional democracy of the rule of law where capital exercises such a right, labor's right to strike could never be constitutionally infringed.

To return now to the situation of Canadians: It will be noted that none of the civil rights and democratic freedoms just outlined are 'absolute' rights or 'absolute' freedoms. (No one has the freedom to play jokes by shouting 'Fire!' in a crowded theater, for example.) Rights and freedoms are not things or objects or entities; they are relations, and specifically relations between persons. In other words, rights and freedoms are contextual; and outside their social and political context, they are mere noises in the air. This is where we Canadians come in. Because Canada is not a constitutional democracy, much less an ideal constitutional democracy, the rights and freedoms that make sense in the context of the kind of constitutional democracy we find in the United States do not make the same sense here. It is this change of context—unrecognized as such by Canadians brought up under the authoritarianism of colonial administrations—that makes it so easy for management, whether intentionally or not, to abuse the principles of democracy and civil rights in Canada.

Outside of elections and parliamentary votes and the like, where the rules are very clear, this kind of abuse is both ideological (e.g. in political speeches and arguments) and actual (e.g. in administrative decisions sheltered from review by anyone other than administrators). There are no doubt exceptions to the general rule, but the basic patterns of thought lying behind these witting and unwitting abuses are quite simple. The process begins by abstracting civil rights and democratic freedoms from the real contextual relations in which they are actually expressed and exercised. This makes it possible to treat such rights and freedoms, in 'good faith' and in 'good conscience', as mere abstractions reducible to 'matters of opinion'. By definition, matters of opinion are 'subjective' beliefs that are, if necessary, utterly resistant to any amount or kind of evidence to the contrary. Here lies the refuge of injustice.

It thus becomes possible—and even perversely logical—to define democracy and civil rights in any way at all. An individual has this right, and if he defines democracy as what you or I recognize as fascism, we must nevertheless respect his right to be wrong. The whole situation changes, however, when the individual in question has the power to impose sanctions on other individuals as a result of his being in authority over them. The moment that 'subjective' opinions are expressed in and through the exercise of power, then they cease to be protected by 'free speech' and so forth; they become subject to their context, to the context of informed opinion and to the reasonable evidence of the facts. This is the point at which the abuse of democratic principles and individual rights through the abuse of power can step in. Unfortunately for the victims, however, the official in question is already prepared for this. By the same process of abstraction from the real context, the official has already defined the abuse of power as just another matter of individual opinion.

The same is true in administrative matters involving real or imaginary violations of individual rights. Because of our lack of constitutional traditions spelling out the protection of civil rights in Canada, officials in power are free to interpret individual rights pretty much as they please—and the citizens cannot expect much help from Canadian courts, which have consistently refused to deal with the general constitutional issues involved.

A similar pattern of arbitrariness obtains in non-parliamentary matters involving the votes of a number of individuals. The predominant view of democracy in Canada by management is that it involves an 'either/or' opposition between 'the rights of the majority', on the one hand, and 'the rights of the individual' (or 'the rights of the minority'), on the other. Because we still lack a dominant constitutional tradition of limited powers, the fact that a working democracy protects *both* the rights of the majority *and* the rights of the individual, with each one limiting the other, is rarely recognized. The fact that each is the context of the other is ignored. As a result, when an official in a position of power is required by procedures to consult other individuals, it does not necessarily make any difference which way their judgements fall. If the minority position does not suit the official's purpose, then he will quite naturally call upon the principle of majority rule, calling the decision 'democratic,' whether or not minority rights are violated. Conversely, if it is the *majority* position that does not suit his purpose, then he can—in the same 'good conscience' as before—call upon the principle of minority rights and refuse to be guided by what has now conveniently become 'the tyranny of the majority,' even when the majority position violates no minority or individual right.

In self-justification, the dominant call on an Imaginary liberalism of 'subjective opinion' or 'lifestyle' (repressive tolerance). They treat racism, sexism, and classism—and other matters of fact unrecognized as such by the dominant ideology—as if they were matters of personal taste.

Item 57: Britain's Free Gift

Quebec, March, 1807

There is a great deal of misapprehension in Britain relative to this country. It is naturally concluded that, in a British colony such as Canada, a conquered country, those who govern and who give law to it, would be Englishmen. This, however, is by no means the case; for though the governor and some of the [appointed] council are English, the French Canadians are in the majority in the [elected] house of assembly; and no law can pass, if they choose to prevent it. The English (supposing the governor to exert all the influence he possesses) cannot carry a single question; and the Canadians have been in the habit of shewing, in the most undisguised manner, the power of a majority. . . . They carry things with a high hand; they seem to forget that the constitution under which they domineer over the English, was a free gift from Britain; and that what an act of parliament gave, an act of parliament can take away.

—Hugh Gray: *Letters from Canada* (1809)

[In Lower Canada in 1834] Adam Thom had organized an armed band, the Doric Club, with the express purpose of using violence to beat down the French Canadians if the government granted them their repeated demands for an elected Legislative Council. Five months before his promotion to be an adviser to Lord Durham [in 1838], and while the prisons [of Lower Canada] were filling up with Canadians, Thom had written: 'The punishment of the ringleaders may well be pleasurable to the English population, but it will not make as deep and useful an impression on the minds of the people as the sight of strangers established on the farms and in the houses of every agitator in every parish. The spectacle of their widows and children parading their destitution amidst the fine houses and lands that have been taken from them, would have the right effect. There must be no hesitation in putting this measure into execution. Special Commissioners must immediately be named and charged with bringing to a close the trial of the gang of traitors now in prison. It would be ridiculous to fatten them up all winter only to send them to the gallows later on.'

—Louis-Joseph Papineau: *Histoire de l'Insurrection du Canada* (1839)

CHAPTER TWELVE

The Division of Powers

Legislative, Executive, Judicial

A basic principle which distinguishes 'constitutional democracies,' such as the United States, from 'parliamentary democracies,' such as Canada and Britain, is the division of powers within the government as a whole. Many people may be familiar with this distinction; but to judge from our local newspapers and from what is generally taught in school, the innovations introduced into capitalist democracy over the past two centuries by the American system of government are not always well understood in Canada. This chapter is probably going to sound like an American high-school civics course, but we cannot fully appreciate the tyranny of the executive in the Canadian system without this kind of comparative information.

The basic consideration underlying the division of powers under constitutional democracy is that each major function of government should be related to other functions of government in such a way that each area of power can act to curb excesses and abuses of power by any of the others.

All democratic systems involve the following three major governmental functions and powers: the *legislative* power (concerned primarily with the making of law); the *executive* power (concerned primarily with the carrying out of the law); and the *judicial* power (concerned primarily with the interpretation and the application of the law in particular and general instances).

The way the system of constitutional democracy actually works in the United States is more complex than we can attend to here (we cannot, for instance, go into the details of why the dominant tradition in the U.S. is a two-party system). Nevertheless, enough of an outline can be given to serve our purposes in comparing this system with our own.

In the U.S. system, the sovereign power, according to the constitution, is the people of the United States; in contrast, under the British tradition, the sovereign power is the Parliament. In the U.S. system the power of the people is delegated to their elected representatives: the legislative power of the House of Representatives (elected proportionate to population for two-year terms) and the Senate (elected every six years, on a staggered basis, with two Senators representing each of the 50 states). The executive power, the President, is elected every four years, for a maximum of eight years, by a peculiar system of indirect voting (through the Electoral College), which nevertheless ordinarily results in a straight popular vote in which the President is chosen by a majority of the voters. At the federal level, judges are appointed by the President with the advice and consent of the Senate and hold their terms during good behavior (like the President, judges may be removed from office by impeachment and trial).

Except under certain special circumstances, legislation passed by the U.S. Congress cannot become law without the separate consent of the President. The executive power can veto a law passed by Congress. In its turn, Congress can overturn a presidential veto by a vote of a two-thirds majority. Thus, while the executive power in this system is commonly the source through which many laws and appropriations are brought to Congress for examination (in Committee), discussion (on the floor and in the back rooms), and approval, the executive power cannot *make* laws as such. Indeed, many of the executive proposals to Congress do not become law at all; and many become law in significantly altered form.

In their turn, all laws agreed on by the legislators and the executive are required to be *constitutional.* No law may in principle or in practice violate the rights, freedoms, privileges, and protections inscribed in the written (codified) constitution and in the various amendments to it.

It is the duty of the third branch of government, the judiciary, to see that both the spirit and the letter of the laws enacted are in accord with the democratic principles laid down in the constitution, in its amendments, and in the ongoing process of the interpretation of the constitution by the courts (ultimately the Supreme Court of the United States)—the process by which the constitution is kept up to date with changes in society. It is also the duty of the courts to make sure that the enforcement and application of the laws by the executive power and its agents (e.g. the police) is itself a constitutionally correct process.

The written (codified) constitution is thus a set of *laws about law,* a set of general principles which the laws, the lawmakers, the courts, and the executive power are forbidden to violate.

One of these constitutional principles is the principle of the *due process of law,* which is intended to protect every individual against abuses of power by the government and its agents in the application and the enforcement of the laws. This principle—that *the law may not be enforced by breaking the laws*— is central to constitutional democracy. It embodies the principle that no one can set themselves above the law—except under conditions of emergency, such as war. This principle applies to the President, to the police and other executive agents, to individual legislators, to judges, to government departments, and to the entire government itself.

The rule of law and of due process does not significantly constrain the Canadian system. Nor does the principle that *laws must be legal* (constitutional) find much of a place in our political arrangements.

The legislators (and/or the executive) in the U.S. system may object to the overturning of a particular law as illegal (unconstitutional) by the courts. If so, then they will ordinarily attempt to reformulate the law so as to meet the constitutional objections made by the courts. (Two common grounds used by the courts to overturn a particular state or federal law are that the law is *discriminatory* or that the law is so *vague* or so poorly worded as to lead to possible abuses.) If the legislators meet the objections of the courts, then the law in question will become a legal law.

The process of the judicial review of the laws in the U.S. may be begun by any individual or group who wish to test the constitutionality of any law. But this process does not end with the wording and obvious intent of the law itself. It also includes the most significant aspect of the law as it affects the individual citizen or resident: the way in which the law is actually carried out by the executive power and its agents. In other words—again to emphasize an extremely important lack of protection for individuals and minorities in the Canadian system as compared with the American system—under constitutional democracy, a law must not only be constitutional in itself, but it must also be applied and enforced in actual daily practice in a constitutionally correct and legal manner. (Incoming presidents are required to swear that they will uphold the constitution and 'faithfully execute' the laws.) Without this protection against the abuse of power in the enforcement of the law, constitutional protections are mere political humbug—just as the so-called Canadian Bill of Rights is at present humbug.

To protect the citizenry and the residents of the country against the abuse of the constitution so prevalent in countries with 'unwritten' (uncodified) constitutions—where the daily passage of ordinary statute law can continue to encroach on, or outlaw, the constitutional protections the people thought they had—the written constitution is made relatively difficult to change in the United States; and any such amendments must be ratified throughout the country by the representatives of the people. In the constitutional democracy of the

United States, amendments to the constitution require a two-thirds approval by both House and Senate, as well as ratification by three-quarters of the fifty state legislatures.

(Compare this actual process of constitutional amendment with the version provided to Canadians by *Quick Canadian Facts*— a traditional high-school 'crib'—in the 1979 edition (p. 150): 'Minor changes in the [American] Constitution are achieved easily and naturally by legislation, but major changes may require years to pass the House of Representatives, the Senate, and finally the judiciary.')

The British system is very different. It provides no procedures for ratifying constitutional changes. It includes no general statement of rights and protections for the individual—nor for groups of individuals—similar to that of the United States. Moreover, in the British system, Parliament (in principle), the Majority Party (in principle), and the Executive of the Majority Party (in practice) are almost omnipotent as regards the making of law, the interpretation of law, and the enforcement of law. (The main reasons for this peculiarity are discussed later in this chapter.)

In so far as we have a constitution in Canada—and allowing for the division of powers between governments as laid down in the British North America Act of 1867—both the Federal and the Provincial governments can act in their respective spheres, by a simply majority of the party in power, to overturn, remake, or reinterpret almost any law in the land (including statutes that provide the people with certain protections against the government and the law). This they can do without any necessary reference to the courts (which tend to remain too close to the government in Canada), and without any necessary reference to the people, or to the Opposition representatives of the people.

Indeed, the Canadian system does not include any working notion of limits, constitutional or otherwise, on the powers of government as a whole. The actual working limit on the abuse of power by government(s) in Canada is, in practice, whatever the Executive thinks it can get away with—and given the complexities of the law, given the lack of political education even at the level of elementary 'civics' in Canada, and given the way the laws can be worded in Canada, what the provincial Premiers and Prime Minister and Cabinet can get away with in practice is very considerable indeed.

The 'Protection of Privacy Act' of 1974, and its associated statutes, provide us with a good example of the game the Federal Government plays with us in such matters. Current law supposedly makes wiretapping illegal, and it includes all sorts of penalties for such 'illegal' activities. But this 'protective' law against trespass into our private lives also contains the provision that legal authorization to wiretap is *not* required when *one* of the parties to a conversation consents to being recorded (Bolton, 1976: pp. 106-9). This violates the principle of contract.

The BNA Act could theoretically protect us here against the Federal government. An invasion of our privacy is obviously an invasion of our civil rights. Because the BNA Act makes 'civil rights' a concern of the provinces, then the wiretapping law is probably unconstitutional as an Act of the Federal government. (It is a violation of the so-called Bill of Rights.) Not that this technicality is worth counting on, however, because the same law would not violate the BNA Act if it were passed by the provincial governments—and in any case the provinces' jurisdiction over 'civil rights' is meaningless in a system which does not in reality recognize such rights, and which in any case makes the Criminal Code a Federal matter.

Under the British and Canadian system, then, there is no effective division of powers between the legislative, the executive, and the judicial powers. Under our system, potential and actual abuses of power by the executive power (called 'the Crown' in court and 'the government' outside it) are not in practice overseen by anyone or by any other part of the system.

The theory which is propounded to rationalize this dictatorial situation (and to construct irrelevant arguments against the U.S. system) is the principle of so-called 'responsible government.' Whereas a constitutional democracy actually has the most responsible of present political systems in the world today, it is ordinarily said by historians and jurists who ought to know better that the U.S. system does not involve 'responsible government' because the American executive and the American legislators are not 'continuously' responsible to the people while in office.

This argument, still heard in Canada today, depends on one technical point: that in Canada, the Executive may display its so-called 'responsibility' to the 'will of the people' at any time by calling an election or by being forced to call one by a no-confidence vote in Parliament. The U.S. system is said not to display such 'responsibility to the people' because its elections are fixed in their timing by the constitution. Therefore, goes the argument, the responsibility of the government to the people in the U.S. system is not 'continuous' but 'periodic.' We will return to this point in the next chapter. For the moment, all that needs to be said is that even if we did have responsible government in Canada, the legislative and the judicial branches of government, under the Parliamentary system, would still be lacking the power, the capacity, and the resources to act in practice as real checks on the Executive power.

Constitutional Democracy: The Competition of Powers

The division of powers under constitutional democracy (not the separation of powers, as the relationship is sometimes incorrectly called) involves three domains of power that are indeed *functions* of government, which is to say that they interrelate and overlap. These functions may be represented by particular persons and by specific legal or governmental bodies in any particular instance. But the three processes involved—the 'making of law,' the 'carrying out of the law,' and the 'overseeing, interpretation, and application of law'—are not necessarily neatly divided up between the three main agencies of government.

For example, when the courts reinterpret a law so as to modify its effect, its enforcement, or its application in the United States, then the courts are co-operating (or competing, as the case may be) with the legislative power in the making of law. Similarly, when the courts direct that a specific law or principle is to be applied in a specific manner in a specific place, they are instructing the executive power in the enforcement of the law.

By its prerogative of proposing laws and appropriations to Congress (e.g. the annual budget), the executive power is even more closely involved in the making of law. Depending on the vagaries of the power of the president as it is permitted by the legislative power to exert itself (cf. Item 63) this involvement may be very considerable indeed. (In the United States, the Congress has recently responded to the increasing power of the president as it developed out of the depression, the world war, the Cold War, and the war in Vietnam, by reasserting its constitutional powers so as to be considerably less amenable, as a whole, to manipulation by the White House.) Besides this involvement in lawmaking, the executive power in the United States, as in every other government in the world, becomes involved in producing administratice regulations concerning the application of laws, policies, and principles. (This making of administrative law by the bureaucracy of the executive is one of the fuzziest areas of government today, and one that is still not adequately subject to review procedures by courts and legislators in most countries.)

In its turn, the legislative power may instruct the executive in the use of the powers that have been delegated to it; or the legislative power may seek to supervise closely the constitutional powers of the executive. In the United States, the executive is normally required to secure the approval of Congress in a considerable number of matters, including ambassadorships, the appointment of Justices of the Supreme Court, and the appointment of the Secretaries of the various departments in the federal bureaucracy. (Such people act as advisors to the president, can be required to testify before Congress—the legislative power—and make up the various executive councils or cabinets in the U.S. system.) The executive is also required to secure the approval of the legislative agency of government for the use of its emergency powers after a specific period of time; and it must also secure the approval of international treaties by the Senate. In these and other ways, the legislative power exerts considerable influence on decisions that are initiated by the executive. (Remember also that the majority in the Congress may not be of the same party affiliation as the president.)

Mention these relationships to the average Canadian Tory, however, and the knee-jerk response will probably be: 'But it doesn't really work that way.' This may well be true—just as true as the reality that the Canadian system doesn't actually work the way it says it does, either. This kind of all-to-common objection to the explanation of the basic patterns of differences between political systems is thus largely irrelevant to the comparative discussion we are concerned with here. Moreover, given the long Tory tradition in Canada (is there any other political tradition in Canada?) of misunderstanding and misrepresenting the American system to Canadians, especially in school, the best answer to such objections is to suggest that the reader conduct an independent investigation of the differences between the various systems, without relying on Canadian or British material seeking to show how wonderfully superior the British (colonial) tradition is to everyone else's.

Indeed, the crucially important characteristic of the American tradition of constitutional democracy, with the division of powers as outlined, is in general practically invisible to our Tory friends—used as they are to the British tradition of *monopolies* of political and economic power.

In contrast, the basic principle that the American colonists decided to apply to government might have come straight out of the anti-monopolistic theory of liberal capitalism laid out in Adam Smith's *Wealth of Nations* (1776). The principle the colonists applied in reforming the British version of the division of powers in government was the principle of *competition*.

In a constitutional democracy like that of the United States, each arm of government overlaps in different ways with the others. Each arm of government has a generally defined area of responsibility and power; but in many instances another branch of government may also be

Item 58: Subversion in Government

In dutiful imitation of that glorious Constitution of the mother country, with its division of power among kings, lords, and commons which, though it really died with William III [1688-1702], still exists in devout imaginations, the Constitution of the Canadian Dominion has a false front of monarchy. The king who reigns but does not govern is represented by a Governor-General who does the same, and the Governor-General solemnly delegates his impotence to a puppet Lieutenant-Governor in each province. Everything is done in the names of these images of royalty.... Each of them, to keep up the constitutional illusion, is surrounded by a certain amount of state and etiquette, the Governor-General, of course, having more of it than his delegates....

... The Governor-General now appears to feel himself bound to dissolve Parliament at the bidding of his Minister, without any constitutional crisis requiring an appeal to the country, or cause of any kind except the convenience of a [Prime] Minister who may think the moment good for snapping a verdict [by means of an election]. We see here that a political cipher is not always a nullity, but may sometimes be mischievous. That the existence of a Parliament should be made dependent upon the will and pleasure of a party leader, and should be cut short as often as it suits his party purposes, is obviously subversive of the independence of the legislature.... An American or Canadian politician in playing his game uses without scruple every card in his hand; traditions or unwritten rules are nothing to him; the only safeguard against his excesses is written law.... The politician in Canada, not less than in the United States, requires the restraint of written law.

—Goldwin Smith: *Canada and the Canadian Question* (1891)*
Goldwin Smith, D.C.L., was a rather unpleasant Anglo reactionary — anti-Semitic, anti-Irish, anti-Catholic, anti-union, and so forth. See, for example, his essays: 'Social and Industrial Revolution'; 'Woman Suffrage'; 'The Jewish Question'; and 'The Irish Question'; published in New York, London, and Toronto in 1893 as Essays on the Questions of the Day.

operating—or wish to operate—in the same area. Since no one branch of the division of powers can operate without the others; since no two can operate effectively without the third; and since each power can be counted on in the long run to seek every means of protecting itself from encroachment by any of the others; then the resulting system of government behaves as a system of *competing vested interests.* At the same time, each division of power retains the basic prerogatives and the sources of strength which keep it distinct from the others in mutually recognized ways.

With all its many faults, the American system feels like a breath of fresh air when compared with the fetid and secretive atmosphere of our system. Because it is much more open to the people and to competition for power than ours, the U.S. system allows many of the economic and other vested interests in the nation at large to engage in open battle with each other in government. The more that these various interests fight it out, the more information about each of them becomes available to the public. *Public* information about real economic and political interests— that alone, for a start, would be absolutely revolutionary—in the eighteenth-century sense—for the system of government in Canada.

It will of course be argued that in the United States, the laws are enforced differentially for and against different social and economic groups; that the system is often a pork barrel of bribery and corruption (especially at the state levels); that business is protected by the law in ways that no one else is; that the system is dominated by a certain race, a certain class, and a certain sex; that the more money you have, the safer you are; and that the privileged still keep getting away with it under the American system.

True again. But these realities do not alter the plain truth that in countries like Canada, where economic and political power is intensely concentrated in even fewer hands than elsewhere (except for more direct forms of dictatorship), the differential enforcement of the law is *even more* differential; bribery and corruption is *even more* widespread; business is *even more* immune from political and legal scrutiny; the rich and the dominators have *even more* power; and the privileged are *even more* protected....

Parliamentary Democracy: The Monopoly of Power

Whether by accident, incompetence, or design, the Tory tradition in Canada has seen to it that much of the information we need about our own governmental traditions is unavailable to us in easily acquired ways, and that much of the information that we hear and read about the American development of the British tradition of government is distorted or misrepresented. It appears now that some of these absences of information and some of these distortions and misrepresentations are beginning to be properly supplied and rectified by younger Canadian teachers and historians, especially in the 1970s. Be this as it may, however, it is still the case that most Canadians today are living with an Imaginary picture of our own political traditions.

Let us return to the question of the division of powers. Apart from the system of ministerial coercion, deadlock, and 'divide and rule' between the federal government and the provincial governments produced by the BNA Act, the principle of competing and mutually constraining governmental powers does not exist in any significant way (nor at any significant level) in our country.

This is hardly an accident. The American colonists reformed the British system when they took it over in the late eighteenth century. In contrast, Canada was not simply forced to retain the British system but also to retain an unreformed version that remained in general considerably behind the reforms that the British were themselves obliged to make because of popular agitation and the influence of the rising industrial bourgeoise in the nineteenth century.

Perhaps the most important aspect of the reform of the British system by the American colonists was the reform and reinterpretation of the divison of powers as it existed under the British constitutional tradition. This radical change in the 'internal' relations of government resulted from the way the American bourgeoisie and petite bourgeoisie in the eighteenth century decided to protect themselves in the future, against their own government in their own country, from any abuses similar to the abuses of power they had experienced at the hands of the British monarchy, its ministers, and its government agents.

Significantly enough, British and Canadian jurists, political theorists, and historians have been claiming for years that the American colonists misunderstood the British system of the division of powers in 1787 and later. They usually blame this supposed misunderstanding on the French political theorist, Montesquieu (1689-1755), who enlarged on the political theory of the British philosopher, John Locke, to state unequivocally, in *The Spirit of the Laws:*

> When the legislative power is united with the executive power in the same person or in the same body of magistrates, there is no liberty at all; for it may be feared that the same monarch or the same senate will make tyrannical laws to be tyrannically executed (Book II, Chapter 6).

This the American colonists understood in practice as well as in theory, since they had been on the receiving end of a combined executive and legislative tyranny at the hands of the 'mother country' for quite long enough. And since they could do nothing to reform the government in England, they set about reforming it abroad, in America.

In contrast, the division of powers for which the 'mother of parliaments' fought the British monarchy over many centuries was not in essence a division of powers between the executive, the legislature, and the judiciary. The division of powers being fought for in Britain emerged in the seventeenth century as a division of powers between *kings, lords,* and *commons* (between the monarchy, the House of Lords, and the House of Commons).

A fourth power in the British struggle, and the one that eventually emerged as the primary repository of the 'English' constitution, was the power of the Common Law, a written, but uncodified series of acts, statutes and precedents which define in relatively vague and jargon-laden ways what ought and and ought not to be done in the name of the Law. Typically, constitutional aspects of the Common Law remain a secret cipher for the majority of the British people, a cipher that has always required paid experts to explain, and one that has been so complex in its historical evolution that few of us can ever be sure what it actually means for us in any particular situation.

The American tradition depends on the precedents of Common Law, just as ours does, but one of the great and lasting innovations in government introduced into the American system was a constitution written in plain English. As for the battle between kings, lords, and commons in the British tradition, this battle was originally defined and undertaken as a fundamental struggle between Parliament and Monarch. It is this characteristic of the struggle that has resulted in the dictatorial system of government under which we live.

The struggle in British history did originally begin as a struggle over *spheres* of power. But since the eighteenth century, and especially since the emergence of more and more powerful political parties in the nineteenth century (along with the emergence of the institution of the monarch's 'first' or 'prime' minister), the struggle soon took on new characteristics. Rather than being a struggle between the different *functions* of government for their own *spheres* of power (executive, judicial, legislative), it gradually became a struggle between the existing *institutions* of government (kings, lords, and commons) for *all* of the power.

Originally, because every minister of the crown was conceived to have a personal and individual responsibility to the monarch, the Prime minister was merely a 'first among equals.' By the twentieth century, the advantages enjoyed by the Prime Minister over and above the Members of Parliament, and, eventually, over and above the Cabinet, had been converted into various styles of autocracy (Lloyd George and Winston Churchill provide powerful examples).

Item 59: Dangers Inherent in the British Tradition

...My purpose here is to show how Parliament has come to be the Sovereign Body in the United Kingdom and how its sovereignty is actually exercised. Here, in the doctrine of Parliamentary omnipotence, lies the unique and characterizing element of our Constitution, and it is, as all jurists know, an element which might in certain circumstances be employed for the subversion of the Constitution itself. We do well, I think, at times to remind ourselves that there is no power—no legal power—on earth, to restrain the Parliament of the United Kingdom from passing an Act giving the Government of the day authority to raise such taxes as it chose, and spend them as it liked, to make such orders as it saw fit, and generally, to rule us at its own sweet will. If this prospect seems fantastic, many other things have seemed fantastic, and yet for want of due care and vigilance they have come to pass....

...In countries of the most diverse history, we see the same experiment, of constitutional government under forms not unlike our own, violently repudiated in favour of one for which we have no general name, but which perhaps might be described as the Dictatorship of the Party....

...I confess I see no barrier, in our institutions themselves, against the establishment even here of a Dictatorship of the Party, employing as its instrument of government, that very power of delegated legislation which the omnipotence of Parliament has created....

G.M. Young: *The Government of Britain* (1941)

There are a number of reasons for this change. These include the power of the Prime Minister to put the future of every member of the party in jeopardy by calling an election. (In Canada, the Prime Minister has only to send an 'instrument of advice,' rather than an 'order in council' agreed on by the full cabinet, to the Governor-General if he wants to dissolve parliament.) They include the development of a powerful central bureaucracy in the 'Prime Ministers Office,' which in practice in Canada is responsible to, and representative of, nobody but the reigning Prime Minister. They include the failure of the system as a whole to provide funds for a powerful and useful set of legislative committees to offset the power of the executive. They include the development of the professional bureaucracy of the many departments, none of whose heads (ministers or deputy ministers) are in real practice truly answerable to the legislators, but only to the Prime Minister. They include the practice whereby the members of the Cabinet now hold office at the pleasure of the Prime Minister alone. Perhaps the most important of these developments as regards the ordinary members of the party in power, is the control, by the 'inner' cabinet, and the economic interests it listens to, of the Party Machine and party funds. Any party member who steps out of line can expect to have trouble being re-elected.

The general pattern of what has happened to the British system over the past two centuries can thus be summed up in a sentence or two. Parliament originally struggled against the monarchy, and won; the House of Commons struggled against the House of Lords, and won; the Prime Minister and Cabinet struggled against the ordinary members of the party in power, and won; the Prime Minister struggled against the power of the Cabinet, and won. The people lost.

This process, briefly summarized as it has to be within the limits of this book, is the process by which the Prime Minister of Canada and the Prime Minister of the United Kingdom have arrived at a position from which they exercise more domestic political power in their own countries than the President does in the United States.

The monopoly of economic and political power originally exercised by the monarch in the British tradition thus passed into two sets of hands in Canada. The Prime Minister inherited the visible monopoly of political power and business took over the monopoly of economic power behind the throne.

There is, moreover, one particularly dangerous way in which the Canadian federal tradition—the most authoritarian, the most unresponsive, the most unrepresentative, and the most irresponsible of the three traditions discussed—has failed to develop beyond its essentially nineteenth-century character. Unlike the British system and the American system, both of which recognized in this century that without labor, capital is nothing at all, Canadian politics at the federal level have persisted in the effective exclusion of the voices of labor from the dominant political parties. Without suggesting that either the British or the Americans have produced a just, truly representative, and truly responsible political reality in their form of government—for they have

Item 60: The War on Labor

The Social Credit government [of British Columbia] performed mischievous work at the emergency session of the [provincial] legislature, but the labor movement would be unwise to react hastily to it. . . .

Granted the government could not allow the West Kootenay schools dispute—the ostensible reason for summoning the legislature—[to continue] much longer. But why the urgency to legislate the Canadian Union of Public Employees back to work [in] the week that schools break up for Christmas vacation? . . . .

[Labor Minister] Williams now says a study is necessary to determine if [Bill 46] should become law, which is another way of saying that the government doesn't need it and doesn't want to proclaim it [as law]. It only wants to use it as a political weapon. . . .

. . .Even the people on the employers' side admit [that Bill 46 was unnecessary].

But what the Socreds really want to do is to convince the rabid right wing of their party, which has not stopped screaming for right-to-work laws,* that they are going to stomp on the labor move-

ment. And they want to provoke a violent response from labor. . . .

The new bill is a dangerous piece of legislation, because it allows the [provincial] cabinet to make decisions that properly belong to the legislature. In effect, it gives one man, [Premier] Bennett, the power to revoke the right to strike.

—Editorial in the *Vancouver Express,* Edition of December 13, 1978

So-called 'right-to-work' laws are designed to increase the competition of workers with each other, with the aim of keeping wages down. Amongst other things, such laws mean the end of the democratic shop. In businesses where a majority of the workers have decided to unionize, and where the union represents all the workers in collective bargaining, the imposition of 'right-to-work' laws would mean that individual workers can refuse to join the union. The result is that these individuals obtain all the benefits of unionism and collective bargaining (decided on by the majority), without incurring any of the accompanying responsibilities. Divide and rule.

not—it is of some importance to note that at least organized labor has a powerful voice in political decisions, through the left wing of the British Labor Party and through the left wing of the American Democratic Party. In contrast, the voices of Canadian labor in the left wing of the New Democratic Party of Canada have even less say in politics than the NDP does as a whole.

In Canada, both the Liberal Party and the Progressive Conservative Party remain the representatives of monopolistic and multinational capital—both foreign and Canadian capital. The Canadian tradition thus remains locked in the nineteenth century in one notably formidable way. It has left most of the war between capital and labor—including the original working class, Women—to be fought out in the streets.

A Note to Chapter Twelve

SSF, SAS, SS: Le Temps de Léopards au Canada? [1]

While considering the dictatorial State Democracy under which we live, we should pay careful attention to the latest way in which the 'special connection' between the 'English-speaking peoples' of Canada, Great Britain, and the United States is being used these days. The following extract from a report written by Roy MacGregor in the November 6, 1978 issue of *Maclean's* magazine, entitled 'The Armed Forces: In from the Cold,' will give at least some idea of what kind of war measures acts may

---

[1] *Le Temps des léopards* is the title of the second volume of Yves Courrière's history of the Algerian War of Independence (1954-62). *Léopards*—from the camouflage battle dress of the elite French parachute corps, who applied the terrorist tactics and methods of torture developed in Indochina against the Viet Minh to the French colonial war against the Algerians—accurately portrayed in the 1966 film by Gillo Pontecorvo, *La Bataille d'Alger* (good enough to be banned in France). Of course, nothing remotely similar can happen here, unless you happen to believe the Major-General Mans already quoted, who also said in his report on Canada: 'Traditional Canadian complacency, the open society, and a feeling generated by its geography that "it cannot happen here," help to create the troubled waters in which the revolutionary fish can swim and propagate.' It is not explained how it is that 'complacency' and the supposed 'open society' create 'troubled waters'—but reactionaries have never been noted for their capacity to use ordinary logic.

possibly be being contemplated behind the scenes in the Canada of the late nineteen-seventies.

> ...A cloud of suspicion continues to linger over the 3,500-member [Canadian] Special Service Force....Formed [in 1977] by combining crack Petawawa units with the elite Canadian Airborne Regiment...the SSF's lack of any specific task has led to continuing rumors concerning the military and the possible separation of Quebec. Though the force was planned for more than a decade, its inopportune announcement—just two weeks after the 1976 Parti Quebecois victory—and opportune location directly across the river from Quebec have given rise to questions that are...without answers. And it is this lack of a 'defined role' that has Defence Minister Barney Danson announcing a specific SSF task this week, which insiders hint may be a detailed NATO commitment to the defence of Norway.
>
> But that will hardly stop the rumors. There will still be those who wonder why the force has 2,500 pairs of handcuffs and 17,800 gas masks despite the fact that no Canadian soldier has come under gas attack since 1918. And further questions will arise next month when the first of some 50 special armored vehicles arrives on the Petawawa [Ontario] base....
>
> The most startling SSF story, however, has remained a secret since the early hours of July 5, 1978, when a plane loaded with British commandos—estimates vary widely between 30 and 190—stole out of Petawawa. Fully two months earlier, also in the dead of night, the same commandos had come [secretly] into the country....On July 3, the commandos took over a cottage on Petawawa Point where they invited several women....Alcohol and high hopes naturally led to bragging, and the soldiers thoughtlessly let it slip that they were members of the mysterious British SAS [the Special Air Service]....
>
> ...The Canadians are, as one officer put it, merely 'lethal boy scouts' compared to the cream of the British army.... Photographing [the British SAS] is forbidden even for the official military magazines and the British ministry of defence attitude toward them is simply, 'We don't mention them—*ever.*'
>
> However, the SAS is known to operate extensively in Northern Ireland where they parachute in at night in small groups and work undercover to disrupt the Irish Republican Army. How they actually operate is guesswork—one ex-SAS told *Maclean's* London bureau that being a member is 'automatically a license to kill'....

Obviously, this clear tie with [the Irish] civil war adds further intrigue to the SAS visit to Canada. The only comparable force to the SAS, the United States Rangers, was also quietly here...in January [1978] when some 175 of them trained with the Special Service Force....

Item 61: One of the Voices
of Domestic Counterinsurgency in the Sixties

The recurrent nature of Canada's basic problems emphasizes both the urgent need for moderation and the striking degree to which this quality has been applied in Canadian affairs. Time and again, Canada has faced the gravest kind of dilemma in her relations with the two great English-speaking nations with whom her destiny is so inextricably bound up. Time and again, economic difficulties or racial antagonisms have threatened her internal structure with deadlock or collapse. Yet on each occasion Canadians have turned from extreme courses to seek a middle ground on which cooperation was possible, and outside of which lay disaster. If the difficulties have never been completely removed, they have never become completely irreconcilable. It is this sound sense of the possible that has enabled Canada to surmount each successive crisis; and each one has uniformly been followed by a new period of progress in Canadian independence and Canadian unity, and by a fresh growth in economic strength and political stature.

Edgar McInnis: *Foreword* to:
*Canada: A Political and
Social History*
(1947; reprinted 1959, 1963)

CHAPTER THIRTEEN

The Tyranny of the Executive in Canada

The 'Crown' in Canada

Our long tradition of colonial authoritarianism and irresponsible and unrepresentative government is now dangerously ensconced, not simply in 'government,' but in the 'Crown' as an administrative and executive entity. By the 'Crown,' we refer neither to the Monarchy (at its level), nor to the Queen (at another level). Our Tory ideologists, however, confuse the Crown with both the Queen and the Monarchy, and quite deliberately so—because they use the pomp and circumstance of the British monarchy as a mythological smokescreen to hide what the 'Crown' actually means in Canada: i.e. the power of the Executive.

Indeed, in the summer of 1978, when Her Majesty made a brief visit to this country, we in British Columbia were subjected to an organized campaign of articles, letters to the editor, guest editorials and the like, obviously calculated to accomplish two main objectives: first, to tap the many sources of British nostalgia, and indeed, love for the Monarchy; and secondly, to confuse all that love and mythology with our political realities in such a way that any criticism of the form of constitution or the form of government in Canada could be—indeed, would be—interpreted as an attack on the Monarchy, or worse, as a personal attack on Her Majesty the Queen.

This campaign was in other words one more replay of the same old Imaginary game of anti-Americanism and anti-republicanism.

It is necessary, therefore, to try to emerge from this smokescreen by pointing out once again that political and constitutional reform in Canada does not involve the person or the majesty of the monarchy or the Queen. Whether Canada remains a monarchy or not in the future is a matter for Canadians to decide; and this matter is one to be decided quite separately from the matter of radical reforms in the political order.

The Crown in Canada is the locus of extraordinary power, not simply in 'national emergencies'—some of our Tories like to call it 'our constitutional fire extinguisher'—but also in the day-to-day operations of all our governments. The Crown in Canada is what on the surface distinguishes the executive arm of the governments in Canada from the executive powers in the federal and state governments of the United States. However, the way the 'Crown' is used in political discussions in Canada leads to the exposure of some significant contradictions about the responsibility of the executive in Canada to the people of Canada.

If you look for the final governmental responsibility for executive decisions in the United States, you will find it somewhere in the White House; and if that executive power exceeds its constitutional limits, provisions for redress are already written into the American system of laws about law: the U.S. constitution. In contrast, if you look for the executive agency and the 'responsibility' called the 'Crown' in Canada, you will not find it anywhere at all—certainly not in the office of the Governor General.

Moreover, you will not be able to localize the responsibility of the executive power symbolized and put into effect by the 'Crown' in any particular person in government. Professor Frank MacKinnon was reported as having answered the neccessary question, in the *Vancouver Sun* of June 29, 1978: 'Does this mean that there is no single person in the entire structure of government who actually possesses and wields at his own discretion the executive powers of the state? It means exactly this.' What could possibly be the point of this peculiar state of affairs, a state of affairs which suggests quite directly that we have never had responsible government in Canada? A moment's thought, and we realize that it is the now rather antiquated 'anti-presidential' argument. This argument depends on a strange kind of logic which goes approximately as follows: 'We have a *real* Queen in Canada, who does not rule; the Americans have a *real* Ruler who is but the shadow of a King. The one reigns, but does not rule; the other rules but does not reign. Therefore we have more freedom in Canada than the Americans do in the United States.'

It is the same argument as the nineteenth-century argument quoted at the end of Chapter Seven, the same century-old muddle about the real relationships on both sides of the 49th parallel.

To some people, then—to those who have presumably neglected to notice (for example) how the power and the secrecy of the operations of the Federal government have repeatedly been protected and increased by the Liberal expedient of moving Cabinet Ministers from post to post, so that each new appointee can allow the government to escape responsibility by denying knowledge of the actions of his/her predecessors—to some people, the fact that the buck never seems to stop anywhere in Canada is apparently what 'fortunately' distinguishes us from the United States.

Try suing a 'Crown Corporation' in Canada, such as Air Canada, the

Canadian National Railway, the Insurance Corporation of B.C., the B.C. Hydro and Power Authority, or Teleglobe (formerly the Canadian Overseas Telecommunications Corporation), for example. Without the permission, in effect, of the provincial or federal government in power, the governments which decide the policies and aims of these so-called corporations, you can't.

In a word, as a result of the way the power called the 'Crown' has evolved directly out of our colonial past, the 'Crown' in Canada has remained effectively *above the law.*

What this constitutional anomaly signifies, in effect, is that whenever our 'invisible Crown' chooses to exert itself, Canadians have no usual or customary constitutional redress against its arbitrary powers beyond that of writing letters to the government and the newspapers, or that of attempting to force an election.

These are illusory alternatives, given that it is the daily and often apparently trivial operations of monopoly government and corporate capital which prepare the system and its people for totalitarianism; and that under the Canadian system of government, it is traditional for the majority party or dynasty in power to do more or less what it wants, no matter what the Opposition or the people say.

This the Government can do because members of the majority party are not permitted by party 'discipline' to diverge from the government's Party Line—except when the Party Line is that they must vote their 'consciences,' e.g. on capital punishment; or when the Party Line forces many members to stay away from the House when the vote is taken.

This last is precisely what occured when the Executive of the ruling Liberal Party rammed through the House of Commons the 'Post Office Continuation Act' in October, 1978. This piece of legislation forced the Canadian Union of Postal Workers back to work without a contract, did nothing to alleviate conditions in the Post Office (which include numerous and persistent violations of the previous contract by the management of the postal system), and deprived the postal workers of the right to strike which they had fought for and won in previous battles. This piece of executive chicanery and failure to abide by contractual agreements included threats of huge fines against individual workers—besides threats of prosecution for conspiracy to defy an Act of Parliament, accompanied by RCMP raids on union offices all over Canada. Moreover, this highly significant bill was forced through the House of Commons in thoroughly 'democratic' style: with only *one-third* of our elected representatives present and voting. Where were the rest of them?

Item 62: O, Canada! Glorious and Free!

Jean-Claude Parrot, president of the Canadian Union of Postal Workers and one of the arrested union officials, said the labor movement 'must mobilize its strength against a government which has proven that is has no respect for human rights and civil liberties.'

'If we stand silently by while the government picks off each union, one by one, we will not only fail as we did in 1975 in the fight against wage controls, we will also be guilty of helping the government to murder our collective rights.'

Parrot, who faces criminal charges in connection with continuation of the postal strike after Parliament ordered an end to the stoppage, touched care-

fully on his own union's battle.

At one stage, he was publicly thanking those who supported CUPW after the back-to-work law was passed [and said] 'we maintained our legal right to strike.'

He quickly corrected himself: 'I'm not supposed to call them legal rights.'

Just a day earlier, Parrot had to issue a court-dictated statement declaring that Parliament's back-to-work bill invalidated the postal workers' right to strike. That kept him out of jail until his trial on a charge of violating a Criminal Code provision which forbids defiance of an Act of Parliament.

Vancouver Sun: Edition of October 28, 1978

In other words, the very real powers over the present and the future of Members of Parliament wielded by the Prime Minister and the Party Machine—and the same principle of course extends at a different level to the members of what is all too accurately called the 'Loyal Opposition'—these real powers are exercised in order to refuse to our elected representatives the right to vote as individuals, as individuals who represent different constituencies with different interests across the country.

The Myth of Responsible Government

The irresponsibility of government in Canada—and the irresponsibility of executive bodies of all kinds—has been referred to many times in this book. Let us consider now how the combination of irresponsibility and rigid party coercion has a direct and useful pay-off to Canadian politicians of all stripes, both in and out of power—for it is by this combination that the whole pseudo-democratic system reproduces itself year by year and election by election.

We can consider this Canadian set-up most easily by means of a brief comparison with the significantly different relationship between party members, the executive, the various party leaders, and the constituents in the United States.

On any important or controversial question which arises in the Senate or the House of Representatives in the U.S., there is generally a roll-call vote. The American Senators or Representatives will vote according to conscience, party pressure, special-interest lobbying, presidential strong-arming, various forms of bribery, party wishes, and often in the interests of (important or noisy) constituents. The point is that 'somewhere out there' at least one group of people will be watching and recording that vote, recording it as the vote of an individual who can be personally and publicly taken to task for that vote in the next election. Since U.S. Representatives are elected to Congress every two years, this system of individual voting makes every Representative very sensitive indeed to what their constituents (and others) want, and very sensitive to what some group or other may or may not do to them the next time around.

In contrast, under the 'unwritten' practices of the Canadian system, the major debates and pressures are expressed and dealt with in the Cabinet, in the 'inner' Cabinet, and in party caucuses on policy. These are not open to the public. Once the Executive of the majority party has decided what to do, the party members all troop into the House of Commons, throw a few insults, perhaps, at the Opposition, and then proceed to 'vote.' The important payoff in this rather clever and obviously self-perpetuating political system is that *not one of the legislators can be held personally responsible for the vote s/he casts.* In practice and in principle, the responsibility for that vote belongs to the Party Executive, not to the individual legislator.

This *tyranny of the executive* in Canada has the rather inflexible effect of turning practically every question, however complex, into one colossal 'either/or' question: e.g. either the Liberals (or the Conservatives) will or won't. Particular MPs or MLAs simply aren't involved as individuals at this level. The 'either/or' question gets even bigger and more simplistic at election time—when the Party Leader can take tactical advantage of the national context by timing the election to correspond with favorable polls, or with economic recoveries.

In practice, the government in power votes as a monolith. The opposition will ordinarily do so as well. But the Canadian people are not a monolith, or even three or four monoliths. We are infinitely more diverse than that. Nevertheless, our system of party 'discipline' tends inevitably to reduce the amount and type of *variety* or diversity that is actually expressed in the parliamentary positions and activities of our representatives.

The system of elections under the British and Canadian systems is one of the most obvious ways in which the voters and the legislators are manipulated by the Party Executive. The whole Tory argument about the supposedly 'continuous responsibility' of the Canadian Government to the Canadian people rests on this one happenstance: that every once in a while the Prime Minister takes tactical advantage of everyone by calling an election.

In Canada the Executive still controls the gerrymandering of electoral districts so as to divide and rule the vote as it pleases in important areas. The principle of 'one person, one vote' has never been properly applied in Canada. The Executive in power can literally demolish the constituencies of powerful opponents. The Executive still controls access to information about what they have actually been up to while in office. Individual Members are ordinarily completely beholden to the same Executive.

Above all, perhaps—apart from the control over the timing of the election—the most significantly manipulative feature of the Canadian system is the short time allowed for the election itself (a few weeks). Reams of paper and miles of video-tape in Canada are expended on whether and when the election will be called (a ridiculous and futile waste of time and money)—but when it actually arrives, there is little, if any time at all for any of the fundamental issues or useful quarrels (useful to the voters) to be properly examined, debated, argued, and fought over. The whole business works most strongly in favor of the incumbents. What the whole exercise ultimately means is an election on mere 'gut issues,' an election devoid of any really useful consideration of just what we want the incoming government to do.

In Canada, then, the structure of responsibility is upside-down. Members of Parliament and Members of the provincial Legislative Assemblies, as we soon discover at election time, are not representing our interests in Government, nor are they in reality responsible to us. Rather than primarily being our representatives, responsible to us, MPs and MLAs in Canada represent the Party Executive, and are primarily responsible to it.

Furthermore, a constituent may possibly differ on only a few issues with the Party in power—but if the differences are important, the choice we effectively end up with is not the elective nomination of an opposing member of the same party (as is possible in the U.S. system of elective primaries), nor a possible split-ticket defeat of a particular Representative, and so on. No. The basic electoral decision in Canada is much more simplistic: We vote *either* to throw them *all* out of power *or* to keep them *all* in.

Item 63: Responsible Government: The Old Twist

'As a principle...the particular minister of the day should not have a right to know what the police are doing constantly in their investigative practices...If the government, the minister, or myself had begun asking the RCMP in any detail about their operations...we would certainly have been accused by the Opposition...of having undue political influence and interference in the RCMP.'

—Prime Minister Trudeau:
News Conference,
December 9, 1977

Oversight of the CIA, both executive and congressional, must be clear and rational. Until the CIA came under attack, the President was able to evade responsibility for covert actions even though he had initiated them. Currently the President is required by law to approve all covert actions.... [This] is probably the only workable system in the U.S. today.

—Edwin Warner:
'Strengthening the CIA.'
Time Magazine. Issue of
April 30, 1979

We are also not permitted as a people to decide who we wish to elect as the leader of any given party, the leader who will become Prime Minister (or provincial Premier) if that party wins a majority.

One other important feature of the U.S. system should be remarked on. In the United States, an unpopular or ill-conceived or even tyrannical measure or bill introduced into Congress by the 'government' (i.e. by the executive power, the Administration) can be roundly defeated in either House or Senate or both without bringing the 'government' down and precipitating a crisis. In Canada, in contrast, following the Party Line is much more necessary and protective for individual MLAs and MPs—because the prevailing custom is that if an *executive* bill is defeated, all the *legislators* go down with it as well.

Item 64: Tyranny in Westminster

It is my belief that the office of the Prime Minister has indeed undergone changes, that its holder now enjoys more power in Great Britain than the President does in the United States, and that this stems, in part at least, from . . . two points . . . that a Minister has no fixed term of office, and that there is no clearly laid down separation [i.e. division] of powers. . . .

My six and a half years in Parliament [as a Conservative] have convinced me that our parliamentary institutions, particularly when the myth is distinguished from the reality, are insufficient by themselves to safeguard our freedom. Indeed, the absence of any defined separation of powers between the executive and the legislature has enabled already strong Governments to use Parliament only too easily as an instrument of tyranny. Paradoxically, the British have been attempting to export the Westminster parliamentary system and use it as the sole protection of the consent of the governed in Africa and Asia at the very point when it has ceased to provide a similar safeguard at home. . . .

The central cause [of the Prime Minister exercising more power than the American President] is that the United States has a written constitution, with a Congress that cannot dismiss the President, other than by the exceptional process of impeachment, and a President that cannot dismiss Congress. . . . [This system] has proved a better safeguard against supra-Presidential rule, than the British system in which in theory Parliament can dismiss the Prime Minister, yet in practice does not, while in theory the Prime Minister can dismiss Parliament, and in fact does. . . .

The hallmark of an unwritten constitution is unperceived change. . . .

—Humphrey Berkeley:
*The Power of the
Prime Minister* (1969)

The Monarchy

We should never underestimate the power of a symbol; and the Crown in Canada (not the Monarchy and not the Queen) has evolved practically unimpeded from its colonial authority to camouflage the Executive power in Canada. Arbitrary, irresponsible, and unrepresentative power. Power over the courts, power over the legislators, power over the people.

Consider the following statement by Michael Valpy in the *Vancouver Sun* of June 27, 1978: '... We separate the *possession* of power from the *wielding* of power: one institution, the monarchy, possesses the power without wielding it; the other institution, government, wields the power without possessing it.' Translated into its logical consequence, this argument implies that the 'institution' which is *responsible* for the exercise of power (i.e. the one that 'possesses' it), here called 'the monarchy,' does not exercise it; whereas the institution which *does* exercise the power, the government, is *not responsible* for it—because it supposedly does not 'possess' it. If this argument seems difficult to follow, we can do no more than refer to its original sources. Mr. Valpy is an associate editor of the *Sun,* based in Ottawa.

Item 65: A Word From Those Who Are Supposed To Know

Former Prime Minister John Diefenbaker says, 'I believe, simply and honestly, that if Canada did not have a Queen, we would now be part of the United States. We would have been taken over... absorbed.

'The Crown is above politics; it has no party affiliations which could in any way demean its value. It endures. Governments and political parties come and go, but the Crown is a symbol of continuity and unity. We have a head of state who has no political bias. The head of state can remove a government and force an election whenever it sees what it feels to be an abuse of power, without fear of party criticism.'

Senator Eugene Forsey, a leading Canadian constitutional expert, agrees. 'To substitute a republic would mean a political organ transplant; cutting out part of ourselves and transplanting into our body political something alien, borrowed from other peoples with a different history, different traditions, different institutions, different needs.'

Tam W. Deachman: *What Every American Should Know About Canada* (1977)

Perhaps the following response to Mr. Valpy's article in a letter by Mark Jowett (July 15, 1978) will help to clear up some of the difficulties. Mr. Jowett says, in part: 'Although I am a teenager and have therefore grown up in an age when the monarchy's role has greatly diminished, I still feel a sense of love and oneness with the Queen.' After asserting that this love is shared by the majority of Canadian

Item 66: Technological Superiority I

The above represents a small-sized Gatling Gun, mounted on a tripod ; it can also be mounted on the gunwale of a ship or in the bow of a small launch, etc. It is a very light and effective arm and is recommended for the suppression of riots, etc.

From: Charles Pelham Mulvaney, A.M., M.D. Formerly of the Queen's Own Rifles: *The North-West Rebellion of 1885*. . . . (1885)

teenagers today, the letter continues: 'Because we are really only the first or second true generation of Canadians, since previous generations consisted primarily of immigrants, the need to establish roots and a Canadian identity is most crucial to the youth of today.' Our parents and grandparents 'developed roots growing up in their homeland; we have none and therefore live with a sense of insecurity and a lack of self-identity.' 'We feel we know our roots a little better when we see the Queen, thus helping us to dispell the insecurity and identify ourselves in the present.' The writer deserves especial credit for putting this matter so clearly before us.

Along with the whole ramshackle edifice of 'law and order'—principally order, and order outside the law—that has been erected over the past 150 years in Canada, the 'Crown' is the symbol of what is still praised today in public and pulpit as the 'distinctively Canadian' entity which keeps us from becoming Americans.

This fleabitten fairytale depends on an argument that traduces the principles of what we know as democracy—an argument that is little short of a treasonable betrayal of the Canadian people. As an open invitation for governments to set themselves above the law in matters both petty and portentous, the reality of the 'Crown' in this country—as a very real symbol of very real socioeconomic power—is the 'internal' colonial *representative,* not of what prevents us from becoming Americans, but rather of *what prevents us from becoming a nation.*

Professor MacKinnon again, author of *The Crown in Canada,* as quoted in the *Vancouver Sun* of June 27, 1978:

> The crown in government resembles the soul of man in philosophy and the algebraic x in mathematics—the one powerful and the other useful.

God save the Queen from such Imaginary flights of fancy! But they nevertheless betray a truth. We have just been told that, in one way, the Crown—the Executive Power—in Canada is an *unknown quality;* and in another way, an *unknown quantity.* Take your pick.

CHAPTER FOURTEEN

Resources

I

A colony, yet a nation—words never before in the history of the world associated together.
　　—Prime Minister Sir Wilfrid Laurier: Speech in London, England,
　　　　　　　　　　in 1897 (Queen Victoria's Diamond Jubilee)

It is an old political and educational maxim that the best way to learn a subject is to explain it to someone else—someone who insists on being persuaded by proper argument and evidence, and especially someone who does not share the specialized vocabulary of your trade. The holes in the argument and the evidence soon show up. This is all the more true if what you are trying to explain is a perspective on a subject, rather than the subject as such.

Let us say that you are trying to explain oppression and you use the word 'girl.' Your companion asks whether you mean 'girl' or 'woman,' and you suddenly realize that you are unconsciously using an oppressive term. You soon find out that if you start using the term correctly to describe female children, rather than women in general, a whole series of other terms are also put into question. You discover that you cannot legitimately use the term 'man' or 'mankind' to refer to the human species or to people in general. It is not a question of just using one expression instead of another one. What happens is that old and well-worn sentences suddenly become unsayable, and very often you cannot at first work out how to rephrase them. You become confused between what you are used to saying and what you now mean.

The change goes further yet. The words and the sentences are not just isolated elements in conversation, but rather the markers of an unconscious attitude. They are all linked to a pattern, and unless you change the pattern, you are stuck with a tokenism which contradicts what you have been taught to think and feel, in this instance, about women. In other words, your perspective on women is inadequate, and consequently your perspective on oppression is also inadequate.

You are now facing a really profound change in attitudes, and this change in attitude cannot be real unless it is accompanied and supported by a change in behavior. Now comes the really hard part. We have been brought up with behavior that stereotypes women. We see women through the Imaginary. As we strive to see the real woman, and to cancel the stereotyping out of our behavior, we soon find ourselves in a state of conflict and confusion. In the process of trying to change our behavior in relation to a person who is 'out there,' as it were, we suddenly find that it is not 'woman' who is in question, safely over there, it is 'man.' The result is that whether I am male or female (but especially if I am male), it is one essential aspect of my own sense of self, my personal identity in relation to social gender, that is under attack. And the attacker is me.

Once you come out the other side of this dilemma and put your own gender identity back together again, in real terms, you will have made a truly fundamental change in political perspective, and you will never be the same again.

I chose this example because I know from my own experience that it is the most difficult political change of all (and not all of one's sexist identity can be changed, so powerful is the conditioning). It is the best test of the radical humanity of one's politics I know of. If we don't make our way out of the dilemna, we   end up as politically and ideologically schizophrenic as Laurier was: 'A girl, yet a woman—words always before in the history of man associated together.'

There is a technical term for this kind of change, one that is however so often misused and misunderstood that it requires using with caution. The change is 'dialectical.' This means that there is an emergence, out of an old position and behavior, of a new position and behavior—and that nothing in the old position's conflicts could have provided enough information to predict what the new position and behavior would be. The personal example of sexism is relatively simple, because it describes the emergence of a real (gender) identity out of an Imaginary one. But the crucial factor in this dialectical change is very similar to a crucial factor that occurs in the socioeconomic change we call revolution: as a result of its own behavior, the formerly dominant system comes into conflict with its environment, and the conflict will not be resolved by the emergence of the newly dominant system until the system-environment contradiction is resolved. The relationship between the two has to become 'recoded,' as it were.

This kind of repunctuation—of the contradiction between colonizer and colonized, for instance—has of course been the major goal of this book. But it is important to recognize that this book itself has also followed the dialectical pattern of unpredictable, yet (in retrospect) logical and understandable change. At the beginning, I had little idea of where the analysis would take me; I did not expect to find such strong evidence for the principal argument; and I could never have predicted the changes that the writing of this text would bring to my own attitudes and understanding.

Item 67: Technological Superiority II

The dangers of the Dalkon Shield IUD were well known before the dump began in 1972. [Shortly] after the Dalkon Shield went on the market in 1971, reports of adverse reactions began pouring in to...the manufacturer, A.H. Robins Co. .... There were cases of pelvic inflammatory disease (an infection of the uterus that can require weeks of bed rest and antibiotic treatment)... blood poisoning...pregnancies resulting in spontaneous abortions...tubal pregnancies and perforations of the uterus. [In some cases, emergency hysterectomies were necessary.] There were even medical reports of Dalkon Shields ripping their way through the walls of the uterus and being found floating free in the abdominal cavity far from the uterus... [By 1974, there had been 200,000 cases of serious infections in the U.S. alone, and 17 known deaths clearly attributable to the Shield.]
...Physicians found insertion was difficult; patients found it almost unbearable. [In February 1971] a physician wrote to A.H. Robins [about] insertion of the Dalkon Shield: 'I have found the procedure to be the most traumatic manipulation ever

perpetrated on womanhood, and I have inserted thousands of other varieties.'
Sometime in 1972...Robins decided to expand its exports. R.T. Ravenholt [Director of the U.S. Agency for International Development] was known to be a population control enthusiast who would ask few questions about a good deal on Dalkon Shields....
Robert W. Nickless, Robins' director of international marketing,...sweetened the deal [by offering] AID the Shield in bulk packages, *unsterilized*, at 48 percent off.
...Nickless emphasized that AID could not distribute the nonsterile...Shields in the U.S. [In 1973, he wrote to AID that the nonsterile form] 'is for the purpose of reducing price' [and] 'is intended for restricted sale to family planning/support organizations who will limit their distribution to those countries commonly referred to as "less developed." '
...The company attached only one set of instructions for each pack of 1000 Shields, [printed in only] English, French and Spanish—although the devices were destined for 42 countries

from Ethiopa to Malaysia. Worse still, only ten inserters were provided per 100 Shields, adding immeasurably to the possibility of infection.

...Hundreds of...cartons [of] unsterilized Dalkon Shields paid for by the U.S. treasury left the shores of America for clinics in Paraguay, Israel, Tunisia and 39 other countries....

—Barbara Ehrenreich, Mark Dowie, and Stephen Minkin: 'The Charge: Gynocide. The Accused: The U.S. Government,' *Mother Jones,* November 1979

After 'urging' from the Federal Drug Administration, Robins finally gave up their lobbying for the Shield in 1974. In 1975, AID recalled the Shields still in storage with major international agencies, but could not recall the estimated 440,000 already in use. In 1979, Ravenholt confided to *Mother Jones* his own theory about IUD-induced pelvic infections: 'Women who frequently change sexual partners have these intercurrent low-grade infections. The IUD can't cause an infection. The body tolerates anything that is sterile [sic].' The Shield is still being inserted, certainly in India and Pakistan, and possibly in South Africa.

In Chapter One we began by recognizing Canada to be an authoritarian, undemocratic, and Imaginary nation, shackled by colonial ignorance and consequently unaware of its powers and potential. We came across strange and unexpected information which eventually made sense, not so much because our knowledge of the real Canada changed, although it certainly did, but rather because our perspective became transformed as basic patterns emerged and became recognizable as connected—through their contexts.

As we proceeded, we began to realize that we are not alone in our predicament—that many of our problems differ only in degree from those of every third-world neocolony struggling to make a living out of its natural resources. We, too, must confront the most powerful and the most sophisticated system of exploitation that has ever arisen on this planet.

The highly trained multinational experts who serve this global economic system know only too well that it is fundamentally unstable. Capitalism is merely three centuries old, and throughout its brief existence it has managed to survive the chaos it creates only by constant expansion, repeatedly finding new environments to exploit.

There is hardly a single imaginable environment in space or time that capitalism will not seek to conquer and to expand into. (Computers, for instance, allow capitalism to expand in time by speeding up the production of profit per unit of time.) Historically, as the capitalist revolution made capitalism increasingly dominant over other kinds of economic systems (*c.* 1600-1800 Common Era), it invented the distinctly Western ideology of 'progress'—the infinite conquest of seemingly limitless new frontiers—to justify the expansion of production it depends on in order to survive.

A strange kind of progress this has turned out to be. With the possible exception of specific acts of genocide in this century—e.g. the Armenians in Turkey, the Jews in Europe (especially Eastern Europe), Stalin's massacre of Russian peasants—and the recent massive famine in Africa south of the Sahara, there are probably more people dying at this moment—of torture, political and racist pogroms, military repression, agricultural poisons, contaminated foodstuffs, unsafe medications, various forms of pollution, and malnutrition and starvation—than ever before in history.

All this in an economic system that could have ended poverty around the globe—and still could, were it not more profitable for capital to produce and reproduce poverty from generation to generation.

What makes capitalism capitalist, and thus fundamentally unlike other systems of production, is that it can turn all kinds of relations, and specifically all human relations, into commodities to be sold on the market. The 'commercial revolution' of the 'age of discovery' (*c.* 1500)—the organized piracy of mercantile capitalism—gradually made both capital and land into commodities, where previously these two components of the means of production had not generally been bought or sold. As it became industrialized (*c.* 1650-1820), the capitalist economic revolution—a revolution in the basic structure of society and social and economic relations—progressively made more and more of the different kinds of labor into a single quantified commodity, largely through its invention of the factory system. (The later extension of this system to farming made agriculture into the 'agribusiness' it is today.) By commoditizing labor, capitalism turned work and creativity—and even play—into wage labor. Forced dependence on wage labor became the principal weapon this imperialist system used to subvert other economic systems. Along with increasingly energy-intensive farming of cash

¹Capitalist farming methods, especially those forced on the Third World by the so-called Green Revolution,' require huge material and energy subsidies in the form of fuel and machinery, fertilizers and pesticides—mostly petrochemical products. Many of the new hybrid strains of plants now used require forced feeding and protection from the environment (e.g. by pesticides) to produce larger crops. By the time one takes a can of peas out of the cupboard, a great deal more non-renewable energy has gone into the product than the energy one gets from eating it.

crops,[1] wage labor controlled by the capitalist market eventually enabled capitalism to subjugate most of the world.

The capitalist system is dominated by short-range survival values. As it oscillates from crisis to crisis, it expands, not for the sake of progress, but for the sake of (ever fleeting) stability. Without expansion, in fact, capitalism is so unstable that it is threatened by structural collapse. Like the constantly escalating arms races and the orgies of destruction its economic values have produced and reproduced in this century, capitalism escalates all forms of production and consumption, including consumption by means of destruction. (Not to be outdone, however, capitalism has now gone on to invent its own 'ultimate weapon'—the neutron bomb—which destroys people, but not capital.)

The most important kind of growth for capitalism is also the most dangerous in the long range: the constant escalation of the system's capacity to produce, as if without limit. The inherent tendency towards unlimited production generates more and more useless and non-essential consumption in the rich nations—consumption that is purchased at the direct expense of the poor countries. At the same time, empire-building within the imperialist system itself concentrates in fewer and fewer hands power over the production of commodities in the quest for profit, and for continued profitability.[2]

Capitalist 'productive capacity'—created by labor and controlled by capital—expands exponentially, like money (finance capital) at compound interest. Because it does not significantly deplete or overtax

---

[2]Labor (creative capacity) creates *use values* out of energy and raw materials—e.g. shoes. Under capitalism, these useful qualities of the product become the basis for *exchange values* quantified like money—e.g. shoes made of alligator skin, whose use value is entirely subordinate to their exchange value in the market. These two fundamental forms of value appear in the surface structure of capitalism as 'wages, price and profit,' expressed in terms of money (the 'general equivalent of exchange').

Before the arrival of capitalism, and in hundreds of societies, some dating back thousands of years, use values occupied a more important position than exchange values. In these economic systems, most of them extraordinarily well-adapted to their natural environments, overall use values constrained the expansion of exchange values. Under capitalism, however—which wages war on its environments—exchange values, as well as their (temporarily) unconstrained multiplication, are dominant over use values. In order for the production of exchange values to keep growing, it becomes necessary to invent practically useless use values—and to create and recreate an environment of consumers who think they need them. Capitalism ignores constraints on such growth invented by non-capitalist societies in their quest for long-range survival, the ultimate use value. Unfortunately, these other societies did not know how to survive capitalism—and we don't know either, as yet.

its environments, money capital (Imaginary capital) can expand indefinitely. In contrast, because it may dangerously deplete or overburden its natural and human environments, real capital—e.g. factories, farms—cannot escalate production exponentially for very long.

Exponential escalation of the capacity to produce is also called 'positive feedback' (where 'output' is added to 'input'): the more capitalism grows today, the more it will grow tomorrow (like an arms race). This kind of growth is most easily envisaged in terms of doubling times. In 1650, for example, the world population of roughly half a billion was growing at a rate of about 0.3 per cent, corresponding to a doubling time of nearly 250 years. By about 1970, the world population was estimated to be about 3.6 billion, and growing at a rate of roughly 2.1 per cent, corresponding to a doubling time of 33 years. Not only did the world population increase, therefore, but the *rate* of increase also increased: the growth has been 'super--exponential.' Encouraging population growth has been a previously essential condition for capitalist growth: the more people, the more workers; the more workers, the more consumers; the more consumers, the more production; the more production, the more profit; the more profit, the more productive capacity; the more productive capacity, the more power.

Capitalism has sown the whirlwind; the peoples of the world are forced to reap it. Capitalism is closer to being totally out of control than it has ever been before. It is a system that can never be satisfied, no matter what we do. The colonization of the wretched of the earth continues to increase. Feudal, slave, and other kinds of fascist relations—in the family, in the factory and the field, in the corporation, in the schools—wax ever more oppressive. At the same time, capitalism's suicidal attempt to colonize nature proceeds as yet unchecked. There is no longer any doubt that the short-range survival values of capitalism are in direct and violent conflict with the long-range survival—as human beings—of everyone on earth.[3]

But the environments of capitalism are finite. There are limits to the expansion of production and consumption under capitalism—limits that not even capitalism can change. It is true that technological innovations and further explorations may effectively increase the natural resources available to feed the existing economic system with energy and raw materials. But little, if anything, can be done to increase the limited

[3]For a well-documented account of specific biological crimes against humanity by American and European corporations, see 'The Corporate Crime of the Century,' *Mother Jones,* November 1979, pp. 22-49.

ecological capacity of the natural environment to absorb, recycle, and detoxify the noxious wastes[4] poured into it by the system's economic output. This waste output continually accumulates even in our own flesh and blood.[5] Thus, should the capitalist and state capitalist system somehow learn how to use some inexhaustible source of energy at its inputs, such a discovery would not necessarily solve the ongoing crises of this kind of economic system. It would not allow capitalism to escape the ecological and human limits on its output into its environments—the limits on the future expansion necessary to its continued survival as a *capitalist* system.

Capitalism as a system is of course adaptive; indeed, it has so far successfully adapted—in the short term—to many of the changes its operations have brought about in its environments. But it is utterly dependent on the survival of the living environments it is exhausting at ever-increasing rates. Any system whose continuing existence depends on the destruction of its environments is self-destroying by definition. Its very organization and behavior threaten it with extinction.

As yet, no one knows just what it means to say that capitalism threatens its own survival. In the colonies making up its geographical context, however, we know that this imperial system threatens us—and that when times get tough the colonies are always the first to go.

This was clear to many of us from the outset. But in the process of seeking to understand this country and its possible futures, we discovered

---

[4]Besides regular garbage and pollution, these wastes include junk commodities, as well as the waste heat of energy conversion. (Roughly 60 per cent of the output of a nuclear generating plant is waste heat, for example.) An economic system takes one kind of order from its environment—e.g. iron ore, coal—then reorganizes this order into other kinds useful to the system—e.g. steel—and in the process injects the disorder left over—e.g. acid rain—into its environment. When the system is rapidly depleting the available varieties of order in the 'resource environment' (or depleting renewable resources—e.g. trees in B.C.—at a rate greater than the natural rate of replacement), and also by its waste output rapidly increasing the disorder of the 'waste-sink environment' (nature in general), it is behaving as if it has repealed the second law of thermodynamics.

[5]Originally useful products, such as antibiotic drugs, may be made lethal to us in their effects by the overproduction and consequent overprescription of antibiotics. Overuse of the drug creates strains of bacteria that are resistant to it. (The same is true of pesticides and resistant strains of insects. And while the agribusiness keeps escalating its war on the 'pests' its own practices have created, thousands of farmworkers around the world are subjected to increasing amounts of increasingly more dangerous toxins.) In Mexico in 1972-3, a catastrophic epidemic of typhoid fever afflicted some 100,000 persons. The typhoid bacteria were resistant to the standard antibiotic (itself capable of lethal 'side effects'); doctors were largely helpless; 20,000 people died.

far more than we ever expected to. We realized how three centuries of being someone else's environment has colonized us, and how deeply this fact has penetrated into every sphere of life in Canada. We discovered 'law and order or else.' We saw that the structures of colonialism in Canada are all too similar to the general structures of oppression and exploitation by class and race and sex. We began to recognize how the colonizers and their agents use the Imaginary image of the *other* as a scapegoat in the divide-and-rule which keeps the colonized 'in their place.' We touched on the national nightmare of 'inferiority,' the 'Canadian complex'— and recognized it to be Imaginary.

Item 68: De-Development

[Under international capitalism] various fractions within a class may make alliances more readily than others. For example, Canadian financial capitalists at the beginning of this century had to choose an ally in moving Canada into the industrial era. They had the choice of the nascent Canadian industrialists, the counterpart of today's middle-range indigenous [sic] capitalists, or their powerful U.S. competitors, the counterpart of today's dominant comprador capitalists. Consistent with their philosophy of stable investments, they chose the latter. In some instances compatible with the movement from entrepreneurial to corporate capitalism, they chose to enter industrial activities themselves, not as entrepreneurs or industrialists but as financiers, by consolidating existing small-scale industries into corporate complexes.

The upshot is that the power of Canadians to make decisions about specific economic activities in Canada has regressed to a state of underdevelopment (although not total underdevelopment of 'material' well-being), with control over future development and stability lost because of the lack of an indigenously controlled base in manufacturing and resources. In the overdeveloped finance, transportation and utilities sectors originally built on U.K. portfolio investment, the dominant indigenous capitalists now in control still remain powerful components of the total class. In other words, the process of compradorization has been sector specific and took place in the presence of traditionally powerful Canadian capitalists rather than displacing them. The effect on weak capitalists in production was, of course, to bring about their downfall.

—Wallace Clement:
Continental Corporate Power
(1977)

We uncovered more than expected about our colonization at the economic level, and we saw more clearly than before into the tyrannical system of government that passes for 'democracy' in Canada. But the most unforeseen and most important discovery of all was the revelation of our country's secret history. We had all been persuaded that there was nothing there to find, that the Tory interpretation of Canadian history was as true as it was deadening and lifeless, that even after all these years Canadians in history had had nothing to say. We had been convinced that our history was alien to us—with some justice, we see, because what we were taught lay like a huge camouflage net over our past, hiding from us a story we had been coerced into believing we didn't want to hear.

What our Tory historians and cultural ideologues were hiding from us is indeed important. Whether 'liberal' or 'conservative,' they were depriving us of any true awareness of the radical democrats of our past, the Radical-National tradition of both English-speaking and French-speaking Canada. This is the proud heritage that comes to us from all the many refugees from European oppressions, the political heritage from Irish, Scots, and Welsh Rebellions; from the radicals in the English Revolution of 1642-88; from the American Revolution beginning in 1776; and from the French Revolution beginning in 1789.

That anglophone Canada has a tradition of political resistance and revolt is news to most of us. That in 1837-39, francophones and anglophones were fighting on the same side against the Empire is more surprising yet. It will take us some time to get used to the real Canada that emerges from our past. We will have to become accustomed to thinking historically—and therefore contextually—about our country, our compatriots, and ourselves.

Item 69: Memory Hold the Door

British Columbia and Japan, 1979
The 'New Manuchuria syndrome.' Not a new movie but Japan's attitude to trade with B.C.

Prewar, resource-rich Manchuria on the Asian mainland fueled Japan's industry. Today, resource-rich B.C. is seen in industrial circles in Japan as 'Shin Manshu,' or 'New Manchuria,' with enough raw materials to keep its mighty industrial machine in top gear.

The parallel between prewar Manchuria and present-day B.C. is borne out by the facts. Of the $3 billion worth of Canadian exports to Japan in 1978 (B.C. accounted for half that figure), materials shipped in bulk form and at a stage where they constitute an 'input' to an industry in Japan

made up more than 90 per cent . . .
—Rod Nutt, Sun Business Writer,
Vancouver Sun, October 25, 1979

China, Manchuria, and Japan, 1938

As this is being written [the Imperial Japanese Army] has 1,000,000 soldiers and huge quantities of war materials in China; millions of innocent people are being slaughtered, milliards of dollars worth of property destroyed. But the real torture and rape of a people is just beginning. If the Japanese succeed in enslaving China, as they have enslaved Manchuria [beginning in 1932], that system of loot, pillage, murder, kidnapping, brigandage, racketeering and degradation of a great people, which they call 'the way of the gods,' will then proceed in earnest. It will follow an even more vicious pattern than the ones which these pages describe, and which, for years, I witnessed with my own eyes.

—Amleto Vespa:
Secret Agent of Japan (1938)

II

I have probably talked too much politics in my letters, but it should be remembered by the reader that politics is the science which teaches the people of a country to care for each other.
—*William Lyon Mackenzie:* The Colonial Advocate, *June 27, 1833*

Apart from Dr. Rolph's betrayal of the Patriot attack on the Toronto armory in December 1837, the biggest problem the Patriots had in 1837-39 was a lack of weapons and military expertise. For example, on the very first day, one of their most experienced military men, Captain Anderson, was shot and killed by a prisoner who had not been searched for weapons. The Patriots made the colossal strategic mistake of accepting conventional battle against the Government troops. At Montgomery's Farm, those who had arms faced mounted troops, a far superior force of infantry, and two field pieces firing grape and canister shot. They presumably knew nothing of the Canayen partisans' harassment of Wolfe's troops in 1759, nor of the successful tactics of the

Spanish and Portuguese against Napoleon's occupying French Army in the Peninsular War between 1809 and 1813. The Iberian *guerrillos* did not invent guerrilla warfare, but they gave it its name (the diminutive of *guerra:* 'war').

We are in a vastly different situation today. Our allies in the anti-colonial struggles around the world have bequeathed to us a rich legacy of tested theory and tested practice by their wars of independence. Above all, we find that nature has provided us with the ultimate economic weapon in the world-wide warfare of the 1980s: an abundance of strategic natural resources.

We don't have much choice if we want a future for our country and our children. We have to learn how to defend ourselves and our destiny from economic and political exploitation. Our resources give us all the power and potential we need to begin this enterprise of collective self-defense—once we assert, as a first step, that our resources must now be placed under our own *political* control—by which we mean real control by the Canadian people.

Forget the nonsense about 'Canada buying back its resource and manufacturing industries' (Note 2 to Chapter Eight). Even if the 'buy-back' scheme were possible, it is not necessary (cf. Item 37), and such a foolish approach to the problem would in all likelihood prove disastrous.

We cannot 'Canadianize' our industries overnight. We will still need foreign technology and expertise in the resource industries, and in the creation of our own large-scale manufacturing concerns, for some considerable time to come, because too many Canadians have been deprived of the opportunity to use their talents in these areas. Nor can we afford to turn these present and future industries over to our present governments and their bureaucracies. If our ruling politicians ran their businesses the way they run the 'nation,' they would be bankrupt within a week. If we try to take control of Canada in this way, without the equivalent of a revolution at the same time, we can expect to fall flat on our faces. We have to train ourselves to take over our own country, and that takes time.

Item 70: Making Imaginary Information Real

Much has been made of the allegation that Canadians are... heavy and, by implication, wasteful users of energy, even making allowances for this country's climate and geography.

For instance, a recent study from the Canadian Energy Research Institute by Z.C. Slagorsky finds that in 1976 Canadians 'consumed' more energy per capita and per dollar of gross domestic product than the residents of any of the other eight countries in the comparison. Our per capita 'consumption' was 5% higher than the American, 40% higher than the Swedish and more than twice as large as the West German.

But the same factors that make Canada a heavy user and net exporter of energy* (we are net importers of coal and oil, but more than compensate by net exports of natural gas and electricity)—[i.e.] relatively abundant and cheap sources of energy—are almost certain to make the energy content of our exports on average larger than the energy content of our imports.

[Thus] it is nonsense to argue that a country that makes energy-intensive goods for the rest of the world [e.g. aluminum] thereby consumes a lot of energy and that those who buy these products do not consume the embodied energy!

Calculations seem to proceed as if this did not matter... An earlier study... showed that our exports [are] nearly twice as energy-intensive as [our] overall gross domestic product (GDP).

[Moreover, as long as internal energy prices for industrial users are kept below the world price] we could be selling [non-ferrous] ingots for less than we could get for the embodied energy alone, to say nothing of the raw materials, capital, and labor. [This is believed to have occurred in the 1950s with the steel exports of Poland, another colony.]

...A very important national debate is [therefore] taking place on the basis of some very shaky data and some less than adequate analysis.

—Stephen Kaliski,
The Financial Post,
December 8, 1979

We have always been self-sufficient in energy. Our 'shortfall' is the result of government collaboration with the multinational energy companies to supply the U.S. (which is not energy self-sufficient). U.S.-based energy companies are among the largest importers of capital into that country, and pay few Canadian taxes. James Laxer provides an excellent analysis: Canada's Energy Crisis *(Lorimer, 1975).*

In using contextualized information to rediscover our real history and to recognize our actual position in the world, we may well feel shame and anger at our historians, our politicians, our educators, and our ruling class, race, and sex. But our shame at their ignorance, their incompetence, their collaborations, and their corruption is countered by our pride in our struggles against the colonial system they have supported and used against us.

When we were defeated in the past, it was not because of some supposed inadequacy in our 'natures.' We were defeated, as many others were, because our efforts towards radical change in an oppressive system were met by overwhelming displays of often vengeful force—military, political, and economic. The dominant ideologues of our colonial 'intelligentsia' then censored our public and private memories by falsifying the truth, and by repressing, omitting, and ignoring it. The result has been a scrambled social memory, a garbled account of values and events, a collective memory made up of contradictions and inconsistencies—all apparently inexplicable, and most of them apparently unrelated. Worse yet, this enforced amnesia is then blamed, individually and collectively, on those who have been brought up to suffer from it and its effects.

In the face of such repeated manipulations of our consciousness and our feelings about ourselves, it is hardly surprising that we have had so much difficulty in bringing our 'leaders' under our control. Information is a major source of power, and sensible, well-sighted action requires the best information obtainable. Without a properly informed social memory—both personal and collective—informed action in the present is made impossible.

Throughout the 1970s, however, we have experienced an outpouring of real information about our present and our past, and the political temper of the country has continued rapidly changing. This change is even visible in the advertising of foreign corporations and multinationals. They are sufficiently in touch with our changing values and perceptions as Canadians (as we would expect them to be) to be putting out publicity designed to convince us that they have always had our *national* interests at heart. The old con-game of 'free trade' with the U.S. is also in the air,[6] and their politicians, eyeing our energy supplies

---

[6]Free trade is impossible between a colony and its colonizers. Consider the supposed 'reciprocity' of the Auto Pact with the U.S. It has recently cost Canada its largest ever six-month deficit, the total deficit on the 'pact' amounting to $1.5 billion in late 1979.

For reasons that are unclear, Carl Beigie of the C.D. Howe Institute in Montreal raised the 'annexation' issue in 1979 on the CBC program *Fortunes* (February 13). Not surprisingly, the issue was raised in Imaginary terms: *Either* 'we join the U.S.' (as if we were not an economic annex) *or* 'we go it alone' (as if the U.S. and the rest of the world will disappear overnight). Peter Reynolds, the writer-producer of the program, carries the nonsense further by saying that Beigie 'fits into the nationalists' conspiracy that the Liberals [sic] plan [sic] to sell the country out by stealth' (*TV Guide*, February 10, 1979). C.D. Howe was the U.S. born Liberal who gained practically dictatorial power in Canada during World War II, using and retaining most of it until 1957. See Robinson, 1957.

especially, are talking about the 'need' for a 'closer relationship' between Canada and the United States. Such defensive offensives are useful signs of change.

But there are other and much more important signs of our changing reality. A colony we may be, but the paradox of capitalism today is that the traditional power relations it is based on are now being subverted by the very system that created them—and not just in Canada. The very economic 'needs' of the system that exploits the world are transferring to the resource-rich colonies of the superstates greater and greater power. Properly constrained and responsibly directed, this new power can be used to do good, not just for Canadians, but also for the peoples of the most exploited countries of the world.

III

If there is one thing that worries Canadians more than economic domination, it is that someone, sometime, will try to do something about it.

    —*George Bain:* The Toronto Globe and Mail *(November 4, 1969).*

    Quoted in Colombo's Canadian Quotations *(1974)*

We cannot reconstruct our national identity and our personal dignity simply on the basis of trees, water, hydropower, gas, oil, ores, and minerals—however essential to the power of our new identity these natural resources will certainly be. Human identities are based originally and primarily on relationships to persons, not simply to things. In fact, when personal and public identities derive their primary nature from the mediation of things—rather than primarily from the mediation of persons in the true sense—they are alienated identities in a pathological relationship to human reality.

Our political identity as Canadians—and our political consciousness— therefore remain impoverished and incomplete as long as we do not know and feel the heritage of courage and pride bequeathed to us by the Canadians who fought against oppression in our past. In particular, the radical-democratic popular consciousness that emerged over the years leading up to 1837-39 is still a relatively untapped resource of political education and identity. Nevertheless, along with the memory of past and present struggles for freedom and justice by Canadian minorities,

Canadian workers, and Canadian women, this radical tradition continues to endure.

This tradition is all the more strengthened and invigorated when we look around us. The French, the British, and the Americans have all been beaten in anti-colonial wars. Christian and Moslem guerrillas are still fighting U.S. imperialism in the Philippines. Watching on television today the tremendous, visible power of the outpouring of national pride in Zimbabwe, as the exiled commanders of the Patriotic Front returned to their homeland after seven years of war, we are reminded that since 1945, not one war of liberation supported by the colonized people has been lost, and most have led to Independence. As conscious as we may be that Independence is the first step down a difficult road, the setting of that goal promises a state of being for which we in Canada have yearned these many long years: the recognition that we are fighting *for* mutual goals, not just *against* obstacles.

Today we live in the era of the 'war of the flea' (Taber, 1969): the political, psychological, popular, ideological, and economic warfare of the colonized against their masters. The 'war of the flea' is the *strategic*[7] response of the colonized peoples against the original imperial aggression, the original act of war by which the imperial powers occupied the corporate and management levels of the colony's economic base. Canadian partisans in the labor movement are already doing battle on this strategic front.

In order to gain control of our own economic base, we must begin by building and strengthening our national base. The national base is the crucial principle and practice that enables us to protect ourselves from national or multinational invasion. We have to begin to deal with our foreign exploiters in ways that will oblige them to cease draining away our natural resources at bargain prices; to cease interfering with our life, liberty, and happiness; and to cease robbing us of the vast profits they make out of Canada and Canadians. In other words, we have to begin the

---

[7] The theory of warfare conceives of the structure of war as a hierarchy of four levels, plus the domain of logistics. *Logistics* refers to every type of mobilization and supply required by each of the levels seen separately and all four of them together. *Grand Strategy* is the highest level. This is the level of overall policy, objectives, and priorities, including the selection of realistic war aims (offensive and defensive) and the building and maintaining of alliances. Such decisions are taken at the national level. *Strategy* is 'the art of distributing and applying military and other means to fulfil the ends of policy' (to paraphrase Sir Basil Liddell Hart). Strategy decides the how, the when, and the where of operations, in cooperation and consultation with allies. It is ordinarily the province of the chief of staff. *Grand Tactics* concerns the actual planning of major operations in all their complexity. (The distinction between this level and strategy is often quite blurred;

process of obliging our colonizing exploiters to help us take them over. After that will come time to see about dealing with capitalism in Canada as we see fit.

The national base draws its fighting strength from three major resources, besides the resources represented by the people. These three are political resources, economic resources, and ideological resources.

The political resources for anti-colonial warfare are the democratic organizations of all the many people's alliances: from day-care units to tenant and community associations; from immigrant, feminist, and gay groups to unions and confederations of unions; from student and teachers associations and political clubs to civil, legal and human rights groups; from the radical and independent media to patients' and prisoners' rights organizations—as well as the constant interchange of support and information between them. The political base is the active and unifying arm of the base in the people. It must therefore also include a political organization, from grass roots to provincial Assemblies to Parliament Hill—as well as outside the country—which is adequately staffed, funded, and informed to develop and put into practice strategies and tactics designed to bring us to the overall goal of independence. The political base will be all the stronger when it is supported by political and economic alliances with other colonies, countries, peoples, and groups facing similar enemies and similar threats.

How quickly and how strongly the support for independence grows depends on organization, strategy, and many other matters with which the colonized people have to deal. We should not forget, however, that this support also depends on the actions of the colonizers. In practically every war of national liberation since 1945, it has been the colonizers' attempts to hang on to what they thought they had forever, that turned the majority of the people against them. By definition, such a majority is an informed majority—they recognize what is really happening—and the power of an informed national majority is one of the strongest weapons

---

indeed, all of the four levels are in reality closely connected.) It involves the seizure of the initiative, speed, and concentration of forces, as well as the maintenance of a reserve sufficient to deal with unexpected emergencies or advantages, and the maintenance of a safe base of retreat and the means of getting there. *Minor Tactics* govern the actual methods of fighting and manoeuvre, and involve every combatant in the field. It will be noted that this hierarchy of levels forms a 'thought structure' (with real referents), a structural map of the system of war which can be applied to any type of warfare, as well as to other goal-seeking activities, in order to understand how decisions made at different levels affect each other. (This outline is taken from David Chandler, *The Art of Warfare on Land,* London and Toronto: Hamlyn, 1974.)

in the armory. The colonizers remain dependent, like parasites, on the people and the colonies they exploit; and their colonial power can be exercised only so long as the people remain ignorant of their actions and divided over how to deal with them.

Item 71: Collective Self-Defense

The following is the report of a motion put forward by James Baird and Owen Garrity at a meeting of the Patriots of Caledon Township in Upper Canada. It was published in William Lyon Mackenzie's second newspaper, The Constitution, *on August 16, 1837.*

If the redress of our wrongs can be otherwise obtained, the people of Upper Canada have not a just cause to use force.

But the highest obligation of a citizen being to preserve the community—and every other political duty being derived from, and subordinate to it—every citizen is bound to defend his country against its enemies, both foreign and domestic.

When a government is engaged in systematically oppressing a people, and destroying their securities against future oppression, it commits the same species of wrong to them which warrants an appeal to force against a foreign enemy.

The history of England and of this continent is not wanting in examples, by which the rulers and the ruled may see that, although the people have been often willing to endure bad government with patience, there are legal and constitutional limits to that endurance.

The glorious revolutions of 1688, on one continent, and of 1776, on another, may serve to remind those rulers who are obstinately persisting in withholding from their subjects adequate securities for good government, although obviously necessary for the permanence of that blessing, that they are placing themselves in a state of hostility against the governed; and that to prolong a state of irresponsibility and insecurity, such as existed in England during the reign of James II [1685-1688], and as now exists in Lower Canada [as a result of the British parliament's Coercion Bill and its refusal to be guided by the wishes of the elected representatives of that colony], is a dangerous act of aggression against a people.

A magistrate [i.e. any executive or judicial agent] who degenerates into a systematic oppressor, and shuts the gates of justice on the public, thereby restores them to their original right of defending themselves, for he withholds the protection of the law, and so forfeits his claim to enforce their obedience by the authority of law.

Our economic resources consist of our natural and human resources; unified control over the workplace by pro-Canadian Canadians; and political control over the use of the natural resources whose strategic role make possible the decolonizing war. Here, as elsewhere, the first string to our bow is the demand for democracy: the economic democracy of resources controlled by the people for the people.

Our first steps in the right direction begin with the destruction of the ideology of the Imaginary Canadian, i.e. with the full utilization of our real ideological resources. Ideological matters concern what we say, how we say it, and who we say it to. They include all the real facts and figures, all the assistance of history, all the real agreements and disagreements, all the real political, economic, and ecological arguments, and all the plain human understanding that, guided by a properly contextual perspective, enable us to demonstrate an utterly convincing case for liberation. The ideological arguments must make themselves heard through every available means of communication—even the CBC. The basic arguments and facts, which are not at all complicated, have to become as familiar as possible throughout the restive nation, improved on and strengthened by contributions from throughout Canadian society. God knows we need them. We must come to recognize that we are much less alone in the world than we have been, that our perspective on Canada and the world is changing radically for the better, that it is possible to find representative and responsible Canadians we can trust with our delegated power, that we ourselves have the power to change the future, that *we* are finally beginning to take over.

It is not enough, however, to direct our arguments towards each other. They must become part of our foreign affairs, deployed to inform and convince all potential allies in the rest of the world. They must be deployed also against the psychological warfare and ideological intimidation—coupled with real threats—that the Imperial Corporations and their Nation States use to keep the producer countries of the Third World divided from each other. We must use our ideological resources to explain our aims and actions to friends in other countries— ultimately the population of the planet—including those in the nations of the colonizing powers, where repression is increasing too.

Our ideological resources form a perspective for strategic research and education. We and our children have been exposed to arguments on behalf of colonization for quite long enough. It is time to teach the arguments against it. To this end, our own intelligence and communicational networks must be mobilized in our own service, and given priority in our schools, our places of employment, our political life, and our press. Without accurate, properly analyzed, and co-ordinated information, one doesn't just lose battles, one loses wars.

This then is the general and strategic perspective for which I have tried to clear the way by writing this book. Detailed discussions of specific actions in our self-defense[8] are matters for other times and places.

Let us not forget, above all, that the very process of recognizing our own colonization is itself an enormously liberating advance. The fact of having been colonized ceases to be a personal skeleton in the Imaginary closet. As we turn to face the future realistically, the fact of colonization becomes a shared and public ground for pride in continuing to survive it—and a source of determination to end it. Recognizing how colonization works provides us with the means to say No!—the means to choose *not* to be its dupe or its accomplice. Every such informed refusal of the oppressor is an act of political resistance, political resistance that nourishes our self-respect. Resistance in the common cause provides our identity with dignity, and dignity with strength.

Sentry: 'Alt, who goes there?
Reply: Scots Guards' night patrol. Password 'Victoria.'
Sentry: Advance and be recognized. . . Pass, Scots Guards.
Sentry: 'Alt, who goes there?
Reply: Mind your own goddam business.
Sentry: Pass, Canadians.
                                          —*Traditional Military Joke* (c. 1915)

[8]Such as the strategic riposte of placing restrictions on the export from Canada of capital made in Canada.

Readings and References

A. RECOMMENDED READINGS

Bergeron, Léandre. *The History of Quebec: A Patriote's Handbook* (1978).

Berton, Pierre. *Hollywood's Canada: The Americanization of our National Image* (1975).

Clement, Wallace. *Continental Corporate Power* (1977).

Colombo, John Robert. *Colombo's Canadian Quotations* (1974).

Commoner, Barry. *The Closing Circle* (1971).

Ehrenreich, Barbara, and English, Deirdre. *Complaints and Disorders: The Sexual Politics of Sickness* (1973); and *Witches, Midwives, and Nurses* (1973).

Fanon, Frantz. *Black Skin, White Masks* (1952); and *The Wretched of the Earth* (1961).

Furhammer, Leif, and Isaksson, Folke. *Politics and Film* (1968).

Keilty, Greg. *1837—Revolution in the Canadas* (1974).

Lindsey, Charles. *The Life and Times of William Lyon Mackenzie and the Rebellion of 1837-8* (1862, reprinted 1971).

MacCormac, John. *Canada: America's Problem* (1940).

Moore, Jr., Barrington. *Social Origins of Dictatorship and Democracy* (1966).

Myers, Gustavus. *A History of Canadian Wealth* (1914, reprinted 1972).

Newman, Peter C. *The Canadian Establishment* (1975); and *The Bronfman Dynasty* (1978).

Persky, Stan. *Son of Socred* (1979).

Postman, Neil and Weingartner, Charles. *Teaching as a Subversive Activity* (1971).

Red Star Collective. *Canada: Imperialist Power or Economic Colony?* (1977).

Robinson, Judith. *This is on the House* (1957).

Ryerson, Stanley Bréhaut. *The Founding of Canada: Beginnings to 1815* (1960); and *Unequal Union: Roots of Crisis in the Canadas, 1815-1873* (1968, Second edition, 1975).

Sartre, Jean-Paul. *Anti-Semite and Jew* (1946, 1965).

Watkins, Mel (ed.). *Dene Nation: The Colony Within* (1977).

Watzlawick, Paul et al. *The Pragmatics of Human Communication* (1967).

B. General

Abbott, Edwin A. *Flatland* [1884]. Oxford: Blackwell's; New York: Barnes & Noble, 1963.

An Observer. A Glimpse of the War in Spain. *Canadian Defence Quarterly,* Vol. 15, No. 2, January 1938.

Anon. *British Empire Series.* Nottingham: John Player & Sons, Imperial Tobacco Company. Series of 50 cards, 1904.

———*Canadian History Series.* Imperial Tobacco Company of Canada. Series of 48 cards, 1926.

———*Great Deeds in Canada.* Kellogg's All-Wheat. Series of 15 cards (c. 1955).

———*Military Uniforms of the British Empire Overseas.* Nottingham: John Player & Sons, Imperial Tobacco Company. Series of 50 cards, 1938.

———*Our Colonial Troops.* London: W. & F. Faulkner Ltd. Series of 90 cards, 1900.

———*Overseas Dominions (Canada).* Bristol and London: W.D. & H.O. Wills, Imperial Tobacco Company. Series of 50 cards, 1914.

———*The Agreement of the People* [1647]. In: Aylmer (ed.), 1975, pp.88-96.

Aylmer, G.E. (ed.). *The Levellers in the English Revolution.* London: Thames & Hudson, 1975.

Bateson, Gregory. *Steps to an Ecology of Mind.* Los Angeles: Chandler; New York Ballantine, 1972; London: Paladin, 1975. (Paperback editions slightly abridged.)

———The Cybernetics of 'Self': A Theory of Alcoholism [1971]. In: Bateson, 1972, pp. 309-37.

Bateson, Gregory, et al. Toward a Theory of Schizophrenia [1956]. In: Bateson, 1972, pp. 201-27.

Baynes, Ken. *Art and Society One: War.* Boston: Boston Book and Art Publishing Co., 1970.

Bell, William. The Way of a White Man: A Thrilling Tale of the Canadian Lumberlands. *The Pip & Squeak Annual for 1936.* London: The Daily Mirror Ltd., 1936, pp. 200-03.

Bengough, J.W. *A Caricature History of Canadian Politics. Events from the Union of 1841. . . .*Toronto: The Grip Printing and Publishing Company, 1886. Two volumes. [One-volume version published by Peter Martin Associates Ltd., Toronto, 1974.]

Bergeron, Léandre. *The History of Quebec: A Patriote's Handbook.*

Tr. by Baila Markus. Toronto: New Canada Publications, 1978. Updated edition.

Berkeley, Humphry. *The Power of the Prime Minister.* London: George Allen & Unwin; New York: Chilmark Press, 1969.

Bernstein, Basil. *Class, Codes, and Control.* London: Routledge & Kegan Paul, 1971.

Berton, Pierre. *Hollywood's Canada: The Americanization of our National Image.* Toronto: McClelland & Stewart, 1975.

Blackburn, Robin (ed.). *Ideology in Social Science.* London: Fontana, 1973.

Bliss, J.M. (ed.). *Canadian History in Documents, 1793-1966.* Toronto: The Ryerson Press, 1966.

Bolton, P. Michael. *Civil Rights in Canada.* North Vancouver, B.C.: Self-Counsel Press, 1976.

Bourinot, Sir J.G. *How Canada is Governed.* Toronto: Copp Clark, 1918. Revised edition.

Broadfoot, Barry. *Years of Sorrow, Years of Shame: The Story of the Japanese-Canadians in World War II.* Garden City, N.Y. and Toronto: Doubleday, 1977.

Brown, Lorne, and Brown, Caroline. *An Unauthorized History of the RCMP.* Toronto: James Lewis & Samuel, 1973.

Burke, Stanley, and Peterson, Roy. *Frog Fables and Beaver Tales.* Toronto: James Lewis & Samuel, 1973.

Cade, Toni (ed.). *The Black Woman.* New York: Signet, 1974.

Callan, Les. *Normandy and On With the Fighting Canadians.* Toronto: Longmans, Green & Co., 1945.

Canadian Pacific Railway Co. *Canadian Pacific Facts and Figures.* Montreal: Canadian Pacific Foundation Library, 1937.

Chance, C.B., Dickinson-Starkey, Peter, Jowett, Mark, and Weeks, Thos. H. Letters to the Editor. *Vancouver Sun,* July 15, 1978.

Chesler, Phyllis. *Women and Madness.* New York: Avon, 1972.

Chrimes, S.B. *English Constitutional History.* London and Toronto: Oxford University Press, 1960. Second edition.

Clement, Wallace. *Continental Corporate Power.* Toronto: McClelland & Stewart, 1977.

Clyne, J.V. The National Will and the Constitution. *Vancouver Sun,* July 21, 1978.

Colombo, John Robert. *Colombo's Canadian Quotations.* Edmonton, Alta.: Hurtig Publishers, 1974.

Commoner. Barry. *The Closing Circle.* New York: Bantam, 1972.

Courrière, Yves. *Le Temps des léopards* (La Guerre d'Algérie, II). Paris: Fayard, 1969.

Coutts-Smith, Kenneth. CBC's 'Riel.' *Centerfold*, June-July, 1979, pp. 228-36.

Culhane, Claire. *Why is Canada in Vietnam?* Toronto: NC Press, 1972.

———*Barred from Prison.* Vancouver, B.C.: Pulp Press, 1979.

Davin, Nicholas Flood. *The Irishman in Canada.* London: Sampson Low, Marston & Co.; Toronto: Maclear & Co., 1877.

Deachman, Tam W. *What Every American Should Know About Canada.* Markham, Ont.: PaperJacks Ltd., 1977.

Dempsey, Hugh A. (ed.). *Men in Scarlet.* Calgary, Alta.: McClelland & Stewart West, 1973.

Dickie, Francis. A Unique Frontier Road. *Meccano Magazine*, Vol. 67, No. 6, June 1962, pp. 236-7, 258.

Dostoevsky, Fyodor. 'The Double' and 'The Eternal Husband.' In: *Three Short Novels.* Garden City, N.Y.: Anchor, 1960.

Douglas, William O. *A Living Bill of Rights.* Garden City, N.Y.: Doubleday, 1961.

Dunham, Aileen. *Political Unrest in Upper Canada, 1815-1836* [1927]. Toronto: McClelland & Stewart, 1963.

Durham, Lord. *Lord Durham's Report* [1839]. Ed. by Gerald M. Craig. Toronto: McClelland & Stewart, 1963.

Eayrs, James. *In Defence of Canada.* Toronto: University of Toronto Press, 1964.

Edwards, Richard C., Reich, Michael, and Weisskopf, Thomas E. (eds.) *The Capitalist System: A Radical Analysis of American Society.* Englewood Cliffs, N.J.: Prentice-Hall, 1978. Second edition.

Ehrenreich, Barbara, and English, Deirdre. *Witches, Midwives, and Nurses: A History of Women Healers.* Old Westbury, N.Y.: The Feminist Press. Glass Mountain Pamphlet No. 1. [Box 334, Old Westbury, N.Y. 11568.]

———*Complaints and Disorders: The Sexual Politics of Sickness.* Old Westbury, N.Y.: The Feminist Press. Pamphlet No. 2.

Eisenstein, Sergei M. The Twelve Apostles [1945]. In: *The Battleship Potemkin.* Ed. by Herbert Marshall. New York: Avon, 1978.

Ellison, Ralph. *Invisible Man.* [1951]. New York: Vintage, 1963.

Elstob, Peter. *Condor Legion.* New York: Ballantine, 1973. Ballantine's Illustrated History of the Violent Century.

Engels, Frederick. *The Role of Force in History* [1888]. London: Lawrence & Wishart, 1968.

Fanon, Frantz. *Black Skin, White Masks: The Experiences of a Black Man in a White World* [1952]. Tr. by C.L. Markmann. New York: Grove Press, 1967.

———*The Wretched of the Earth.* [1961]. Tr. by C. Farrington. New York: Grove Press, 1968.

Faribault, Marcel, and Fowler, Robert M. *Ten to One: The Confederation Wager.* Toronto: McClelland & Stewart, 1965.

Farrow, Moira. Believe it or Not, We're Running Out of Trees. *Vancouver Sun*, June 20, 1978.

Fetherling, Doug. Conflict of Interest: A Canadian Tradition. *Financial Post Magazine*, May 1979.

Franklin, Stephen. *The Heroes: A Saga of Canadian Inspiration.* Toronto: McClelland & Stewart, 1967. The Canadian Illustrated Library.

Freire, Paulo. *Pedagogy of the Oppressed* [1969]. Tr. by M.B. Ramos. Sommers, Ct.: Seabury Press, 1971.

Furhammer, Leif, and Isaksson, Folke. *Politics and Film* [1968]. Tr. by Kersti French. New York: Praeger, 1971.

Garcia, John. IQ: The Conspiracy. *Psychology Today*, September 1972.

Garrett, Richard. *Clash of Arms: The World's Great Land Battles.* London: Weidenfeld & Nicolson, 1976.

George, Susan. *How the Other Half Dies: The Real Reason for World Hunger.* New York: Universe Books, 1977.

Godelier, Maurice. Structure and Contradiction in *Capital* [1966]. In: Blackburn (ed.), 1973, pp. 334-68.

Gray, Hugh. *Letters from Canada.* London: Longman, Hurst, Rees, and Orme, 1809. Toronto: Coles Canadiana Series, 1971.

Halton, Matthew. *Ten Years to Alamein.* Toronto: S.J. Reginald Saunders & Co., 1944.

Harris, C.J. (ed.). *Quick Canadian Facts 1978-9.* Toronto: Quick Canadian Facts Ltd., 1978. Thirty-third annual edition.

Heller, Joseph. *Catch-22.* New York: Dell, 1955.

Hill, Christopher. *Reformation to Industrial Revolution.* Harmondsworth: Penguin, 1967.

Hoar, Victor. *The Mackenzie-Papineau Battalion.* Toronto: Copp Clark, 1969.

Hobsbawn, E.J. *Industry and Empire.* Harmondsworth: Penguin, 1968.

Holland, Ray. *Self and Social Context.* London: Macmillan, 1977.

Howard, Joseph. *Strange Empire.* New York: Wm. Morrow & Co., 1952.

Howison, John, Esq. *Sketches of Upper Canada, Domestic, Local and Characteristic.* London: G. & W.B. Whittaker; Edinburgh: Oliver & Boyd, 1821. Toronto: Coles Canadiana Series, 1970.

Hutchison, Bruce. Canada's War Effort. *National Geographic*, Vol. 80, No. 5, 1941, pp. 553-90.

Idris-Soven, Ahmed, Idris-Soven, Elizabeth, and Vaughan, Mary K. (eds.). *The World as a Company Town: Multinational Corporations and Social Change.* The Hague: Mouton; Chicago: Aldine, 1978.

Kafka, Franz. 'The Burrow' [1931]. In: *Metamorphosis and Other Stories.* Harmondsworth: Penguin, 1964.

Kahn, Leon. *No Time to Mourn: The True Story of a Jewish Partisan Fighter.* Vancouver, B.C.: Laurelton Press, 1978. [1194 Wolfe St., Vancouver, B.C.]

Keilty, Greg (ed.). *1837: Revolution in the Canadas, as told by William Lyon Mackenzie.* Toronto: NC Press, 1974.

Knelman, Martin. *This Is Where We Came In: The Career and Character of Canadian Film.* Toronto: McClelland & Stewart, 1977.

Knight, James (ed.). *C.W. Jefferys: The Formative Years: Canada 1812-1871.* Toronto: The Ryerson Press, 1968.

Knightley, Phillip. *The First Casualty: The War Correspondent as Hero, Propagandist, and Mythmaker.* New York and London: Harcourt Brace Jovanovich, 1975.

Kramer, Heinrich, and Sprenger, James. *The Malleus Maleficarum* [The Hammer of the Witches, 1486]. Tr. by the Rev. Montague Summers. New York: Dover, 1971. Reprint of 1928 edition.

Kruger, Rayne. *Good-bye Dolly Gray: The Story of the Boer War.* London: Cassell, 1959.

Lacan, Jacques. The Mirror-Phase [1949]. Tr. by Jean Roussel. *New Left Review*, Vol. 51, 1968, pp. 71-7.

―――*The Language of the Self: The Function of Speech and Language in Psychoanalysis.* Ed. and tr., with notes and commentary, by Anthony Wilden. Baltimore: The Johns Hopkins Press, 1968; New York: Delta Paperbacks, 1975.

Laing, R.D. *The Divided Self.* Harmondsworth: Penguin, 1960.

Landon, Fred. *An Exile from Canada: The Story of Elijah Woodman, Transported Overseas for Participation in the Upper Canada Troubles of 1837-38.* Toronto: Longmans, Green & Co., 1960.

Lehrer, Tom. National Brotherhood Week [1965]. *That Was The Year*

That Was. Reprise Records, WEA Music of Canada Ltd., A Warner Communications Company, n.d.

Lilburne, John. *Englands Birth-Right Justified Against all Arbitrary Usurpation, whether Regall or Parliamentary, or under what Vizor soever* [1645]. In: Aylmer (ed.), 1975, pp. 56-62.

Lindsey, Charles. *The Life and Times of William Lyon Mackenzie. With an Account of the Canadian Rebellion of 1837, and the Subsequent Frontier Disturbances, Chiefly from Unpublished Documents.* Toronto: P.R. Randall, 1862. Two volumes in one. Toronto: Coles Canadiana Series, 1971. Two volumes.

Lister, Ardele. Hewing the Wood and Drawing the Water: Women and Film in Colonized Canada. *Heresies,* Vol. 1, No. 2, May 1977, pp. 103-5.

McClelland, Bob. Controlling Those Who Can't Control Themselves. Excerpts from the Health Minister's Speech on the Heroin Treatment Act. *Vancouver Sun,* June 21, 1978.

MacCormac, John. *Canada: America's Problem.* New York: Viking, 1940.

McEwen, Jessie, and Moore, Kathleen. *A Picture History of Canada.* Thomas Nelson & Sons (Canada) Ltd., n.d. Revised edition (c. 1950).

McInnis, Edgar. *Canada: A Political and Social History.* New York and Toronto: Holt, Rinehart & Winston, 1963. Revision of 1947 and 1959 editions.

MacLaren, Roy. *Canadians on the Nile: 1882-1898.* Vancouver, B.C.: University of British Columbia Press, 1978.

McNaught, Kenneth. Stiff, Royalist—and Very Canadian. *Vancouver Sun*, July 24, 1978. [Originally from the *Toronto Sun*, July 1, 1974.]

Malcolm X. *The Autobiography of Malcolm X. As told to Alex Haley.* New York: Ballantine, 1976.

Malone, Col. Dick. *Missing from the Record.* Toronto: Collins, 1946.

Malone, Lt.-Col. Richard (ed.). *The Maple Leaf Scrapbook: Souvenir Book Printed in Belgium at Cost Price to Forces Overseas.* Brussels: No. 3 Canadian Public Relations Group, 1944.

Mandel, Ernest. *An Introduction to Marxist Economic Theory* [1964]. New York: Pathfinder Press, 1970.

Manvell, Roger. *Films and the Second World War.* South Brunswick and New York: A.S. Barnes & Co.; London: J M Dent & Sons, 1974.

Marcuse, Herbert. *One-Dimensional Man.* Boston: Beacon; London: Routledge, 1964.

Marquis, T.G. *Canada's Sons on Kopje and Veldt: A Historical*

Account of the Canadian Contingents. Toronto: Canada's Sons Publishing Co., 1900. Introduction by the Very Rev. George Monro Grant of Queen's College, Kingston.

Mercer, John. *The Squeaking Wheel.* Montreal: Rubicon Press, 1966.

Miller, Craig. The Ugly Face of Highschool Racism. *Burnaby Times,* March 14, 1979.

Monopoli, William. Justice Delayed, Justice Denied. *Financial Post,* May 26, 1979.

Moore, Barrington, Jr. *Social Origins of Dictatorship and Democracy.* Boston: Beacon Press, 1966.

Morgan, Robin (ed.). *Sisterhood is Powerful.* New York: Vintage, 1970.

Mulvaney, Charles Pelham. *The History of the North-West Rebellion.* Toronto: A.H. Hovey & Co., 1885. Toronto: Coles Canadiana Series, 1971.

Myers, Gustavus. *A History of Canadian Wealth* [1914]. Toronto: James Lorimer, 1972. Introduction by Stanley B. Ryerson.

Nasmith, Col. George G. *Canada's Sons and Great Britain in the World War.* Toronto: John C. Winston Co., 1919.

Newman, Peter C. *The Canadian Establishment.* Toronto: Seal Books, 1975.

———*The Bronfman Dynasty.* Toronto: McClelland & Stewart, 1978.

Nicolaus, Martin. The Unknown Marx. In: Blackburn (ed.), 1973, pp. 306-33.

Norris, William. *The Canadian Question.* Montreal: Lovell Printing and Publishing Co., 1875.

Partridge, Eric. *A Dictionary of Slang and Unconventional English.* London: Routledge & Kegan Paul, 1951. *Supplement,* 1974.

Persky, Stan. *Son of Socred.* Vancouver, B.C.: New Star Books, 1979. [2504 York Avenue, Vancouver, B.C.]

Pimentel, David, et al. Food Production and the Energy Crisis. *Science,* Vol. 182, 1973, pp. 443-9.

Pollard, Sidney. *The Idea of Progress.* Harmondsworth: Penguin, 1968.

Posner, Michael. The Man Who Knew Too Much. *Maclean's,* Vol. 91, No. 10, May 15, 1978, p. 66.

Postman, Neil, and Weingartner, Charles. *Teaching as a Subversive Activity.* New York: Delta; Harmondsworth: Penguin, 1971.

Pugsley, Lieut. William H. *Saints, Devils and Ordinary Seamen.* Toronto: Collins, 1945.

Raemakers, Louis. *Raemakers War Cartoons.* London and Montreal: Carreras Ltd. Series of 140 cards, 1916.

Rappaport, Roy A. Ritual Regulation of Environmental Relations. In: Vayda (ed.), 1969, pp. 181-99.

———The Flow of Energy in an Agricultural Society. *Scientific American,* Vol. 225, No. 3, 1971, pp. 116-32.

———Nature, Culture and Ecological Anthropology. In: *Man, Culture and Society.* Ed. by Harry L. Shapiro. Oxford: Oxford University Press, 1971. Only in the second edition.

Raskin, Marcus G., and Fall, Bernard B. *The Viet-Nam Reader.* New York: Vintage, 1967. Revised edition.

Read, Conyers (ed.). *The Constitution Reconsidered.* New York: Columbia University Press, 1938. Revised edition: New York: Harper Torchbooks, 1968.

Red Star Collective. *Canada: Imperialist Power or Economic Colony?* Pamphlet No. 1, March 1977. [P.O. Box 65723, Station F, Vancouver, B.C.]

Reiter, Rayna (ed.). *Toward an Anthropology of Women.* New York: Monthly Review Press, 1975.

Robertson, Heather (ed.). *A Terrible Beauty: The Art of Canada at War.* Toronto: James Lorimer, 1977.

Robertson, Peter (ed.). *Relentless Verity: Canadian Military Photophotographers since 1885.* Ottawa: Public Archives of Canada; Québec: Les Presses de l'Université Laval; Toronto: University of Toronto Press, 1973.

Robinson, Judith. *This is on the House.* Cartoons by Grassick. Toronto: McClelland & Stewart, 1957.

Rowan, Mary Kate. Our Disappearing Farmland. *Vancouver Sun,* July 26, 1978.

Ryerson, Stanley Bréhaut. *French Canada: A Study in Canadian Democracy.* Toronto: Progress Books, 1943.

———*The Founding of Canada: Beginnings to 1815.* Toronto: Progress Books, 1960.

———*Unequal Union: Roots of Crisis in the Canadas, 1815-1873.* Toronto: Progress Books, 1968. Second edition, 1975.

Sartre, Jean-Paul. *The Transcendence of the Ego* [1937]. Tr. by F. Williams and R. Kirkpatrick. New York: Noonday Press, 1957.

———'L'Enfance d'un chef' [1939]. In: *Le Mur.* Paris: Livre de Poche, 1962, pp. 151-245.

———*Anti-Semite and Jew* [1946]. Tr. by G.J. Becker. New York: Schocken, 1965.

Schatzman, Morton. *Soul Murder: Persecution in the Family.* New York: Signet, 1974.

Schoenberner, Gerhard. *The Yellow Star: The Persecution of the Jews in Europe 1933-45* [1969]. Tr. by Susan Sweet. New York, London, and Toronto: Bantam, 1979.

Schreber, Daniel Paul. *Memoirs of my Nervous Illness* [1903]. Ed. and tr. by Ida Macalpine and Richard A. Hunter. London: Wm. Dawson, 1955.

Shapiro, Evelyn (ed.). *PsychoSources: A Psychology Resource Catalog.* New York and Toronto: Bantam, 1973.

Shumiatcher, Morris. The Kingdom, the Power, and the Glory (Perspective on the Nation). *Vancouver Sun,* August 4, 1978.

Sluzki, Carlos E., and Ransom, Donald C. (eds.). *Double Bind: The Foundation of the Communicational Approach to the Family.* New York: Grune & Stratton, 1976.

Smith, Alfred G. (ed.). *Communication and Culture.* New York: Holt, Rinehart & Winston, 1966.

Smith, Goldwin. *Canada and the Canadian Question.* Toronto: Hunter, Rose & Co.; London and New York: Macmillan, 1891.

————*Essays on Questions of the Day.* Toronto: Copp Clark; New York and London: Macmillan, 1893.

Stanley, George F.G. *Canada's Soldiers.* Toronto: Macmillan, 1960.

Stewart, Roderick. *Bethune.* Toronto: New Press, 1973.

Stewart, Walter. *As They See Us.* Toronto: McClelland & Stewart, 1977.

Sweezy, Paul M. The Future of Capitalism. In: *The Dialectics of Liberation.* Ed. by David Cooper. Harmondsworth: Penguin, 1968, pp. 95-109.

Taber, Robert. *The War of the Flea: Guerrilla Warfare Theory and Practice* [1965]. London: Paladin, 1977.

Tanner, Ogden (ed.). *The Old West: The Canadians.* Alexandria, Va.: Time-Life Books, 1977.

Taylor, A.J.P., Roberts, J.M., and Cross, R.W. (eds.). *20th Century.* Milwaukee, Toronto, Melbourne, and London: Purnell Reference Books. Volume 1.

Teeple, Gary (ed.). *Capitalism and the National Question in Canada.* Toronto: University of Toronto Press, 1972.

Thomas, Keith. The Levellers and the Franchise. In: *The Interregnum 1646-1660.* Ed. by G.E. Aylmer. London: Macmillan, 1972.

Tiffany, Orrin Edward. *The Relations of the United States to the Canadian Rebellion of 1837-1838.* Buffalo, N.Y.: Buffalo Historical Society, 1905; Toronto: Coles Canadiana Series, 1972.

Vallières, Piere. *The Assassination of Pierre Laporte: Behind the*

October '70 Scenario. Tr. by Ralph Wells. Toronto: James Lorimer, 1977.

Valpy, Michael. Why the Queen is Essential to Canada. *Vancouver Sun,* June 27, 1978.

———Our Constitutional Fire-Extinguisher. *Vancouver Sun,* June 29, 1978.

Vayda, Andrew P. (ed.). *Environment and Cultural Behavior.* New York: Natural History Press, 1969.

Wallace, W. Stewart. *The Growth of Canadian National Feeling.* Toronto: Macmillan, 1927.

Wallon, Henri. Comment de développe, chez l'enfant, la notion du corps propre. *Journal de Psychologie,* 1931, pp. 705-48.

Ward, Olivia. Is Canada a Haven for War Criminals? *Sunday Star* (Toronto), March 25, 1979.

Watkins, Mel (ed.). *Dene Nation: The Colony Within.* Toronto: University of Toronto Press, 1977.

Watzlawick, Paul, Beavin, Janet, and Jackson, Don D. *The Pragmatics of Human Communication.* New York: W.W. Norton, 1967.

Wicker, Tom. Watergate's Lessons Do Not Travel Well. *Maclean's,* Vol. 91, No. 20, September 25, 1978, pp. 22-3.

Wilden, Anthony. Libido as Language: The Structuralism of Jacques Lacan. *Psychology Today,* Vol. 5, No. 12, May 1972, pp. 40-2, 85-9.

———Piaget and the Structure as Law and Order. In: *Structure and Transformation.* Ed. by Klaus Riegel and G.C. Rosenwald. New York: Wiley Interscience, 1975, pp. 83-117.

———The Scientific Discourse: Knowledge as a Commodity. *Mayday* Vol. 1, No. 1, 1975, pp. 69-77.

———Ecology and Ideology [1973]. In: Idris-Soven et al. (eds.), 1978, pp. 73-98.

———Changing Frames of Order: Cybernetics and the *Machina Mundi.* In: *Communication and Control in Society.* Ed. by Klaus Krippendorff. New York and London: Gordon & Breach, 1979, pp. 9-29.

———Culture and Identity: The Canadian Question, Why? *Ciné-Tracts* (Montreal), Vol. 2, No. 2, Spring 1979, pp. 1-27.

———*Le Canada imaginaire.* Tr. by Yvan Simonis. Quebec: Presses Coméditex, 1979.

———*System and Structure: Essays in Communication and Exchange.* London: Tavistock; New York: Methuen, 1980. Social Science Paperbacks. Revision of 1972 edition.

Wilden, Anthony, and Wilson, Tim. The Double Bind: Logic, Magic, and Economics. In: Sluzki and Ransom (eds.), 1976, pp. 263-86.

Wills, Garry. *Nixon Agonistes: The Crisis of the Self-Made Man.* New York: Signet, 1969.

Willson, Beckles. *Romance of Empire: Canada.* London: T.C. & E.C. Jack Ltd., 1922.

Wormser, Rene A. *The Law.* New York: Simon & Schuster, 1949.

Young, G.M. *The Government of Britain.* London: Batsford Books, 1941.

Zaretsky, Eli. *Capitalism, the Family and Personal Life.* New York: Harper Colophon, 1976.

C. Video

Bethune (National Film Board, 1964). 60 minutes.

Black Tide (*Nova,* Public Broadcasting System, 1979). Escalating tanker spills. 60 minutes.

Buster Keaton Rides Again (NFB, 1965). 55 minutes.

The Dionne Quintuplets (Canadian Broadcasting Corporation—NFB, 1978). 90 minutes.

Dreamland: Canadian Film, 1895-1939 (NFB-CBC, 1974). 90 minutes.

Grierson (NFB, 1972). 60 minutes.

Has Anybody Here Seen Canada; The Canadian Film Industry, 1939-1952 (NFB-CBC, 1978). 90 minutes.

The Image Makers (NFB, 1979). History of the NFB. 90 minutes.

The Killing Ground (American Broadcasting Corporation, 1979). Pollution dumping. 60 minutes.

Los Canadienses (NFB, 1975). The Mackenzie-Papineau Battalion. 60 minutes.

Paul Jacobs and the Nuclear Gang (Center for Documentary Media, 1979). Victims of radioactive pollution (military and industrial) in the U.S. 55 minutes.

There Never Was an Arrow (CBC, 1979). Destruction of the Avro Canada CF-105 and the industry associated with it. 60 minutes.

Acknowledgments

The immediate source of the ideas developed in this book was the revision of an earlier text, *System and Structure* (1972), for a forthcoming second edition.

Many people have contributed to the process of political education that made this book possible. I cannot thank them all by name. It could not have been written without the help of numerous communications students at Simon Fraser University since 1974. Bruce Byfield, Gwen Kallio, and Jane-Anne Manson made particularly helpful direct contributions to this text. Larry Johnson hunted up information I would not have known enough to look for on my own. Many of the central ideas could never have taken their present form without the aid of Patrick Palmer and Rhonda Hammer.

I am most grateful to Bob Brown, Paul Heyer, and Klaus Rieckhoff for other kinds of assistance, and to Rowland Lorimer, who has been fighting our imaginary Canadians longer than anyone else I know.

I must also thank the following people: D.S. Roberts, Michael Cherniavsky, and G. Van Praagh of Christ's Hospital, West Sussex; Bob Seeds of Prince George, B.C.; Philip T. Rogers and Walter Gage of Vancouver, B.C., and Neal Lawson of London; Edith E. Lucas, Harry Hickman, Dorothy Cruickshank, and Peter Smith of Victoria, B.C.; Ned Larsen, Graham Anderson, and Derek Hyde-Lay of Shawnigan Lake, B.C.; Nathan Edelman, Chester Wickwire, Maxine Judd, and Dennis Judd of Baltimore, Maryland; Robert Elliott, Newton Harrison, and many students at the University of California at San Diego; Godwin Assogba of Lomé, Togo; Massimo Piattelli-Palmarini of Paris, France; Bill Cooper and Hermann Koenig of Michigan State University and Harley Shands of New York. Especial thanks to Yvan Simonis, Université Laval, Richard M. Coe, UBC, and Anthony Read of Vancouver, B.C.

Rosemary Bakker and Rhonda Whitwell spent considerable time typing the early drafts; Carol Knight both typed and criticized; Linda Clarke has pursued her impeccable way through many, many such pages over the past four years.

My thanks also to the Vancouver Foundation (H.R. MacMillan Family Funds) for a graduate fellowship (1965-68).

Pulp Press first saw this text in the late summer of 1978, when it was a short essay. As a result of their support for the central ideas, it gradually turned into a book. Linda Field, Steve Osborne, Norbert Ruebsaat, and Don Fraser took firm and patient charge of a manuscript riding off in all directions. In the process they gave me a crash course in the discipline and the craft of writing. The result, however, is not their fault.

Acknowledgment is gratefully made to the following for the use of extracts from their work or publication.

John Howison, Esq., G. & W.B. Whittaker, Oliver & Boyd, and Coles Publishing Co. Ltd. *Sketches of Upper Canada* (1821, 1970);

Eric Partridge and Routledge & Kegan Paul, *A Dictionary of Slang and Unconventional English* (1951), *Supplement* (1974);

Michael Posner and *Maclean's,* © 1978 by Maclean's Magazine, reprinted by permission;

Stephen Franklin and McClelland & Stewart, The Canadian Publishers, *The Heroes: A Saga of Canadian Inspiration* (1967);

William Lyon Mackenzie, Charles Lindsey, and P.R. Randall Ltd., *The Life and Times of William Lyon Mackenzie* (1862);

Sir Francis Bond Head, J.M. Bliss, and The Ryerson Press, *Canadian History in Documents* (1966);

Edgar McInnis and Holt, Rinehart and Winston, *Canada: A Political and Social History* (1947, 1959, 1963);

Arthur R.M. Lower, The Ryerson Press, and Imperial Oil Ltd., *C.W. Jefferys: The Formative Years: Canada 1812-1871*, edited by James Knight, © 1968 by Imperial Oil Ltd., reprinted by permission;

C.J. Harris and Quick Canadian Facts Ltd., *Quick Canadian Facts* (1978);

George Monro Grant and Canada's Sons Publishing Co. Ltd., *Canada's Sons on Kopje and Veldt* (1900);

S.B. Chrimes and Oxford University Press, *English Constitutional History* (1953);

Hugh Gray, Longman, Hurst, Rees, and Orme, and Coles Publishing Co. Ltd. *Letters from Canada* (1809, 1971);

Goldwin Smith, Hunter, Rose & Co., and Macmillan, *Canada and the Canadian Question* (1891);

G.M. Young and Batsford Books, *The Government of Britain* (1941);

Roy MacGregor and *Maclean's,* © 1978 by Maclean's Magazine, reprinted by permission;

Pierre Elliot Trudeau;

Edwin Warner and *Time* (1979);

Humphry Berkeley and George Allen & Unwin, *The Power of the Prime Minister* (1969);

Mark Jowett and the *Vancouver Sun*;

John Diefenbaker and Senator Eugene Forsey;

Charles Pelham Mulvaney, A.H. Hovey & Co., and Coles Ltd., *The North-West Rebellion of 1885* (1885, 1971);

Barbara Ehrenreich, Mark Dowie, Stephen Minkin, and *Mother Jones,* 'The Charge: Gynocide. The Accused: The U.S. Government' (1979);

Rod Nutt and the *Vancouver Sun*, 'B.C. Becomes Japan's "New Manchuria"' (October 25, 1979), reprinted by permission;

H.J. Timperley, Amleto Vespa, and Victor Gollancz Ltd., *Secret Agent of Japan* (1938);

Stephen Kaliski and *The Financial Post* (1979).

Index